With best wishes for
tight lines!

Ed Muljadolshi

THE INQUISITIVE ANGLER

BOOKS BY EDWARD C. MIGDALSKI

Salt Water Game Fishes—Atlantic and Pacific (1958)

How to Make Fish Mounts (1960)

Fresh Water Sport Fishes of North America (1962)

Boy's Book of Fishes (1964)

Fresh and Salt Fishes of the World (1976)

Clay Target Games (1978)

Fish Mounts and Other Fish Trophies (1981)

The Inquisitive Angler (1991)

THE
INQUISITIVE ANGLER

Edward C. Migdalski

Lyons &
Burford,
Publishers

Printed in the United States of America

10 9 8 7 6 5 4 3 2 1

Library of Congress Cataloging-in-Publication Data

Migdalski, Edward C.
    The inquisitive angler / Edward C. Migdalski.
        p.   cm.
    Includes bibliographical references and index.
    ISBN 1-55821-132-2
    1. Fishing.   2. Fishes.   I. Title.
SH441.M54   1991
799.1′2—dc20   91-36355
                                                            CIP

To FOSTER BAM
friend, colleague, and fishing companion

Author's Note

During a lunch meeting in New York City, Nick Lyons proposed that I write a book on fishes and fishing that would follow closely the format employed in two of my earliest publications. I was pleased because today the volumes he referred to, now long out of print, are accepted by book collectors as classics.

My response was a suggestive one. I counterproposed doing something different—a type of book related to fishing done in a style of attitude and information that, to my knowledge, had not been published before.

Nick's response was, "Give it a shot."

It is a challenge to produce a selection of subjects associated with sport fishes and angling that, I believe, is of interest to the knowledgeable rod and reel enthusiast, that is, the *inquisitive angler* or the *amateur ichthyologist* interested in fishing.

Contents

Introduction   *1*

1 GENERAL ICHTHYOLOGY   5
2 THE FISH'S MAKEUP   19
3 THE MOST COMMONLY CAUGHT GAMEFISHES   *81*
4 MARINE FACTORS RELATED TO FISHING   *113*
5 LIMNOLOGY IN ANGLING   *131*
6 ANATOMY RELATIVE TO FISHING   *145*
7 ESPECIALLY FOR THE INQUISITIVE ANGLER   *159*
8 SCUBA AND SUBMERSIBLES IN THE STUDY
   OF FISHES   *183*
9 FISH TAXIDERMY AND THE ANGLER   *199*

Index   *213*

Introduction

In the eyes of sportfishermen I have led an enviable life, fishing around the world and getting paid for it. With all the ramifications of ichthyology at Yale University in collecting fishes for study, manuscript writing, and museum exhibits, the employment of chemicals, nets, traps, spears, and harpoons was necessary. The majority of large specimens, however, including all that are termed game fishes, were taken by rod and reel because that was the only way to capture them. Lest the angler get the wrong impression, traveling to exotic places and working long hours in primitive areas under difficult conditions was not all fun and games. There were many days in boats in turbulent seas; nonstop day-and-night work ashore, sometimes in uncomfortably hot weather under a blazing sun, and other times at near-freezing temperatures at high altitudes. Be that as it may, my job created opportunities for me to use rod and reel to catch just about every well-known game fish, and in such diverse situations as using big-game tackle for marlin off the coasts of South America, Africa, and New Zealand; giant bluefin tuna off Nova Scotia; spin-casting for mahseer in India; fly-fishing for grayling in Alaska, steelhead in Oregon, Atlantic salmon in Canada and Iceland, and blue-gills in Connecticut.

My work has required the accumulation of a significant personal library per-taining to fishing, hunting, and other outdoor pursuits. Often, when I take a volume in hand and read its contents, I wonder how the author first became interested in his subject, or what influence guided him to pursue it.

My love for fishing was inherited from my father, who first introduced me to it through a method now considered primitive. I was too young to handle a drop line, so, perched on a rocky seashore ledge a safe distance away from the forth-coming piece of lead, I watched in admiration as Father prepared to heave out a tarred line armed with two snelled hooks at its terminal end. After unwrapping about two hundred feet of line from a piece of wood and spacing it on the rock by his feet, he spit on the baited hooks for good luck. Then he grasped the line about four feet above the hooks and lead sinker and proceeded to twirl the works above his head with increasing speed before letting the lead fly out, dragging the line behind it as it finally plopped into the green salt water of Long Island Sound.

As the tide advanced and the fish began to find the sandworm bait, Dad was anxious for me to pull in the struggling fish. But it soon became apparent that I had more interest in convincing him to place the live fish in one of the tide pools created in the irregular shelves of rock by the previously receding tide than in inserting them safely into the wet potato sack that served as our creel.

Lying on my belly, I loved to observe the captives as they opened their mouths to take in water and expel it through the alternating opening and closing of the gill covers. I was fascinated by the graceful movements of the fins as they undu-lated while the fish swam slowly, seeking an exit from their entrapment.

The quarry in the tide pool were flounder, cunner, sea robins, sculpins, and small tautog. When it was time to leave for home I was happy to see the undesir-ables (for the table) scooped from the pool and released, to swim slowly away in shallow water between the waves that rolled along the sandy shore. I was sad-dened, however, to see "the good fish," the flounder and tautog, removed and placed in the sack to take home.

Big, slippery eels hooked on the drop line always caused great excitement. Dad absolutely refused to put them into the tide pool. They could not be controlled on the rocks and had to be carried by the line, still hooked, so that the squirming, snakelike forms and fouled rig could be handled with the aid of sand and a dry cloth. A doubleheader was a nightmare. The eels would tangle the line in figure eights, causing Father to let go a stream of cuss words that were new to me.

In the backyard of our home, by a table and water hose, my interest continued as Dad cleaned the catch, including the eels he loved to eat. An ice pick was poked through the eel's head and into a plank to facilitate the skinning. A shallow cut was made completely around the body, behind the head, and with the aid of a pair of pliers the skin was peeled off with one long pull.

That evening the dinner specialty was fried eel, cut into four-inch pieces, covered with cornmeal, flour, and pepper, and cooked in olive oil with the bottom of the pan holding sautéed onion and a touch of crushed garlic. I also developed a taste for pickled eels, produced by Father in a concoction of brine, dill, onion, vinegar, peppercorns, and other spices. He maintained that such a delicacy was far superior to store-bought pickled herring as a tidbit to go along with his vodka before dinner. In later years, as a professional ichthyologist studying the American eel, I reminisced with fondness about those wonderful boyhood experiences.

At Konold's Pond in Westville, Connecticut, I first used a rod, reel, and bobber. Father and I, loaded with fishing gear, lunch basket, and a can of worms, took the trolley to the end of the line (ten cents for adults, three tokens for a quarter, and children rode free). Then we hiked a couple of miles to the pond, which was located in a heavily wooded area considered to be wilderness.

The excitement started when the bobber dimpled the surface of the water and suddenly disappeared. We caught yellow perch, pickerel, sunfish, and bullheads. The bullheads, being a hardy fish that survive when other species expire, gave me an unexpected delight when I found several still alive as the basket of fish was dumped on the lawn and sprayed with water. I immediately placed them in a pail of water. After my pleading, Mother acquiesced to lend me her washtub (those were the days before washing machines). The tub became an aquarium. I set in stone, sand, and grass, changed the water periodically, and fed worms to the bullheads. Without realizing it, by overlooking a tide pool on my belly along the shore of Long Island Sound and caring for bullheads in a washtub in our basement at home, I was practicing ichthyology.

1

General Ichthyology

The Logical Approach

From my experience, and at the risk of offending some readers, I say that the majority of today's college students would have to delve into a dictionary to become acquainted with the word *ichthyology* and its meaning—the branch of zoology dealing with fishes. Many times, when I have been introduced as an ichthyologist, I was considered to be a skin-disease specialist or a preacher of the gospel. Sometimes I was asked, "What the hell is that?" Many of those who know what the word means, pronounce it and spell it as itchyologist. And to my surprise, even in academia and in popular publications, the word is often mis-spelled. Actually, the word is quite simple when broken down, and easy to spell if one remembers that it contains two *h*'s. The first part, *ichthy*, is derived from the Greek *ichthys*, a fish; the second part, *ology*, means a science or branch of learning.

One incident has influenced me to write Chapter 1. I received a call from a fishing buddy of mine, Howie Johnson, who informed me that his grandson, Geoffrey Schroeder, a sophomore at Hamden Hall, a country day school in Connecticut, was showing unusual interest in fishes and the oceans. As a second-term project in his biology class his assignment was to research the study of fishes. I was asked to come to the school to be interviewed by Geoffrey. His questions and my answers were recorded on tape. That incident provided me with the assumption that this chapter would be of interest to the inquisitive angler and others searching for basic information pertaining to the study of fishes.

The Beginnings of Ichthyology

The history of ichthyology is assumed to have begun with Aristotle (384–322 B.C.), a Greek philosopher who documented facts concerned with the fishes of Greece. For many centuries after Aristotle, scholars seemed to be content merely to copy his work, and only a few original observations were added until the middle of the sixteenth century, when the work and interest of five naturalists stimulated the infant science to the first real advances in hundreds of years: Guillaume Rondelet (1507–1566), Ippolito Sylviani (1514–1572), Konrad von Gesner (1516–1565), Pierre Belon (1517–1564), and Ulisse Aldrovandi (1522–1605).

Peter Artedi, however, born in Sweden in 1705, is popularly known as the father of ichthyology because he was the first to specialize in the study of fishes. Carolus Linnaeus, the great Swedish naturalist, was responsible for publishing Artedi's work, *Ichthyologica,* but not until three years after his death. Linnaeus and Artedi were close friends and co-workers. Since Artedi's days, hundreds of scholars have added to his work in contributing to our present vast knowledge of fishes. There are countless fish mysteries remaining to be solved, however, and in the United States and around the world, there continues to be great interest in fishes and fishing.

The Professional Ichthyologist

Although the professional ichthyologist has a comprehensive knowledge of the subject of fishes, he must specialize in a certain phase of it because the science of ichthyology has developed into many branches and it is impossible for any one person to be an expert in all of them.

For example, there are specialists called "taxonomists," whose main interest is the classification of fishes; that is, they arrange them in groups according to their differences and similarities and determine their natural relationships, beginning with the primitive types and then progressing gradually to the modern or more advanced fishes.

The anatomist investigates and compares the internal and external structure of fishes, including the microscopic, embryological, and comparative points of view. The embryologist is concerned with the development of the fish from egg to adult. The paleontologist, interested in evolution, studies the past, the origins of fishes, and the sequence in which modern or present-day fishes evolved from previous types, including fossils. The ecologist's or field naturalist's main interest is in the way of life of fishes and how they fit into their environment. The physiologist studies the functions of organs and tissues. Museum curators collect, preserve, and arrange fishes in an orderly system or collection. They are specialists in the methods of exhibiting mounted or models of fishes for display. The term "fisheries biologist" or manager is usually applied to a scientist working in state or federal fish and game departments who is concerned with producing good fishing for the sportsman. He must be versed in subjects such as fishery statistics and how they apply to fishing laws, control of undesirable fishes in lakes and streams, stocking, hatchery procedures, and improvement of fish environments. The aquarist is a specialist in the principles of correct aquarium management, which includes aquarium construction, display of living fishes, oxygen, light, and temperature control, correct feeding, diseases, breeding, collecting, and transplanting fishes. A fish culturist must be an expert in breeding fishes, hatchery procedures, food and weight relationships, development of desirable characteristics in fishes, and so on.

Although the aforementioned examples are separate or definite categories of ichthyology, some are closely allied, intermingle, and depend one upon the other. Many positions that require an ichthyologist demand also the services of a person versed in associated matters. For example, museum curators should have both the academic and technical knowledge to create fish exhibits and the ability to deal with the public, and the fisheries biologist working in state fish and game departments needs to be an accomplished public speaker well versed in public relations.

The Amateur Ichthyologist

It is not necessary to be a professional employee of a college, state, or federal department in order to study fishes. Many people who developed a love of fishes in their youth have carried on this interest throughout life. Some even made important contributions to the literature concerning fishes and fishing. Actually, anyone who raises bait fishes successfully or makes a collection of preserved specimens or knows why fishing is best at certain times and certain places is practicing ichthyology.

The opportunities to study fishes are everywhere; one need not seek faraway or exotic environments to do so. There are many facts we still do not know about our most common fishes. Much of the literature concerned with fishes has been the work of professional scientists who have made observations on bodies of water located practically in their own backyards. Anyone who has a craving to study fishes can also have fun doing it. The most important pieces of equipment are pencil and notebook. The enthusiast who develops a habit of noting his observations intelligently will find this practice beneficial throughout life. And from a fishing point of view, the person who studies fishes and records observations will, over a period of time, catch more fish than the angler who does not practice ichthyology.

A Fish Defined

In order to answer correctly the question, What is a fish? it is necessary first to understand a fish's relationship to other animals. It may seem awkward to refer to a fish as an animal; nevertheless, a fish is an animal. All living things are either plants or animals, and the two divisions are usually referred to as kingdoms: the plant kingdom and the animal kingdom. Since a fish is an animal, the plant kingdom does not concern us here.

Divisions of Animals

The animal kingdom as a whole is commonly split into two major divisions— invertebrates and vertebrates—that is, animals without backbones and animals with backbones. Examples of invertebrates are worms, clams, oysters, lobsters, crabs, squids, and insects. (Although clams, oysters, shrimp, crabs, and lobsters are referred to as shellfish, they are not fish.) The vertebrate animal kingdom is composed of five distinct living groups—fish, amphibians, reptiles, birds, and mammals. Each of the five groups has definite characteristics that separate it from the others. A fish is a cold-blooded vertebrate that typically possesses gills and fins and primarily depends on water as a medium in which to live and reproduce. Amphibians—frogs, toads, and salamanders—are capable of living in water and on land. They begin life in water where the eggs are hatched and pass through a gill-breathing stage in the water before developing into air breathers. Reptiles are horny, scaled vertebrates that breath with lungs: they are snakes, turtles, crocodiles, alligators, and lizards. Birds are covered with feathers and have wings, and scales are found on their legs. Mammals are warm-blooded, bear their young alive, produce milk, and possess hair and fleshy lips. Man is a mammal, as are most of the common animals familiar to us—horses, cows, tigers, lions, dogs, deer, and so on.

This book is not concerned with porpoises, dolphins, whales, and seals because they are not fishes. Although they live in water, they must come to the surface to breath air; furthermore, they possess all the other mammalian characteristics of significance. In other words, they are seagoing mammals.

Fossil Fishes

Fossils are petrified remains or impressions of the original animals or plants preserved in the rocks of the earth's crust. Dinosaurs, for example, are known as fossils. The word "fossil" originates from the Latin *fossilis,* meaning dug out or dug up. Fossils may be hundreds of years old. The science of study of ancient life and fossil organisms is called paleontology. "Paleo" is derived from the Greek *palaios,* meaning ancient or old. The branch of paleontology that treats of fossil animals is known as paleozoology.

When a fish dies in the sea, its body may slowly sink to the bottom. Although the soft parts may disintegrate or be eaten by small organisms, there is a possibility that the bones of the skeleton may remain undisturbed. In the course of time, the skeleton may be overlaid by an ever-increasing thickness of material called sediment or detritus. After a great many years, this mud or sand may be transformed by chemical and mineral exchanges into a true fossil.

The science of the earth known as geology (taken from the Greek; *geo* equals earth) shows us that rocks seldom remain forever undisturbed. The rocks or rock mass may be left high and dry through the retreat of water. Or the rock mass may be forced upward into folds by the movement of the entire region of the earth's surface; that is why fish fossils are occasionally discovered high up on hills and mountains.

The fossil specimens entombed in the rocks may be destroyed by the pressure or movements of the earth's crust. However, it is also possible that the movement has forced the fossil close to the earth's surface where it becomes exposed; or the elevation or tilting of the layer of rocks in which the specimen lies may expose it to the influence of the wind, rain, frost, snow, and sudden changes in temperature caused by the sun's heat during the day and the contrasting coolness at night.

Fossil fish *Diplomystus denatus* was a Wyoming fish of the Eocene Age, 60 million years ago.

These forces may break or erode the rock to a point where it is possible to dig out the fossils. Rivers, and waves of the sea, cutting their way through land, may also expose fossils. The fish fossil, dug out by nature's forces or by man, may be greatly altered by pressure or by chemical change during its entombment; therefore, museum curators and preparators work on the matrix (the mass in which the fossil is embedded) until the specimen is exposed to best advantage (see illustration).

Identification

Many excellent anglers with whom I am aquainted are not familiar with the correct method of identifying a fish. For example, trout fishermen usually have no difficulty in recognizing a brook, brown, or rainbow trout; but if the fish is not a typical one, their identification is not given with assurance. Yet, it is a simple matter to separate the three species by noting points of anatomy or certain stable color marks. Brook trout have wormlike markings on their backs, and their lower fins are edged with white with a black line or band next to it. The rainbow has small black spots over body, dorsal fin, and tail. If the brown trout has spots on its tail, they are few and are restricted to the uppermost part. There are points of color and anatomy that separate each species, but the above examples are easy to remember.

Generalizations should never be used for identification. For example, a fluke cannot be separated from a flounder because it is bigger or because it has a darker color. One must look for such points as the anatomy of the head and the size of its teeth. Does the head face right or left? Is the lateral line of the body straight or is it curved? Some species of fishes resemble each other so closely that even scientists have to consider other factors before identification can be made. In some cases, such points of the external anatomy as the number of gill rakers or the presence or absence of teeth in the roof of the mouth are enough to determine the species of a fish. In closely related or similar-appearing species, however, the ichthyologist often has to take into account certain aspects of the internal anatomy, such as the color of the lining of the abdominal wall or the number of pyloric caeca attached to the stomach. Every angler should make an effort to observe and remember the points of anatomy in identification; it will add much interest to fishing.

For identification purposes, the original and anatomically correct line drawings by the author in Chapter 2 include the common sport or game fishes taken by rod and reel in fresh water and salt water.

For an inclusive guide to overall identification and distribution of marine fishes I highly recommend two volumes in the Peterson Field Guide Series: *Atlantic Coast Fishes,* by C. Richard Robbins, G. Carlton Ray, and artist John Douglas; and *Pacific Coast Fishes,* by William N. Eschmeyer, Earl S. Herald, and artist Howard Hamman. Both books are excellent. A. J. McClane's two field guides, *Saltwater Fishes of North America* and *Freshwater Fishes of North America,* are also handy productions along the same style as the Peterson guides.

For the angler-ichthyologist who is interested in books that offer a closer or more intimate connection between science and sportfishing, Edward C. Migdalski's *Fresh Water Sport Fishes of North America,* and *Salt Water Game Fishes—Atlantic and Pacific* are out of print but available in libraries. *Fresh and Salt Water Fishes of the World* by the same author is also available in libraries.

Every angler-ichthyologist should be a member of the International Game Fish Association (IGFA). Membership at a nominal cost entitles one to receive a special annual publication titled *World Record Game Fishes.* This highly attractive and voluminous production not only carries a section on species identification but also includes an up-to-date listing of world records of all game fishes, a worldwide inventory of "tag and release" programs for marine fishes, a multilingual guide to common names of saltwater fishes, and other items of interest to the inquisitive angler. For membership, write to IGFA, 3000 East Las Olas Boulevard, Fort Lauderdale, Florida 33316.

Names

The common names of fishes vary, especially in different parts of the country and around the world. For example, the popular sport fish known as the striped bass along the northeastern California and Oregon coasts is called the rockfish in South Carolina. There are a great many such cases among both freshwater and saltwater fishes. One of the most glaring examples is the cutthroat trout. In the literature, it has been referred to by more than seventy different names! Ichthyologists, therefore, use Latin names for fishes. If the scientific name of the striped bass, *Morone saxatilis,* is used, it refers to the same species of fish in Connecticut, California, South Carolina, or any other place in the world.

There is only one Latin name for each kind of fish. The name is composed of two parts (a double word, or binomen). The great Swedish biologist Carl von Linné (Carolus Linnaeus in Latin) introduced this system in 1758 when he produced *Systema Naturae,* in which he attempted to name in Latin all the animals of the world. The system proved a success and is still used today.

The first part of the name refers to the "genus"; the genus is a category into which are placed fishes that closely resemble each other (we might say, close relatives). The second part of the distinctive or scientific name is called the "species," which in Latin means each "kind." Another way of putting it is, the first part is the generic name and the second, the specific name. As an example to illustrate the method, let us consider the Pacific salmons. We place them (the coho, sockeye, chum, pink, and Chinook salmon) in the genus *Oncorhynchus,* but each has its specific name; coho is *Oncorhynchus kisutch;* sockeye is *Oncorhynchus nerka* and so on.

Anglers who wish to pursue further the subject of scientific names can find a full treatment of it in any good textbook on zoology. However, inquisitive fishermen are always interested in knowing to what family a certain fish belongs. The family group (Latin family names always end in *idae*) is composed of fishes that belong to the same genera (plural for genus). For example, the marine bass family is named *Serranidae* and is composed of sea basses, groupers, and rock basses; the family as a whole includes several different but closely related genera. The best guide to correct scientific names of fishes is *A List of Common and Scientific Names of Fishes from the United States and Canada,* published by the American Fisheries Society. This list was produced by fisheries scientists to stabilize common and scientific names of our better-known fishes. Both freshwater and marine fishes are included. (The annual IGFA'S *World Record Game Fishes* follows the same list and is more easily available.)

Classification

As a means of organizing groups of fishes in an orderly fashion, taxonomists arrange the various fishes according to their physical characteristics. This system of listing each species, family, and group in proper relationship to one another is referred to as "classification of fishes." There are a few variations in organization, depending on whose classification one follows. But, generally speaking, the fishes are rated according to their evolutionary advancement. The system begins with the most primitive ones and ends with the most advanced types. The more primitive indications a fish possesses, the lower it is placed in the scheme. For instance, trout possess ventral fins far back on the belly—a primitive trait. Bass, perch, and some others have their ventral fins closer to the throat, which is considered a more advanced condition. The adipose fin of the trout, the small rubbery protruberance between the dorsal fin and the tail, is a relic of ancestors that carried a fin or fleshy fold in its place. Trout have teeth on the maxillaries, erroneously called lips. The fins are soft-rayed; that is, they do not contain spines. Scales are small and of a round type called "cycloid" by ichthyologists. These are all primitive characteristics; by using some of these characteristics, we see that the trout is in a much lower classification than the catfish!

Scientists seldom reach complete agreement on all the technicalities of classification. However, all agree that living fishes can be divided into three major natural divisions: first, the lampreys and hagfishes: second, the sharks, rays, and skates; third, all the higher fishes with true bony skeletons. The third division usually begins with the so-called primitive rayfins—sturgeons, paddlefish, gars, and bowfin—and continues with the soft-ray types, such as tarpon, trout, salmon, and pike. The last group in the division includes the fishes that have spinous fins, such as the perch, bass, bluefish, and flounder.

Criteria for Classification

In constructing various systems of fish classification, renowned investigators since the earliest days of fisheries research have relied heavily on the skeleton, the only organ system available for detailed comparison with fossil fishes. Today, even though the full informational context of skeletal and other morphological aspects are far from exhausted, progressive taxonomists feel strongly that researches on the nervous, digestive, muscular, and vascular systems are greatly needed to enlighten further the mysteries of the evolutionary process in fishes. Therefore, it is not surprising that professionals interested in the taxonomy of fishes do not agree on many points involving the proper alignment of groups of fishes and, in many cases, on the placement of individual species within a group. Modern fisheries workers freely admit that some of the most generally recognized teleostean orders (groups of fishes with true backbones) are simply catchalls for separate lineages that have acquired similar stages of specialization or conformity. The possibility of creating a stable classification of fishes in the near future is further diminished because the discovery of new species and genera is not a rarity; and new forms, especially deep-sea types and fossils that have an evolutionary bearing on the relationships of fishes, are still being found. Consequently, fisheries academicians agree that the available classifications produced by respected scientists are far from perfect.

Past and Present Systems of Classification

The history of fish classification records that the first scientific attempt to produce a classification of recent fishes was made by Johannes Müller (Berlin, 1844). Subsequently, scientists from various countries published their opinions on the subject. Some of the major contributions were made by L. Agassiz (1857), G. A. Boulenger (1904), E. S. Goodrich (1909), C. T. Regan (1909), D. S. Jordan (1923), and A. S. Woodward (1932). In 1940, Leo S. Berg, an eminent ichthyologist at the Academy Museum in Leningrad and a member of the Russian Academy of Science, authored the highly respected *Classification of Fishes, Both Recent and Fossil*. Shortly thereafter (1941), Carl L. Hubbs and Karl F. Lagler, two well-known American ichthyologists, conceived a plan to publish Berg's work in the United States. Consequently, Lagler received permission from Berg to reproduce the book. It contains both Russian and English texts.

In 1945 Alfred S. Romer, in his book *Vertebrate Paleontology* (second edition), produced a comprehensive classification of vertebrates that includes fishes. In recent years, Berg's has been the most widely accepted general classification of bony fishes. Romer's work is also used widely, and fisheries scientists today are not criticized by their peers if they basically employ either Berg's or Romer's system.

The present-day attitude of fisheries scientists concerning classification can best be exemplified by a statement made by Daniel M. Cohen, at that time editor-in-chief of Part Six of *Fishes of the Western North Atlantic*, published in 1973 by the Sears Foundation of Marine Research, Yale University:

> Secure in the wisdom of hindsight we must also call attention to a statement in the introduction to Part One, which notes that a widely accepted general outline of classification will be followed. Although such may have existed in 1948, a decade of research by a number of ichthyologists studying both recent and fossil fishes has demonstrated that there does not presently exist any easy way to chart the family tree of fishes. Although the overall study of fish phylogeny is not an active field, the end

point, an adequately documented and widely accepted classification, is not yet available.

In 1966 four outstanding investigators made a meaningful contribution to the general taxonomy of fishes: P. Humphrey Greenwood of the British Museum of Natural History; Donn E. Rosen, American Museum of Natural History; Stanley H. Weitzman, Smithsonian Institution; and G. S. Myers, Stanford University, produced "Phyletic Studies of Teleostean Fishes, with a Provisional Classification of Living Forms"; it appeared as a bulletin of the American Museum of Natural History. This classification is based on an analysis of what the authors considered to be the predominant evolutionary trends in the largest and most advanced group of bony fishes. They recognized the families and their placement according to Berg's system, but they made emendations based on manuscripts published subsequently and also on unpublished facts contributed by many investigators.

Professional American fisheries scientists today, in forming general organizations of text, that is, the arrangement of families, genera, and species, closely follow the taxonomic order of the 1980 American Fisheries Society's *A List of Common and Scientific Names of Fishes from the United States and Canada.*

Information concerning the classification of fishes is offered here because many readers, I am sure, including inquisitive anglers and budding biologists in schools and colleges, will find it interesting and valuable as an insight as to how the order or alignment of fishes in literature is arranged.

Classification of fishes, however, need not be considered from a strictly scientific point of view. Angler-ichthyologists may prefer to separate fishes into major divisions: fresh water and salt water, and then to subdivide them into categories such as pond and lake, river and stream, coastal and inshore, reef, bottom, open ocean, and deep sea.

In recent ichthyological literature there has been confusion as to the total number of living species of fishes in the world. For example, from 1948 through 1965, six scientists individually declared, in various publications, the following estimates of the number of species of fishes on earth today: 15,000 to 17,000; 20,000; 25,000; 32,000; 33,000; 40,000. One wonders how trained researchers could differ so widely in offering estimates; the difference between 15,000 and 40,000 is not a small divergence.

Daniel M. Cohen, associated with the Bureau of Commercial Fisheries, Washington, D.C., decided that an attempt at producing a rational estimate of the total number of fish species (rather than guesses) should be made. Consequently, over a seven-year period of gathering information, with the cooperation of about fifty specialists, he prepared a manuscript in 1970 that appeared in the *Proceedings of the*

California Academy of Sciences. His paper, titled "How many Fishes are There?" gave the following figures (the estimates are intended to be the actual number of living species rather than the number that have been described): jawless fishes, about fifty; cartilaginous fishes, 515 to 555; bony fishes, 19,135 to 20,980—for a total estimate of 19,700 to 21,585. Cohen's percentages of species living in various habitats indicates that of the total number of fishes, about 40 percent are freshwater inhabitants and 60 percent are marine.

Specific and General Books on Ichthyology

Atkinson, Barry. 1961. *Angling from the Fishes' Point of View*. New York: Sterling Publishing Co.

Bates, Joseph, D., Jr. 1974. *How to Find Fish and Make Them Strike*. New York: Harper & Row.

Bond, Carl E. 1979. *The Biology of Fishes*. Philadelphia: W. B. Saunders Co.

De Latil, Pierre. 1955. *The Underwater Naturalist*. Boston: Houghton Mifflin Co.

Eschmeyer, William N., and Earl S. Herald. 1983. *Pacific Coast Fishes of North America*. Peterson Field Guides. Boston: Houghton Mifflin Co.

Greenwood, P. H. (1975). *A History of Fishes*. New York: John Wiley & Sons.

Herald, Earl S. 1962. *Living Fishes of the World*. rev. ed. New York: Doubleday & Co.

Hoese, Dickson H., and Richard H. Moore. 1977. *Fishes of the Gulf of Mexico*. Texas A & M University Press.

Lagler, Karl F., John E. Bardach, Robert R. Miller, & Dora R. Passino. 1977. *Ichthyology*. 2nd. ed. New York: John Wiley & Sons.

Marshall, N. B. 1966. *The Life of Fishes*. New York: Universe Books.

Migdalski, Edward C. 1958. *Saltwater Game Fishes—Atlantic and Pacific*. New York: Ronald Press Co.

Migdalski, Edward C. and George S. Fichter. 1976. *The Fresh and Salt Water Fishes of the World*. New York: Alfred A. Knopf.

Moyle, Peter B., and Joseph J. Cech, Jr. 1982. *Fishes: An Introduction to Ichthyology*. New Jersey: Prentice-Hall, Inc.

Nelson, Joseph S. 1984. *Fishes of the World.* 2nd. ed. New York: John Wiley & Sons.

Norman, John R., and P. H. Greenwood. 1963. *A History of Fishes.* 2nd ed. New York: Hill and Wang.

Robins, Richard C., and G. Carleton Ray. 1986. *Atlantic Coast Fishes of North America.* Peterson Field Guides. Boston: Houghton Mifflin Co.

Rounsefell, George A., and W. Harry Everhart. 1953. *Fishery Science.* New York: John Wiley & Sons, Inc.

Sosin, Mark, and John Clark. 1971. *Through the Fishes Eye.* New York: Harper/Outdoor Life.

Wheeler, Alwyne C. 1975. *Fishes of the World: An Illustrated Dictionary.* New York: Macmillan Publishing Co.

Willers, W. B. 1989. *Trout Biology.* New York: Nick Lyons Books.

Wilson, Roberta, and James Q. Wilson. 1985. *Watching Fishes.* New York: Harper & Row.

2

The Fish's Makeup

Anatomy and Physiology

Body Form

Of all the vertebrates (fish, amphibians, reptiles, birds, and mammals) on earth, fishes are by far the most numerous. Scientists estimate the number of living species to be about twenty thousand. In this vast assemblage of species, there is found a great diversity of body form.

The classical or typical fish body form is exemplified by such species as the perch, bass, and grouper. Fish forms digress from the typical in three directions; compressed (side to side), depressed (top to bottom), and elongated (end to end). Although all fishes will fit into one of these categories, each form in turn may vary with different adaptations, that is, portions of the external anatomy are adapted for specific environments or certain ways of life. For example, the extremely steamlined tuna is an open-ocean fish that is constantly on the move, takes part in

BODY DIVISIONS

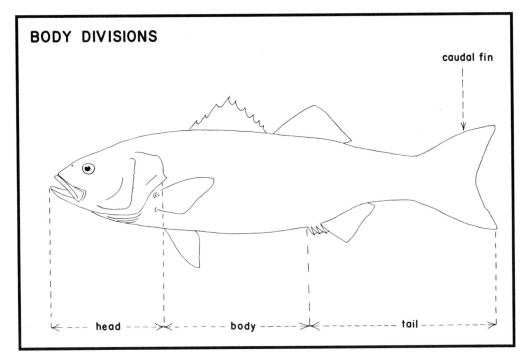

caudal fin

|← --- head --- ×← ----- body ----- ×← --------- tail ----- →|

long migrations, and is capable of feeding on fast-swimming schools of smaller fishes. The tuna does not have a distinct neck (typical of fishes in this respect) as do the land vertebrates; the head merges without demarcation into the trunk and the trunk merges into the tail. The regions of the body may be separated into three sections: tips of snout to gill opening, gill opening to vent, and vent to tip of caudal fin—the head, trunk, and tail, respectively. The bullet-shaped head with its pointed snout is formed efficiently to cut through water. The jaws fit closely together. The surfaces of the eyes are level with the adjoining surfaces of the head; gill covers are close-fitting. Scales, where present on the body, are small and form a smooth surface. The hollow curves of the posterior portion (hind end) of the body are well suited for the passage of water displaced while swimming. All these features compose a body form whose primary function is speed. Incidentally, the tuna, as well as most fishes, is covered with an abundant supply of slime or mucus that is designed to reduce friction with the surrounding water (this enables the fish to move smoothly through the water) and fill up any small irregularities in the surface of the body.

Marlin, sailfish, and swordfish are large fish that possess long bills that are used both as clubs to stun their prey and as defensive weapons. Their body forms are adapted for swift pursuit and long ocean voyages. The smooth, rather rigid form and efficient cutting dentition (teeth) of the bluefish denote that it is a fierce or voracious "chopper" of bait schools, which it swiftly purses. The striped bass, on the other hand, has a body more adapted to life closer to shore where it prefers rocks and sandy areas. Great speed is not required to capture the particular worms, fishes, and crabs on which it feeds. The barracuda's body is suited best for arrowlike darts at other fishes, but not for sustained speed. Groupers live around rocks and reefs; they do not move about much or take part in extensive migrations. They have large mouths and are fat and lazy-looking. There are many species of small, brightly colored reef fishes such as the angelfishes, whose compressed body form enables them to dart and squeeze into narrow spaces in rock and coral formations. The sawfish's compressed body and sawlike bill are admirably suited for its life along shallow sandy areas where it digs up invertebrates to feed on. Fishes such as the skate and flounder spend most of their lives on the bottom; their bodies (depressed) are flat, thin, and difficult to detect. The eel loves muddy areas; its snakelike (elongated), extremely slippery body is capable of negotiating ponds, lakes, and streams as well as marine waters.

Skeleton

A fish's skeleton is composed of either cartilage or bone. The skeleton generally supports the body and fins, protects the brain and spinal cord, and provides an attachment for the muscles. It consists of three main parts: skull, vertebral column, and fin skeleton. One of the principal characteristics that separates the sharks, rays, and skates from the true bony fishes is their cartilaginous skeleton.

Muscles

The substance covering the skeleton of fishes, known commonly as the meat or flesh, is muscle. In humans the muscular system is a complicated one, but in fishes it is fairly simple. Fishes have three major kinds of muscle, as do all vertebrates: smooth (involuntary), cardiac (heart), and skeletal (striated). Functionally, there are two types: voluntary and involuntary. Smooth or involuntary muscles are found in most organs, for example, the digestive tract, air bladder, reproductive and excretory ducts, and the eye. The striated muscles, which run in lateral bands, compose the bulk of the body and are functional in swimming. These muscle segments or bands, called "myomeres," are divided into an upper and lower half by a groove along the mid-body of the fish. The myomeres can be seen clearly if the skin is carefully removed from the body. In locomotion, the fins

SKELETON

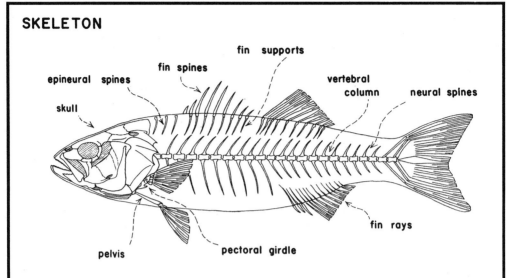

A fish's skeleton is composed of either cartilage or bone and generally supports the body and fins, protects the brain and spinal cord, and provides attachment for the muscles. It contains three main parts: skull, vertebral column, and fin skeleton.

SUPERFICIAL MUSCLES

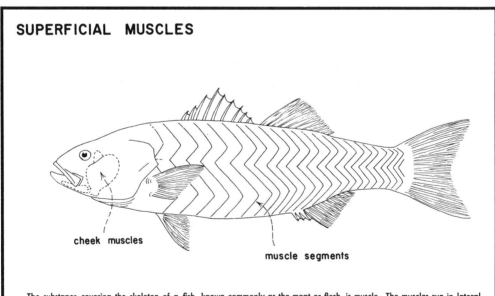

The substance covering the skeleton of a fish, known commonly as the meat or flesh, is muscle. The muscles run in lateral bands and compose the bulk of the body. They are functional in swimming.

are maneuvered by muscles attached to the base of the fin spines and rays. A more complicated muscle system is present in the head, where separate sets of muscles move the jaws, eyes, and gill arches.

Fins and Locomotion

Every angler should be familiar with the names of fins and their location on the fish's body. Fins are divided into two groups: paired fins and unpaired fins. Unpaired fins, often referred to as vertical or median fins, include the dorsal (in the middle of the back), anal (on the underside behind the vent), and the caudal or tail fin. The paired fins are the pectorals and pelvics. The pectoral or breast fins are always located close to the gill opening, but the placement of the pelvics varies in different types or groups of fishes. In the perch, for example, they are found well forward, under the pectorals; in trout, they are located closer to the vent.

In bony fishes, the structures supporting the fins are of two kinds: spines, and soft or segmented rays. Fin spines are individual, unsegmented structures as in the first dorsal of the perch and bass. Soft rays are usually branched or segmented, as in salmon, trout, and the second or soft dorsal fins of perch and bass. Also, caudal fins (tails) of all bony fishes have soft rays. It should be noted that in the carp and catfish families, some of the soft-ray elements in the pectoral, anal, and dorsal fins have fused in the embryo to form a spinous ray; this is not a true spine, though it is commonly referred to as such.

The caudal fin is the dominant fin on the fish's body; it is usually the main propelling force in locomotion (swimming). The dorsal and anal fins act as stabilizers that maintain the body in an upright position or on an even keel, so to speak. The paired pectoral and ventral fins are used for balancing, steering, rising, diving, turning, and stopping. However, the muscles attached to the base of the fins make it possible for different movements to occur in the same fin. Therefore, the pectorals and pelvics in most fishes can also serve as keels to retard rolling. In other words, the function of a certain fin is not restricted to a certain action or resulting position of the fish's body. If one or more fins are removed by experiment or by accident, the remaining fins take up the added burden and the fish continues to have reasonable balance.

Fishes with a fairly rigid body, such as the filefish, trunkfish, triggerfish, manta, and skate, depend mostly on fin action for propulsion. Eels, in contrast, rely on extreme, serpentlike body undulations to swim, with fin movement assisting to a minor extent. Sailfishes, marlins, and other big-game fishes fold their fins into grooves (lessening water resistance) and rely mainly on their large, rigid tails to go forward. Trouts, salmon, catfishes, and others are well adapted for sudden turns an short, fast moves. If water is expelled from the mouth over the gills and out through the gill covers suddenly in breathing, it acts like a jet stream and aids in a fast start forward.

A fish's air bladder, which may serve in some species as a supplementary breathing organ and in others as an amplifier of sounds, also assists the fish in swimming. By varying the amount of gas in the bladder, the fish is able to adjust its body weight so that it equals the weight of water that its body has displaced. This makes the fish become virtually weightless so that it can remain suspended at whatever depth it elects and can then use all its energy in a driving force for swimming. Sharks, flatfishes, catfishes, and others that have no air bladders can dive to the bottom quickly when necessary.

The pectoral fins of a ray are broad "wings" with which the the fish sweeps through the water almost as a swallow does in the air. The sharks, close relatives of the rays, swim swiftly in a straight line but have great difficulty in stopping or turning because their fins have restricted movement.

Flying fishes glide above the surface of the water with their winglike pectoral fins extended. Sometimes they get additional surges of power by dipping their tails into the water and vibrating them vigorously. This may enable them to remain airborne for distances as great as a quarter of a mile. Needlefishes and halfbeaks skitter over the surface for long distances, the front half of their bodies held stiffly out of the water while their still submerged tails wag rapidly. An African catfish often swims upside down, and sea horses swim in a "standing up" position.

Many kinds of fishes jump regularly. Those that take to the air when hooked give anglers their greatest thrills. Often, however, there is no easy explanation for why a fish jumps, other than the possibilty that it derives pleasure from these momentary escapes from its watery world. The jump is made to dislodge a hook or to escape a predator in close pursuit; or the fish may try to shake its body free of plaguing parasites. Some species make their jumps by surging at high speed from deep water. Others swim rapidly close to the surface, then suddenly turn their noses skyward and give a powerful thrust with their tails as they take to the air. Sailfishes and other high jumpers may leap several feet into the air when hooked, often leaping as many as twenty times before being brought to gaff.

The remarkable leaping of a salmon up a falls in its journey from the sea to its spawning grounds is a well-known phenomenon. And when hooked, its superb leaps in resistance to rod and reel rank it as one of the world's greatest game fish. It is this magnificent ability that has given the salmon its name, the Latin *Salmo salar* being from the same root as *salire,* to leap.

Another fish appreciated by sportsmen for its leaping antics when hooked is the tarpon. There are differences of opinion as to the maximum height these fishes reach, but judging from photos and films it seems that seven or eight feet is maximum. I must add, however, that often when I was sitting in a fighting chair aboard a boat trolling for marlin with a surface dancing bait, a kingfish would come up from below with great speed, nip half the bait free of the hook, and continue on into the air for twelve or fifteen feet.

Other denizens of the open sea that are worthy of note because of their leaps into the air and consequent falling back down on the water with a resounding splash that can be heard for a long distance on a calm day are the rays and mantas. While hunting for the giant manta to harpoon for exhibition at Yale's Peabody Museum, I witnessed dozens of these huge fish with a wing spread of a dozen feet clear the water. It was always an electrifying sight.

Fins are also used for purposes other than those mentioned. For example, in North American freshwater catfishes, the leading edge of the pectoral fin is a sharply pointed spinous ray or spine that contains a locking device at its skeletal base. The catfish is capable of erecting and holding erect the spine and using it as an instrument of defense (a hand puncture by the spine is very painful). The sea robin, scorpion fish, and a few others use their pectoral fins almost as legs, for standing or even "walking" on the ocean floor. Many fish, especially trout and salmon, use their anal and tail fins in developing their nesting areas. Others, such as the largemouth bass, fan their nests with their tails so that the eggs will be free of sediment.

The number of spines and rays in the median or vertical fins is often used in identification of fishes. The anal fin is especially useful for that purpose.

Speed

"How fast do fishes swim?" It is a difficult question to answer precisely. First, we must clarify the question: does it refer to cruising speed, maximum sustainable speed, or top speed over relatively short distances?

Cruising (ordinary travel) speed statistics have been taken mostly from tagged fishes released at one point and recaptured at another. For example, some bluefin tuna tagged off Cat Cay, Bahamas, were recaptured in Norwegian waters. Two of these crossed the ocean in less than three months. Another completed the trip in the remarkable time of fifty-two days. (These facts contradict the belief that all bluefin tuna migrating from the Bahamas spend the summer in western Atlantic coastal waters.) The information indicates that bluefins swim swiftly, but obviously we do not know whether the recaptured specimens swam a direct course or indulged in detours. Also, ocean currents can be a help or a hindrance.

Maximum sustainable speed, that is, the speed that a fish can maintain for long periods, is almost impossible to judge unless measured experimentally on small fishes by determinating the length of time they can swim in approximately the same spot when currents of the same velocity are flowing by. Boats traveling alongside big-game fishes have "clocked" their rate of speed. In addition, some anglers have attempted to gauge the speed of game fishes by improvising speedometers on their fishing reels or by using stopwatches to time the runs of hooked fishes. The speed of a sailfish has been estimated to be as high as a hundred yards per three seconds, or sixty-eight miles per hour. All the speeds indicated by such experiments are approximate at best because many factors have to be considered—size of the individual, temperature of the water, currents, the area of the mouth where the fish was hooked, physical condition of the particular fish hooked, and so on.

All members of the tunalike fishes, such as the bluefin tuna, bonito, and albacore, are also extremely fast. Other species that have a reputation for great speed are marlin, wahoo, dolphin, and swordfish. Generally, speeds of forty to fifty miles per hour are attributed to these forms. In fresh water, the top speed of salmon has been estimated at fourteen to thirty miles per hour, and the cruising speed at eight miles per hour. The top speed for largemouth bass has been estimated at twelve miles per hour.

Skin

The skin of a fish, as in all other vertebrates, is the protective covering of the body. It is composed of two layers: the thin layer, called "epidermis," and the inner "dermis." The epidermis contains numerous gland cells that extend into the dermis and secrete the slime or mucus that removes irritants whose accumulation on the skin might be harmful. Mucus is naturally exuded, cast off, and replaced. It also allows the fish to "slip" through the water smoothly. Arab sailors plying the waters of the Indian Ocean realize the importance of such a covering; they brush oil over the hulls of their wooden dhows, thereby reducing water resistance and increasing speed. Mucus also harbors fish odors.

The inner dermis or dermal layer of skin contains blood vessels, nerves, and sense organs. Connective tissue between the skin and the body muscles can easily be seen when skinning a fish. Scales are formed on the dermis.

Scales

Scales are a special, prominent outgrowth of the skin possessed by many types of fishes. The diverse fish families exhibit various kinds of scales, from tissue thinness and microscopic diameter to cardboard thickness and silver-dollar diameter. Some are bony, others are not; some are attached loosely, others are difficult to remove. Generally, scales overlap one another, but they may be separated or they may touch only at the margins. Some species have only part of their bodies covered by scales; others have no scales at all. The paddlefish, for example, is mostly covered with a leathery skin except around the throat, pectoral girdle (breast), and the upper portion of the base of the tail.

Within one species of carp may be found three types: carp that have a complete covering of scales are known as "scaled carp"; those that have patches of large irregular scales on the lateral and dorsal region are known as "mirror carp"; the kind that have no scales or almost none are named "leather carp." Sturgeon possess several longitudinal rows of plates; the rest of the body skin is naked. The freshwater catfishes of our continent, like the lampreys, have a leathery skin minus scales. It is a surprise to most people when they learn that the American eel possesses scales. These scales are microscopic in size, and a square inch holds about 150 of them. Brook trout, too, have tiny scales. Some fishes are liberally sprinkled with spines instead of scales, and some species, such as the sea horses, gars, and armored catfishes of South America, have bony plates over much of their bodies.

Fish scales have four distinct shapes. The platelike (placoid) scale with each plate carrying a small cusp is common among sharks and is considered to be the most primitive type. The diamond-shaped (rhombic) scale is typical of the North American gars whose scales form armored protection. The disclike (cycloid) scale is thin and smooth around the edge. Most soft-rayed bony fishes—trout, salmon, pickerel, sucker—have cycloid scales. Scales with comblike margins (ctenoid) are present on spiny-rayed bony fishes—perch, bass, grouper, snook. Scales are often used for classifying fishes. For example, the major division of bony fishes is split into soft-rayed fishes (cycloid scales) and spiny-rayed fishes (ctenoid scales). Cycloid and ctenoid scales are translucent; they lack the enamel of the other more primitive types of scales. They may be called bony-ridged scales because examination under a microscope clearly reveals the bony ridges that alternate with valleylike depressions. The ridges may be referred to as "circuli." The "annulus," or annuli, if more than one, is more clearly defined and readily distinguished from the circuli. An experienced person can "read" the changes in the growth pattern of the individual by the character and distribution of the ridges.

Usually, a centrally located zone or focus of the scale can be recognized; it is the first part to develop. In some species, grooves (*radii*) radiate from the focus toward the margin. The minute, sharply pointed spines on the exposed edge of the ctenoid scale may be referred to as teeth. Similar to a floating iceberg, only a

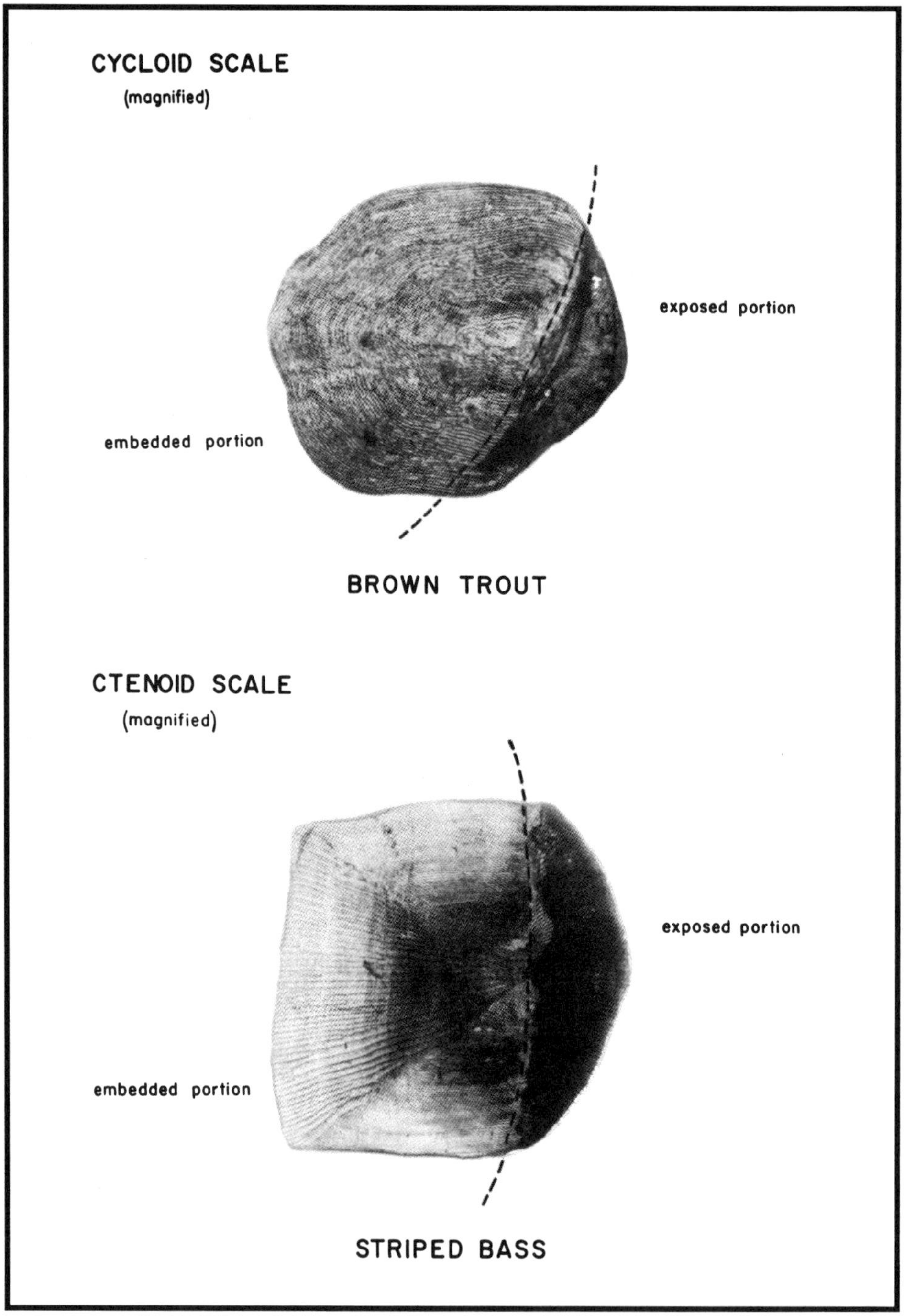

CYCLOID SCALE
(magnified)

exposed portion

embedded portion

BROWN TROUT

CTENOID SCALE
(magnified)

exposed portion

embedded portion

STRIPED BASS

PLACOID SCALE
(magnified)

SHARK

RHOMBIC SCALE
(magnified)

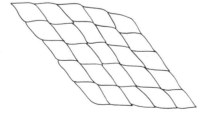

**ALLIGATOR
GAR**

portion of the scale is exposed—one scale laps over another. Scales sometime tell more than just age. In the Atlantic salmon, for example, spawning marks are evident on the scales from which can be deduced the age at which the fish went to sea, its age at first spawning, how many times it has spawned, and its age when captured. Growth is accelerated in the sea; therefore, the time when the fish first migrated to salt water is marked by an abrupt increase in the distance between the circuli.

However, no one can just take any scale from any fish and hope to recite the fish's past history. The scales of some species reveal nothing even to the best fishery scientist. And in the fishes that have readable scales, the information is often difficult to interpret. Some scales may be scarred or blurred. Others may be regenerated, that is, they are replacements for scales that have been lost. Regenerated scales have a blank center, and chances of obtaining accurate information from such scales are slim. A professional fisheries worker requires a large number of specimens in order to discard uncertain cases and obtain accurate averages.

Coloration

A fish that is seen on crushed ice in a market has lost its true coloration. At death, even a freshly caught specimen will quickly lose much of its true color. But anyone who has visited an aquarium or has taken a minute to study a live fish on the hook will agree that fishes are beautiful. Unquestionably, there are fishes that will match or surpass in beauty the most gorgeously colored bird or butterfly. Some of the startling color combinations produced by the color cells in fish skins are impossible to describe with justice.

The color in fishes is produced by skin pigments, and basic or background color is due to underlying tissues and body fluids. Iridescent colors are present in body scales, eyes, and abdominal linings of some fishes. The rainbowlike reflecting hues of certain kinds of fishes are caused by skin pigmentation fragmenting through the irregular ridges of transparent scales.

Not all fishes, however, are highly colored; the range extends from the fish with bright colors to species of coal black or uniform gray. Most of the varieties and shades of color tend to follow the color of the environment and render the fish less visible. In oceanic forms, basic color may be separated into three types: silvery in the water's upper zone, reddish in the middle depths, and violet or black in the great depths. The fishes that primarily frequent the upper layers of ocean water are typically white on the belly, grading to silvery sides, and dense blue or greenish blue on the back. The bottom-dwellers, especially those living close to rocks, reefs, and weed beds, may be intricately mottled or striped. Intensity of color also varies with the shore or coastal species, depending upon the type of area they inhabit. For example, a striped bass taken over a sandy area will be lighter generally than one caught in deeper water or around dark rocks.

The same principals apply to freshwater fishes. A pickerel, pike, or musky is mottled greenish because its habitat is primarily weed beds and lily pads where brightness alternates with shadow; thus, it is camouflaged. A catfish is a dark-backed bottom dweller. Trout taken from different environments in the same stream will differ in coloration to a startling degree. A trout taken in shallow, swiftly running water will be silvery and bright compared to his dark brother or sister, who has lived not far away in a deep pool under a log in slow water. (The color of a trout's flesh depends more on the types of food it devours than on its habitat.) Another good example of the influence of environment is the rainbow trout, which in western rivers migrates to the sea and is called by a different name when it returns—steelhead. When the fish is fresh from the ocean, it is very silvery. However, after a stay in fresh water it develops the beautiful crimson lateral band and the black spots of a typical rainbow.

Coloration in fishes is primarily adapted for camouflage, that is, concealment by blending into the background. In some species the color intensifies perceptibly when excited by prey or by predators. Dolphins, (the fish, not the mammal) a blue-water angler's delight, appear to be almost completely blue when seen from above in a darting school in calm waters. When one is brought aboard, the unbelievable brilliant golden yellows, blues, and greens undulate and flow magically along the dolphin's body as it thrashes about.

A billfish, such as a striped marlin, following a surface-trolled bait is a wondrous spectacle to observe. As it eyes its quarry from side to side while maneuvering into position to attack, the deep cobalt blue dorsal surface and bronze-silver sides are at their zenith; this electrifying dislay of color is lost almost immediately when the fish is boated. At times, however, after losing its intense color the brilliant hues may appear suddenly and momentarily just before the fish expires.

Most types of fishes change color during the spawning season; this is especially noticeable among the trout and salmon tribes. As spawning time approaches, the general coloration becomes darker and more intense. Some examples are surprising, especially in the salmons of the Northwest. All five species are silvery in the ocean, but as they travel upstream to their spawning grounds they gradually alter to deep reds, browns, and greens. The final colors are so drastically different that it seems hardly possible the fishes were metallic bright only a short time earlier. Each type of salmon, however, retains its own color characteristics during the amazing transition.

Size, Weight, Age

Fishes range widely in size, from tiny Philippine gobies less than half an inch long, the smallest of all animals with backbones, to giant whale sharks sixty-five to seventy feet long. Despite their diminutive size—it takes literally thousands of them to weigh a pound—the little gobies are harvested commercially for use in many foods. Equally surprising, the behemoth whale sharks that may weigh as much as twenty-five tons are so docile they even allow inquisitive humans to pull alongside them with boats and then climb aboard to prod and poke as they give the big plankton eaters a close examination. Between these extremes are seemingly limitless shapes and sizes among the estimated twenty-thousand species.

The least darter, a member of the perch family that prefers to spend most of its life hidden in dense vegetation in quiet waters of streams and lakes, is one of the smallest species found in the United States. It matures at about one inch in length. The sturgeon of our West Coast is the largest fish inhabiting the fresh waters of our country. Truly gigantic specimens were reported captured seventy to eighty years ago in the lower Columbia River and in the Fraser River in British Columbia. Photographs have been published of specimens ten, and eleven, feet long, weighing from 800 pounds to over 1,000 pounds. Nearly all these huge fish were taken on set lines baited with a variety of delicacies: lamprey eels, chunks of old beef, mutton, chicken innards, onions, and potatoes.

In May or June of 1912, a giant white sturgeon, measuring twelve feet six inches in length and weighing 1,285 pounds, was captured in the Columbia River after it was entangled in a salmon gill net. This female, whose roe weighed 125 pounds, met its doom near Vancouver, Washington—about 125 miles from the river's mouth. That sturgeon appears to be the largest fish taken in Amerca's fresh waters of which we have definite data. Several records claim sturgeon of 1,500 pounds—one from the Weiser River in 1898 and another caught by Nephi Purcell in the Snake River, near Payette, Idaho, in 1911. I have seen a photograph of the latter; the fish appears to be an emaciated specimen that would have to be of unusual length to weigh 1,500 pounds. The fish was said to be weighed on livery-stable scales, but the ceremony was not witnessed. Fishery workers have fruitlessly tried to ascertain a legend concerning a monstrous sturgeon of over 2,000 pounds. It was caught—so the story goes—near Astoria and mounted for exhibition at the Chicago World's Fair in 1893.

The day of really huge sturgeon was accepted as a bygone phenomenon until a Yakima Indian made a capture that renewed again the old legends. I was visiting Ivan Donaldson, a West-Coast scientist, when he showed me a photograph of this extremely large fish. In the photograph, a Mr. Esterbrook is posing alongside the

This white sturgeon weighed 900 pounds and measured eleven feet, two inches in length. Ten-year-old Ralph Nuñez stands on the shoulders of Wilson Charley.

The gigantic specimen was caught in the Columbia River on set line by Joe Esterbrooke, a Yakima Indian, at The Dalles, Oregon, on August 17, 1951. The baited hook punctured the heart of the fish, making capture possible.

This photo was given to the author by Ivan Donaldson, friend and well-known fishery scientist at the Bonneville Dam, who determined the age of the sturgeon by counting the rings of the annuli in a very thin cross section of the anterior ray of the pectoral fin; it was eighty-two years old.

In the spring of 1912, a giant, measuring 12½ feet long and weighing 1,285 pounds, was captured in the Columbia after it was entangled in a salmon gill net; the huge female, full of roe, appears to be the largest fish taken in America's fresh waters of which we have definite data.

The white sturgeon migrates to salt water and returns to spawn in freshwater rivers. The world's largest strictly freshwater fish is the arapaima or pirarucu, which inhabits South American rivers of Peru, Brazil, and Guyana.

The rod and reel world record for white sturgeon is 468 pounds; Joey Pallotta III caught that fish at Benicia, California.

The arapaima or pirarucu is the world's largest strictly freshwater fish. The Macusi Indian standing by this 148-pound specimen paddled the dugout canoe while the author fought the fish in the Rupununi River in Guyana, South America. The lure was a three-inch, red-and-white-striped spoon and the line was twelve-pound test. The catch was given international publicity as a world's record on rod and reel. Larger specimens have been captured by spear and net in the Amazon River. *Photo by author.*

sturgeon. Ralph Nunez, a ten-year-old Yakima boy, is standing on Mr. Esterbrook's shoulders and just reaches the sturgeon's mouth with his hand. The well-shaped fish weighed 900 pounds and measured eleven feet, six inches in length. The great capture was effected by set line on August 17, 1951, near The Dalles, Oregon, on the Columbia River. The hook had penetrated the heart cavity, quickly killing the fish.

In the fresh waters of the United States, no other species comes close to attaining the huge weight of the white sturgeon. Nevertheless, several other species do grow to huge proportions. Maximum size for the lake sturgeon is about 300 pounds and eight feet in length. Atlantic sturgeon up to 600 pounds have been brought into Portland, Maine. In recent years, there have been reports that paddlefish weighing ninety pounds have been taken at Fort Peck Reservoir, Montana. The literature is sprinkled with old reports of paddlefish weighing over 200 pounds; however, these reports have never been substantiated. The largest specimens (from reliable records) of the fierce-looking alligator gar were a female, with roe, measuring 9 feet, 7½ inches, and weighing 302 pounds; and a 279-pounder, which was taken on rod and reel.

The arapaima, also called pirarucu, of South America, is the largest of the world's strictly freshwater fishes (the white sturgeon enters salt water). The author once landed a 148-pound specimen on twelve-pound-test line in the Rupununi River, Guyana at that time a world's record. There are South American and Asian catfishes that may reach 200 pounds or more.

Among the other giants of the sea is the mola, or ocean sunfish, which goes also by the name of headfish because its fins are set far to the rear on its broad, almost tailless body. Molas, which have the unusual habit of basking at the surface, lying on their sides as though dead, may weigh nearly a ton. In salt water the bluefin tuna, swordfish, and certain sharks and marlins reach weights of more than 1,000 pounds. For example, the world's largest fish taken on rod and reel was a black marlin taken by Alfred Glassell, Jr., off the coast of Peru that weighed 1,560 pounds. Black marlin weighing over 1,000 pounds are now frequently caught on rod and reel off the coast of Australia. A bluefin tuna taken off the coast of Nova Scotia in 1979 weighed 1,496 pounds. Another saltwater giant is the swordfish. The record for a member of that species subdued by rod and reel is 1,182 pounds, landed off the coast of Chile. Although not a true fish, it is worthy to note that the record for the mako shark, an excellent game species, is 1,080 pounds, and the largest great white shark taken on rod and reel weighed 2,664 pounds.

Although the whale shark is by far the largest of the oceanic fishes, there is another that can be truly called a giant. During a Yale University expedition

This replica of a 1,560-pound black marlin, the largest game fish ever taken
on rod and reel, was presented to the National Museum of Natural History
in Washington, D.C., by Alfred Glassell, Jr., who caught the fish off Cabo
Blanco, Peru, on August 4, 1953. *Photo by author.*

along the shores of South America, the university's team harpooned and captured
a Pacific manta that weighed (cut in four sections) 3,300 pounds. The length from
wing tip to wing tip was eighteen feet, six inches.

The following list of close to maximum-size fishes taken on rod and reel gives
an indication of the sizes reached by some of the more common game fishes.

FRESH WATER

SPECIES	*POUNDS*	*OUNCES*
Bass		
Largemouth	22	4
Rock	3	0
Smallmouth	11	15
White	5	14
Yellow	2	4

FRESH WATER (*Continued*)

SPECIES	POUNDS	OUNCES
Bluegill	4	12
Bowfin	21	8
Carp	75	11
Catfish		
Bullhead, Black	8	0
Bullhead, Brown	5	8
Bullhead, Yellow	4	4
Blue	97	0
Channel	58	0
Flathead	98	0
White	17	7
Crappie		
Black	4	8
White	5	3
Drum, Freshwater	54	8
Eel, American	4	7
Gar, Alligator	279	0
Gar, Longnose	50	5
Muskellunge	69	15
Perch		
White	4	12
Yellow	4	3
Pickerel, Chain	9	6
Pike, Northern	55	1
Salmon		
Atlantic	79	2
Chinook	97	4
Chum	32	0
Coho	31	0
Pink	12	9
Sockeye	15	3
Landlocked	22	8
Sauger	8	12
Trout		
Arctic Char	32	9
Brook	14	8
Brown	26	2

FRESH WATER (*Continued*)

SPECIES	POUNDS	OUNCES
Brown	35	15
Cutthroat	41	0
Dolly Varden	12	0
Golden	11	0
Lake	102	0
Rainbow	42	2
Walley	25	0
Whitefish, Lake	14	6

SALT WATER

SPECIES	POUNDS	OUNCES
Albacore	88	2
Amberjack	155	10
Barracuda	83	0
Bass		
Black Sea	9	8
Giant Sea	563	8
Striped	78	8
Tautog	24	0
Bluefish	31	12
Bonefish	19	0
Cobia	135	9
Cod	98	12
Dolphin	87	0
Drum, Black	113	1
Drum, Red	94	2
Flounder, Summer	22	7
Mackerel, King	90	0

SALT WATER (*Continued*)

SPECIES	POUNDS	OUNCES
Marlin		
Black	1,560	0
Blue, Atlantic	1,282	0
Blue, Pacific	1,376	0
Striped	494	0
White	181	14
Permit	51	8
Pollock	46	7
Runner, Rainbow	33	10
Roosterfish	114	0
Sailfish		
Atlantic	128	1
Pacific	221	0
Sawfish	890	8
Shark		
Blue	437	0
Hammerhead	991	0
Mako	1,080	0
Porbeagle	465	8
Thresher	802	0
Tiger	1,780	0
White	2,664	0
Snook	53	10
Swordfish	1,182	0
Tarpon	283	0
Tuna		
Bigeye, Atlantic	375	8
Bigeye, Pacific	435	0
Blackfin	42	0
Bluefin	1,496	0
Skipjack, Black	20	5
Wahoo	149	0
Weakfish	19	2
Spotted (Sea Trout)	16	0
Yellowtail, California	78	0

As with all large game fishes, the maximum size and rate of growth of bluefin tuna is of much interest to anglers and fishery workers. Information from Mediterranean scientists indicates that young fry grow at an astounding rate; fish hatched in June in the Mediterranean reach a weight up to a little more than a pound by September.

One of the most popular questions asked by anglers when they see a large bluefin is "How old is it?" Therefore, I am listing statistics produced by the Italian ichthyologist Sella, who has done much work on tuna. He has made studies of the concentric rings in the vertebrae of fifteen hundred Mediterranean bluefins. (The vertebrae possess annual rings similar to those found in the trunk of a tree.)

SELLA'S AGE-WEIGHT RELATIONSHIPS OF MEDITERRANEAN BLUEFINS

AGE IN YEARS	*WEIGHT IN POUNDS*
1	10
2	21
3	35
4	56
5	88
6	128
7	170
8	214
9	265
10	320
11	375
12	440
13	517
14	616–660

When a fish as large as a giant tuna comes aboard, everybody attempts to guess its weight, and usually wagers are made. Of course, facilities to weigh a fish of this size are not present on sporting boats, but a tape measure is easy to carry. Therefore, I have attempted to formulate a length-weight table that may help anglers estimate the weight of a bluefin when boated. Israel Pothier, amateur scientist and former manager of the Tuna Guides Association at Wedgeport, Nova Scotia, presented me with data covering the landings of tuna for three seasons. This data I modified slightly with bits of information available in a few scientific papers.

LENGTH IN INCHES	WEIGHT IN POUNDS
55– 60	110–140
61– 65	150–185
66– 70	190–205
71– 75	208–250
76– 80	260–290
81– 85	320–400
86– 90	440–500
91– 95	510–560
96–100	570–650
101–105	670–700

The above table can be considered fairly accurate. However, as stated previously, large adults of the same length may weigh up to about one hundred pounds less in southern waters than they do in colder waters two or three months later. Also, it is possible that fish of the same length caught the same day in the same waters may differ as much as 100 pounds. In other words, the angler should take into consideration whether the tuna is slim or fully developed.

WEIGHT DETERMINATION

On many fishing trips, when a scale was not available, I have, with the aid of a tape measure and the foregoing formula, arrived at fairly accurate weights of the fish I have caught. I am sure that other anglers may have found the same formula useful. It is only recently, however, that I discovered how this formula came into being. During my just-arrived retirement years my big trips have been concentrated on fly-fishing for Atlantic salmon on Iceland's Grimsa and Canada's Matapédia, Miramichi, and Restigouche rivers. Consequently, I have been digging out of the literature all the information I could find pertaining to this splendid game fish. From a volume resting untouched for many years in my personal library I discovered the origin of the method of obtaining weights of fish by measurements alone; it should interest the angler-ichthyologist.

The formula and how it originated were documented by Edward R. Hewitt, one of the greatest of fly-fishermen in America, in his book *Secrets of the Salmon*, published in 1922. Here I present it as it appears in this excellent volume.

It is often of interest to know the weight of a salmon when no scales are available. Mr. Wm. H. Ward many years ago worked out a formula for obtaining the weight of any fish by measurements alone. He gave it:

$$\frac{\text{girth}^2 \times \text{length}}{800}$$

This formula is very accurate but it is difficult at first glance to see how it was arrived at. Mr. Benj. F. Kittredge worked out the solution as follows:

The area of the base of a wedge multiplied by half its length gives its cubic volume. The volume of a fish in cubic inches would be the area of his middle section multiplied by half his length, which is the length of two half wedges. If you square the circumference of a given circle or square, you obtain a square which is sixteen times the area of the given circle or square. So the square of the girth of the fish divided by sixteen would give the area of the section of the fish at its girth. Multiply the area of this section by half his length, the length of one wedge, and you have the cubic volume of the fish.

$$\frac{\text{girth}^2}{16} \times \frac{\text{length}}{2} = \text{cubic volume}$$

The specific gravity of a fish is about 1.15 so that twenty-five cubic inches of fish weigh twenty-nine of water, or one pound. So if you divide the number of cubic inches in a fish by twenty-five, you will have his weight in pounds. The formula becomes:

$$\frac{\text{girth}^2}{16} \times \frac{\text{length}}{2} \times \frac{1}{25} = \text{weight in pounds}$$

$$\frac{\text{girth}^2 \times \text{length}}{16 \times 2 \times 25} = \frac{\text{girth}^2 \times \text{length}}{800}$$

Edward Hewitt's prime concern with the weight determination formula involved the Atlantic salmon. Ward however, indicated that the formula can be applied to *any fish* in determining weight by measurements alone. My interest in the extent of accuracy of Ward's formula increased just prior to my serving as chief judge at the U.S. Atlantic Tuna Tournament in September 1990, out of Harwich, Cape Cod. Consequently, I brought along a notebook, tape measure, and a hand calculator.

After the sportfishing boats return to port, the tuna are deposited at a designated dock where they are measured and weighed. In this tournament the bluefins, in order to qualify for scoring, had to reach a length of 70 inches from tip of nose to fork of tail. On the first day of the competition, Jeff Drogen, fishing aboard the boat *Sandy*, caught a tuna measuring fifty-eight inches in girth and seventy-five inches in length. Using Ward's formula my calculator read 315 pounds. Upon weighing the fish on the official scales the weight blinked out at 308 pounds. On the second day of the tournament the same lucky angler brought into dock another bluefin that just made seventy inches. The girth was forty-nine inches. My calculator, according to formula, registered 210 pounds. The digital scale read 213 pounds.

I measured a third tuna caught by an angler not in the tournament who departed immediately after selling his fish. The tuna's girth was forty-two inches and its length was sixty-four inches. The formula's calculation came up with 142 pounds. When the scale read 141 pounds I thought that my arithmetic was off, so I again pressed the calculator buttons and the same figures came up. The measurements and scale readings of the three tuna were witnessed by Sal Cestaro, the tournament weight judge.

The length of the tunas was measured in a straight line from tip of nose to fork of tail, as mentioned previously. If the tape was employed over the curvature of the lateral surface it would have produced an inaccurate measure of several more inches.

Upon arriving home, my curiosity persisted when I looked at the mounted fishes displayed as trophies in my tackle room. They all were cast in polyester resin directly from the plaster molds of the original specimens, and therefore accurate in size and shape. The weights of these fishes when freshly caught were known to me. I compared the original weights to the weights produced by the formula. Here are listed the comparisons in pounds (ounces are discounted).

TROPHY	GIRTH	LENGTH	ACTUAL WEIGHT	FORMULA WEIGHT
Atlantic salmon (Quebec)	21	37	21	20
Atlantic salmon (Iceland)	19	30	14	13

(*continued*)

TROPHY	GIRTH	LENGTH	ACTUAL WEIGHT	FORMULA WEIGHT
Steelhead (Oregon)	20	37	16	18
King salmon (Alaska)	29	31	42	32
Brook trout (Labrador)	12	22	5	4
Brown trout (Connecticut)	16	22	8	7
Largemouth bass (Florida)	18	21	9	8
Striped bass (Rhode Island)	30	49	58	55

Ward's formula works out well when a close approximation of the weight of a fish is desired and a scale is not available. Also, it can be used as a fun de-liar when a friend shows off a mounted fish and exaggerates its weight. I trapped myself into such a position when I measured the mounted salmon that I caught in Alaska's Naknek River. The fish weighed forty-two pounds on camp Skytel's rusty scales. When I used the the formula the weight proved to be thirty-two pounds. I hate to admit it, but now I must accept the latter weight.

Caution: The International Game Fish Association will not accept measurements instead of actual weights in application for record consideration.

WEIGHT LOSS

Before we leave the subject of size and weight, the question of weight loss in fishes after being boated or landed should be considered. A recent occurrence concerning weight loss of a big-game fish, a blue marlin, should be of interest to all anglers. Fishermen generally calculate weight loss to be anywhere from 5 percent to 15 percent of actual body weight after a fish has been out of the water for several hours.

The affair I point to happened during the spring of 1987, when some unusually large blue marlin appeared in the offshore South Carolina fishing grounds. One of these impressive fish was taken on rod and reel, and because of its possible record size, it was transported to the North Myrtle Beach area for weighing. The marlin was boated about noon, but because of engine trouble the boat arrived at the marina late at night. No adequate scales were available at the marina; consequently, the fish was loaded onto a truck and driven to Murrells Inlet, where, after midnight, it was weighed. The scales read 678 pounds—thirty-eight pounds heavier than the state record.

Ten hours later, when a South Carolina Marine Resources Department biologist checked the marlin, it was weighed on state scales at 608.4 pounds—almost seventy pounds less than the original given weight. The biologist did agree with the angler that fish lose weight during long intervals between weighing, but this weight loss seemed excessive, expecially since the fish was iced down between weighings.

During the next eleven days the controversy escalated among the factions concerned with the state-record status of this blue marlin. Both scales were checked and proved accurate. No study regarding weight loss in blue marlin was known. The state biologist, however, solved the problem. Two marlin of similar size (390 and 403 pounds) and caught about the same time were obtained. One fish was left uncovered while the other was iced down and wrapped. The unprotected marlin was exposed to hot sunlight in order to encourage weight loss.

After a two-hour hanging with the head down so that visceral and body fluids could drain, the protected marlin lost 1.8 pounds, or 0.45 percent of its body weight. The abused fish lost 4.4 pounds, or 1.14 percent of its weight. The weight loss of these fish during the fifteen hours of the study was 2.1 percent of the body weight. Applying the study's weight loss to the original weight reported for the North Myrtle Beach blue marlin, a maximum loss of only 14.24 pounds should have been applied. The seventy pounds' difference noted when the fish was reweighed calculated 10.3 percent of gross body weight. Because of this large discrepancy between the weights, as indicated by the study, the application for state-record status was denied.

Although the weight of this marlin was officially rejected as a state record, controversy continued and a finger was pointed at the South Carolina Marine Resources Department. Two days after the Department's official rejection, all questions were put to rest, with some embarrassment I assume, when a freelance photographer delivered to the department's office photos of the original weighing of the marlin. The photos displayed the fact that the scales had been misread by fifty pounds and no allowance had been made to subtract the twenty pounds of block and tackle!

This story brings to light the truth that not much research has been done regarding the loss of body weight of fish kept under different conditions after landing. And it also suggests an opportunity for angler-ichthyologists to contribute original findings on this subject by simple research with different species of fish.

Age and Growth

In contrast to birds and mammals, fishes continue to grow after they reach sexual maturity. Growth is fastest during the first few years of life and continues at a decreasing rate—providing food is abundant—until they die. Growth rate is greatest during the warm months of the year when food is easily obtainable. During winter fishes do not feed much, and their metabolism slows down greatly; consequently, growth is retarded. Because of this unequal seasonal growth rate occurring in temperate zones, the growth deposits on scales, spines, ear bones, opercular bones, and vertebrae are discernible.

The statistics pertaining to age and growth of fishes are of great importance to man. In order to harvest the fish crop wisely—both sporting and commercial— the age of fishes and their rate of growth must be known. Rules and regulations controlling both fisheries are based on the knowledge of life history facts of the fishes.

Generally, fishes reach sexual maturity and grow faster in warm climates because the growing seasons are longer and the food supply is not retarded by cold weather. For these reasons, the southern largemouth bass, for example, grows bigger than its cousin in the north. This phenomenon is so apparent that separate northern and southern divisions have been established in fishing contests in the largemouth bass category. In southern areas such as parts of Florida and Louisiana, the largemouth may spawn after one year; but along the northern portions of the United States, Wisconsin for example, they do not spawn until their third year. Farther north in Canada, bass may not reach maturity until their fourth or fifth year of age.

A pond or lake can hold only a certain number of normal-size, healthy fish, just as a cabbage patch can support only a certain number of normal, healthy heads of cabbage. In some bodies of water, where there are too many fishes for the available food supply, the fishes grow very slowly. This condition is referred to by fisheries biologists as a "stunted population." The yellow perch and some of the sunfishes are often found in such a situation. It usually means that only a few, if any, predators, such as pike, pickerel, or bass, are present. Also, stunted fishes may be the result of no fishing harvest, or of anglers throwing back all the small ones. If enough perch or sunfish are taken by predators or by fishermen, the population will revert to a more natural balance, and big specimens will again be found in those bodies of water.

Numerous articles have been published on the growth rates of bluegills in individual bodies of water around the country. Under normal conditions, the average total length for a one-year-old bluegill is about 2½ inches; two years, 4½ inches; three years, 5½ inches; four years, 6½ inches; six years, 7½ inches; seven years, about nine inches. A six-inch bluegill normally weighs about 2½ ounces; eight inches, six ounces; ten inches, 12½ ounces. Variations in the growth of groups or populations may occur from year to year, and fishes from different localities may vary slightly in growth rate. However, the following examples indicate how age-growth patterns occur in different species.

Brown trout in streams may average four to six inches after the first year of growth, six to nine inches at two years, nine to twelve inches at three, twelve to fifteen at four, sixteen to nineteen at five, twenty to twenty-three at six, and twenty-six to twenty-seven inches at age seven (sea-run browns grow at a much faster rate).

Under average conditions, the largemouth bass will attain three inches in the first five months, five to six inches in one year, and eight to ten inches in two years. By the third year, they are twelve or more inches in length.

The muskellunge is a popular freshwater sport fish that has received much attention by fishery scientists. The following table concerning Wisconsin specimens demonstrates well the age and growth of muskies.

AGE (YEARS)	LENGTH (INCHES)	WEIGHT (POUNDS)
1	8	½
2	16	1
3	23	3
4	28	6
5	30	8
6	32	9
7	35	12
8	38	14
9	40	16
10	43	19
11	45	23
12	46	25
19	60½	42

Muskellunge in the world-record class (vicinity of sixty pounds) reach an age of about thirty years.

Other samples of growth statistics are: grayling, fifteen inches in length, six years old; paddlefish, fifty-six inches, twenty-four years; lake whitefish, twenty-five inches, twelve years. Fishes in their natural state seldom live longer than twelve to twenty years. Some aquarium fishes may reach thirty years of age. Many species of small minnows have a life span of only two years or less.

The white sturgeon of our Pacific Coast has a reputation for long life. Similar to the rest of the sturgeon family, it is a slow-growing fish that has a long life with an estimated maximum of 150 to 175 years. An eighty-two-year-old specimen, eleven feet, six inches long, was captured in the Columbia River. Scientist Ivan Donaldson made the age determination at Bonneville by counting the rings of annuli in a very thin cross-section of the anterior ray of the pectoral fin of the big fish.

The striped bass is one of the few saltwater fishes whose life history is fairly well known. Eugene Scofield, who produced the first important biological treatise on striped bass in California, worked out the following table on the average lengths of various age groups.

AGE GROUP	FEMALE (INCHES)	MALE (INCHES)
I	3.8	3.8
II	10.4	11.3
III	13.6	14.7
IV	18.0	18.2
V	21.1	19.6
VI	23.8	21.3
VII	27.0	24.0
VIII	30.6	27.0
IX	31.3	31.7
X	34.2	30.9
XI	37.3	—
XII	39.0	—
XIII	38.6	—
XIV	40.6	—
XV	41.3	—
XVI	42.5	—

Scofield found that both sexes grow at about the same rate during the first year. "From then on to the fourth year the males are larger, but beyond this point the females continue their rapid growth while the growth of the males is retarded, and at the end of the tenth year they are about seven centimeters shorter than the females. Males older than ten years are quite rare, as are females beyond the sixteenth year."

It must be realized, however, that variations in the growth of classes from year to year may differ. Also, fish from different localities may vary slightly in growth rate. The approximate length-weight relationship is:

INCHES	POUNDS
12–13	¾
18–20	2¾–3
24	5
30–32	10–15
33–36	18–20
43	30
47–48	40
50–51	50

Scientific investigators Gilbert Voss and Donald de Sylva have worked on the life history of the sailfish. Voss is of the opinion that growth of the sailfish is extremely rapid, but that their length of life is short—three to four years. After spawning in southern waters, the larvae and the young are carried northward to Carolina waters. (Larval sailfish are also found in other areas, for example, the Gulf of Mexico, mostly in June.) Then they work inshore—five- to eight-inch specimens are found in this area during the summer—and back southward to Florida, where they arrive as four- and five-foot adults in October and November. Within a year, the fish may be five or six feet in length. The average sailfish, seven feet and twenty-five to sixty pounds, is about two years old.

Donald de Sylva, in further studies on the growth of the sailfish, reports that a fish hatched in June will reach fifty-six inches and a weight of seven pounds by November; one year—seventy-two inches, twenty-one pounds; two years—eighty-five inches, forty-three pounds; three years—ninety-two inches, sixty-three pounds. The average of three-year-old fish is sixty-three pounds, but individuals may weigh from forty-two to 109 pounds. Apparently, three years is old age for the sailfish and few may reach four years. Nearly all its rapid growth takes place in the first two years.

Age Determination

A fairly accurate determination of the age of fishes that live in temperate climates can be made from various bony portions of their anatomy. The definite changes in seasons in the temperate climates cause annual marks to grow. These year-zones of growth are caused by the slowing down of metabolism in winter and the rapid increase in the spring. In some species of fishes, the scales and cheek or opercular bones demonstrate definite or pronounced ridges called "annuli," which can be counted. In fishes that have tiny scales and smooth cheekbones, the annuli are difficult to detect. Therefore, spines, vertebrae, jawbones (dentaries), and ear bones (otoliths) are also used for age determination. The year marks in the cross sections of spines and jawbones, for example, may be discernible just as annual rings may be seen in the cross section of a tree trunk.

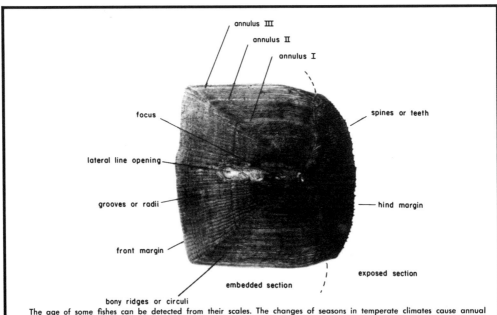

The age of some fishes can be detected from their scales. The changes of seasons in temperate climates cause annual marks to grow. The centrally located focus of the scale is the first to develop. In some species, grooves (radii) radiate from the focus toward the margins. The annulus (or annuli if more than one) is usually readily distinguished from the circuli. The scale above was taken from the lateral line of a striped bass, which was beginning its fourth year of growth.

In the monsoon tropics, the age of some freshwater fishes can be denoted from seasonal growth marks that are laid down according to dry and wet seasons. But in uniformly warm waters, such as the equatorial oceans, fishes show little if any seasonal fluctuations in growth; therefore, age is extremely difficult to determine.

Teeth, Food, and Digestion

TEETH

The dentition (teeth) of fishes exhibits great diversity in size and form. The types of teeth a fish possesses is a clue to its feeding habits and the kind of food it eats. Of all fishes, some sharks undoubtedly have the most spectacular teeth; they are famed for their vicious appearance and built for grasping, tearing, and cutting. The barracuda also draws much attention because of its fearsome teeth, which are flat, triangular in shape, extremely sharp, and closely set. It is obvious that the barracuda-type dentition is ideally adapted to capturing live fish, upon which it primarily feeds. The teeth may cut the victim in two or wound it so that it cannot escape; then it is swallowed whole. The bluefish, well known for its ability to "chop up" a school of baitfish, has teeth of a similar nature but smaller in size.

Musky, pike, and pickerel have sharp, conical teeth (often referred to as canine or dog teeth) that indicate they prey on live fishes. However, they are not capable of cutting; instead, they are adapted for piercing and holding. Fishermen must be careful when removing hooks from the mouths of these fishes.

Some species, for example, perch, catfish, and sea bass, have multiple rows of teeth that are numerous, short, and closely packed. This type of dentition, which resembles the bristle tips of a brush, is well suited for grasping various types of food off the bottom or holding prey in a sandpaperlike grip.

Many species of fishes have sharply edged cutting teeth called "incisors." Some have a saw edge, others resemble human incisors, and still others become variously fused into parrotlike beaks, as in the parrotfishes that feed on small organisms that they "pick" from corals, rocks, and reefs.

Molar-like teeth, sometimes referred to as "molariform," are characteristic of some bottom-dwelling species such as certain skates, rays, and drums. Molariform teeth are well suited for crushing crustaceans and mollusks and other organisms.

Strange as it may seem, some of our most common fishes, including carps, minnows, and suckers, have pharyngeal (throat) teeth. Some species may have pharyngeal teeth that are sharp, others possess the molariform types, while still others have practically lost them completely. Some fishes have teeth on their

The mako is considered by marine anglers to be the best fighter of the big-game sharks. The 321-pound mako pictured above was taken by the author in the Bay of Islands, New Zealand. This specimen cleared the water completely in taking a trolled two-pound mackerel bait.

Nearly all sharks have several rows of sharply pointed teeth; one or more rows are functional. When the useful teeth break off or are worn down, they are replaced by the teeth from the next row. The number and shape of the teeth, especially those in the upper jaw, aid in identification.

The cartilaginous jaws of the same 321-pound mako were cut away from the head, preserved, and mounted. The display served a dual purpose: (1) to demonstrate to students the shark's spectacular teeth famed for their vicious appearance and built for grasping, tearing, and cutting; (2) as a trophy and reason for bragging by the angler. *Photo by author.*

Note: The teeth have been outlined.

vomers and palates (roof of mouth) and on their tongues. Certain trout have comparatively few teeth on these areas, whereas in the pike, musky, and pickerel, the same areas may bristle with teeth. One of the distinguishing features between a true trout and a char (rainbow trout versus brook trout, for example) is the presence or absence of vomerine teeth. The vomerine bone in the center of the char's mouth has a few teeth only, located on its forward end, whereas the vomer of a true trout is longer and has teeth all along it. Some species have teeth on their premaxillary or maxillary, or on both. And many species (for instance, planktonic feeders) have no teeth at all. Their long gill rakers assist in collecting the microscopic organisms drawn into their mouths.

FOOD

All animals require a sufficient amount of nutrition in order to survive. When the food is digested, it affects various functions in a fish's body. It may be used for growth, to supply energy, or to supply substance for restoration or replacement of worn-out cells.

Unlike humans, who have a fairly constant body temperature, fishes cannot regulate their body temperature; it changes with the surrounding environment. Generally, a fish that lives in a temperate zone (where seasons change markedly) will eat much more during the warm months than it will in the cold months of the year. In winter, a fish's metabolism slows down greatly.

As can be expected, fishes, which are a highly diversified group of animals, feed on an extensive variety of foods. Some species feed entirely on plants, others feed on a variety of animals, some feed on both. And there are many types that, when mature, feed almost exclusively on fishes. The sea lamprey indulges in the unattractive habit of parasitic feeding; it attaches itself to the body of a live fish, rasps its host's skin, and sucks out the blood and tissue fluids.

The general food scheme of a fish's life is to eat and be eaten. Such a course of events may be described as a food chain that basically and briefly operates in this way: Nutrients in the water nourish various kinds of free-flowing aquatic plants (phytoplankton) that are consumed by a variety of microscopic animals (zooplankton). A tiny fish feeds on the zooplankton, and a larger fish feeds on the smaller fish, and so on. Many steps may be included in the chain as larger fish eat smaller fish until the chain may end with, for example, a marlin. The marlin eventually dies and may sink to the bottom where it is consumed by worms, crabs, and other bottom-dwellers. Finally, bacteria return the nutrients to the water in a soluble inorganic form that the tiny phytoplankton can once again use. Thus, the chain or cycle is complete.

Some of the most important large invertebrates that provide food for fishes are worms, snails, mussels, clams, squid, crabs, and insects. Fish also eat other vertebrates: amphibians, reptiles, birds, mammals, and other fish. For example, largemouth bass, pike, and musky often take frogs, and occasionally a small turtle or snake may be found in their stomachs. Songbirds have been found in gar stomachs, and a goosefish was found floundering on a Long Island Sound beach with two full-grown gulls in its stomach.

The methods or manner of feeding is also quite diverse in fishes. "Predators" grasp their prey with the aid of their well-developed teeth. Fishes that feed on bottom organisms may be called "grazers" or "browsers." Those that participate in a general type of feeding by straining tiny organisms from the water by use of their long gill rakers may be referred to as "strainers." Types such as the suckers and sturgeons that have fleshy distensible lips and suck food off the bottom could be categorized as "suckers." And the lamprey (mentioned above) and hagfishes that depend on the blood and fluids of other fishes to live on are termed "parasites."

Many types of structural adaptations to assist in feeding are found in fishes; some are interesting and unusual. The paddlefish has a long, sensitive, paddlelike snout that is used to stir up bottom organisms. Sturgeon have heavy protrusible lips on the underside of the head. Gars possess long thin snouts filled with many needlelike teeth. The angler or goosefish and the deep-sea angler fishes have an elongated dorsal tentacle with an irregular piece of skin on its tip that functions as a bait to attract fish on which it may feed.

DIGESTION

As in all other vertebrate animals, the basic job of the digestive system is to dissolve food so that it can be absorbed or assimilated into all the components that make up a fish. This transformation of food into fuel to supply the physical and chemical requirements of a fish's body is referred to as metabolism or metabolic process. The system is also capable of removing some of the toxic properties that may be found in certain substances on which fishes feed.

The basic plan or typical route of food traveling through the digestive tract of a spiny-rayed fish is as follows: As the food enters the oral cavity (mouth), it passes over the tongue (the tongue is not flexible nor does it have striated muscles; it cannot move as does the tongue of higher vertebrates) into the pharynx (throat), down the esophagus (gullet), and into the stomach, then into the pylorus at the lower end of the stomach and into the pyloric caeca (pyloric caeca are blunt fingerlike pouches that have a digestive function); next, the food moves into the small intestine where it moves past the openings of the ducts that bring in bile and pancreatic secretions. The food that is not absorbed goes through an S-curve into the large intestine where it is held until expelled through the anus.

The esophagus in fishes is highly distensible; it generally can accommodate any type of food that a fish can get into its mouth. Rarely does a fish choke to death because of something that it takes into its mouth.

The stomach differs in shape in different groups of fishes. In predatory species such as the pickerel, barracuda, and striped bass, the stomach is elongated. Fishes that eat anything available have, in general, a sac-shaped stomach (as in man). Some species—for example, sturgeon, gizzard shad, mullets—have a stomach

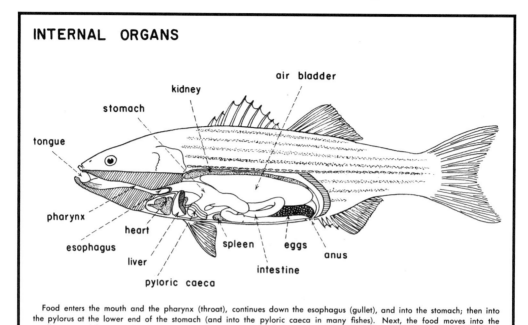

INTERNAL ORGANS

air bladder

kidney

stomach

tongue

pharynx

heart

esophagus

liver

pyloric caeca

spleen

eggs

anus

intestine

Food enters the mouth and the pharynx (throat), continues down the esophagus (gullet), and into the stomach; then into the pylorus at the lower end of the stomach (and into the pyloric caeca in many fishes). Next, the food moves into the small intestine. The food that is not absorbed goes into the large intestine where it is held until expelled through the anus.

with heavily muscled walls—an adaptation for grinding food similar to the gizzard of a chicken.

Some of the deep-sea swallowers have stomachs that are capable of great distention and are thus able to accommodate relatively huge prey. The puffers and porcupine fish can inflate themselves with water or air and take on a balloonlike shape. After removing a puffer from a hook, pat it gently on the belly; it will inflate itself and, if placed in the water, will slowly float away until it feels safe to expel the air and dive. Some fishes have no stomach at all but instead have accessory adaptations such as a gizzard or unusually effective grinding teeth that crush the food so finely that it is absorbed very easily.

The intestine is also not the same in all fishes. In predators or carnivores such as the musky and barracuda it is shortened, because meaty foods can be digested more easily than vegetable foods. On the other hand, it is elongated and sometimes arranged in many folds in the species that may be considered herbivorous (plant-eating). Sharks and a few other fishes have a spiral or coiled valve in their intestines that apparently improves the efficiency of its digestion. Some species depart further from the fundamental plan of the fish digestive system. The lampreys and hagfishes have no jaws and do not have a well-defined stomach or curvature of the intestine.

The various species of salmon never take food during their spawning migrations from the sea far up freshwater rivers and streams. Their digestive tracts shrink greatly and the reproductive organs, eggs, or milt fill up the abdomen.

Respiration

GILLS AND BREATHING

Like all other living things, fishes need oxygen to survive. In humans, the organs responsible for this function are the lungs. In fishes, it is the gills that perform the job. However, in some scaleless fishes, the exchange of gases takes place through the skin. In fish embryos, various tissues temporarily take up the job of breathing. Some fishes are capable of obtaining oxygen directly from the air through several adaptations, among which are included modifications of the mouth cavity, gills, intestine, and the air bladder.

A fish's gills are much-divided thin-walled filaments where capillaries lie close to the surface. In a living fish, the gills are bright red, feathery organs that are prominent when the gill cover of the fish is lifted. The filaments are located on bony arches. Most fishes have four gill arches. Between the arches are openings through which the water passes. In the gills, carbon dioxide, a waste gas from the cells, is released; at the same time, the dissolved oxygen is taken into the blood for transport to the body cells. This happens quickly and is remarkably efficient— about 75 percent of the oxygen contained in each gulp of water is removed in the brief exposure.

Different kinds of fishes vary in their oxygen demands. Trout and salmon require large amounts of oxygen. The cold water in which they live can hold a greater amount of dissolved oxygen than can warm water. Further, many live in fast-flowing streams in which new supplies of oxygen are churned into the water constantly. Most of the catfishes are near the opposite extreme; their oxygen demands are so low that they thrive in sluggish warm-water streams and also in ponds and lakes where the oxygen supply is low. A catfish can, in fact, remain alive for a long time out of water if the fish is kept cool and moist. Like the carp and similar kinds of fish, catfishes can be shipped for long distances and arrive at the market alive.

A few fish, such as the various walking catfishes, climbing perches, bowfins, gar, gouramis, and others, can breathe air. Air-breathers use only about 5 percent of the oxygen available to them with each breath of air. The best-known air-

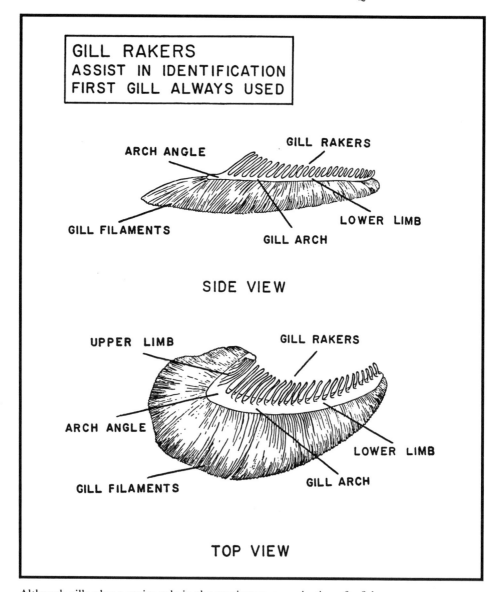

GILL RAKERS
ASSIST IN IDENTIFICATION
FIRST GILL ALWAYS USED

ARCH ANGLE   GILL RAKERS

GILL FILAMENTS   GILL ARCH   LOWER LIMB

SIDE VIEW

UPPER LIMB   GILL RAKERS

ARCH ANGLE

LOWER LIMB

GILL FILAMENTS   GILL ARCH

TOP VIEW

Although gills play a major role in the respiratory organization of a fish, they also serve another purpose. Gill rakers, by projecting over the throat opening, strain water that is passed over the gills. Also, solid particles are prevented from passing over and injuring the gill filaments. The number of gill rakers on the first gill arch is sometimes used as an aid in identifying or separating species of fish that closely resemble one another.

breathers are the lungfishes that live in tropical Africa. Their "lung" is an air bladder connected to the lungfish's mouth by a duct, its walls richly supplied with blood vessels. A lungfish gets new supplies of oxygen by rising to the surface and taking in gulps of air. It will drown if kept under water. When the stagnant pool in which it lives dries up, which happens seasonally, the lungfish burrows into the soft mud at the bottom and secretes a slimy coating over its body. It continues to breathe air through a small hole that connects to the surface through the mud casing. When the rains come again and the pool fills, the lungfish wriggles out of its cocoon and resumes its usual living habits.

The sea lamprey (and all other lampreys) have seven paired gill sacs or branchial pouches. A lamprey does not take in water through its mouth as other fishes do, even when its mouth is not in the act of sucking blood and juices out of its prey. Water, from which the lamprey secures its oxygen, is both taken in and expelled through the gill sacs.

The sea lamprey is a parasitic eellike creature that exists by sucking out the blood of fishes. It attaches itself to the side of its host by means of a funnel-shaped mouth lined with radiating rows of sharp teeth. With its toothed tongue, it rasps a hole in its victim and proceeds to draw out the fish's life blood and body fluids. Fish do not fear the lamprey by sight. The lamprey swims along serenely by the side of a lake trout (or other fish) and simply reaches out, clamping its suction mouth onto the unsuspecting prey. After feasting, it departs and the trout usually dies. If by chance the prey survives, it carries a wound that invites infection.

Rays and skates mostly have five paired external gill slits (rarely six or seven) located on the bottom side of the head. Sharks also have the same number of gill slits, but they are located laterally (on the side). In sharks, the water used for respiration is taken in through the mouth and expelled through the gill slits. Rays and skates, however, draw in water through the spiracles located on top or close to the top of the head (an excellent adaptation for bottom-dwelling fishes). The water flows over the gills and out the gill slits located on the underside of the head.

Because a fish has no opening between its nostrils and mouth cavity as in humans, it has to breathe through its mouth. As the fish opens its mouth, a stream of water is drawn in. During this intake of water the gill cover is held tight, thereby closing the gill opening. Then the fish closes its mouth and drives the water over the gills and out the external openings by the use of special throat muscles. As the water passes over the gills, the exchange of gases takes place; that is, oxygen (which has been absorbed from the air by water exposed to it) is taken in through the walls of the fine blood vessels in the gill filaments and carbon dioxide is given off. The blood, well oxygenated, then travels through the fish's

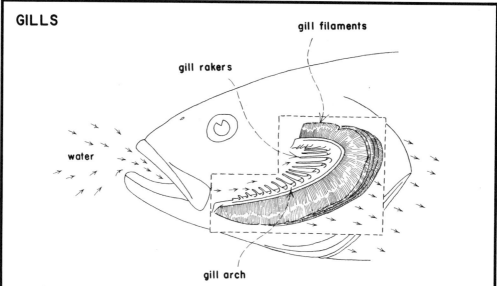

GILLS

gill filaments

gill rakers

water

gill arch

As the water enters the fish's mouth and passes over the gills, the exchange of gases takes place. Oxygen, which has been absorbed from the air by water exposed to it, is taken in through the walls of the fine blood vessels in the gill filaments; and carbon dioxide is given off. (The blood, well oxygenated, then travels through the fish's body.) Most fishes have two gill arches on each side. Each arch has two rows or series of gill filaments.

body. The rapidity with which a fish breathes varies with different species. A human in good health under normal circumstances breathes about twenty to twenty-five times a minute. Some types of fish have a breathing rate as low as twelve a minute, while others take as many as 150 breaths per minute. If the fish is exerting itself, or if the oxygen content of the water becomes low, the rate of breathing will be faster, and the fish "pants" like a runner after finishing the mile.

Although gills play a major role in the respiratory organization of a fish, they also serve another purpose. Gill rakers, located along the anterior margin of the gill arch, aid in several ways. By projecting over the throat opening, they strain water that is passed over the gills. Solid particles are prevented from passing over and injuring the gill filaments. Gill rakers may be short, and knobby, as in the pickerel, which is primarily a fish-eater. The shad, on the other hand, feeds on minute organisms. Its gill rakers are numerous, long, and thin, and they serve to sieve out the tiny organisms on which the shad feeds. In between these two extremes in size and shape, gill rakers of various sizes can be found in different types of fishes. The number of gill rakers on the first gill arch is sometimes used as

This gill structure, cut away from the head of a 640-pound bluefin tuna at Wedgeport, Nova Scotia, about four hours after it was caught, shows well the prominent gill rakers that serve to protect the feathery gill filaments from injury by food passing down the throat.

In a living fish the gills are bright red. The degree of freshness of a fish can be detected by lifting the gill cover. The intensity of the redness, or lack of it, is the clue. *Photo by author.*

an aid in identifying or separating species of fish that closely resemble one another.

AIR BLADDER

The air bladder, located between the stomach and backbone, is also known as the swim bladder, which is misleading because it has no function in the movement of locomotion of fishes in any direction. The mixture of gases that it contains is not normal air, so the correct name should be "gas bladder."

The air bladder is present in most bony fishes; it does not appear in lampreys, hagfishes, sharks, rays, or skates. The air bladder performs several functions. It may be well supplied with blood vessels, as it is in the tarpon, and act as a supplementary breathing organ. The tarpon has an open tube that leads from the upper side of its gullet to the air bladder. (The tarpon also has a set of gills.) Some species of fishes use the air bladder as a compartment in which to store air for breathing. The fish falls back on this reserve when its usual supply of oxygen may be shut off. The air bladder plays a part in aiding equilibrium of density between the fish and the water. (It has no function of adjustment of pressure to changing levels.) In other words, the volume of water occupied by the fish should weigh about as much as the fish does. The air bladder is a compensator between them. For example, the pickerel is capable of "floating," its body motionless, anticipating its prey. The catfish, on the other hand, has no air bladder; it spends most of its life on the bottom. The saltwater flatfish also has no air bladder, and it dives to the bottom swiftly if it escapes the hook near the surface of the water. (A fish does not raise or lower itself by increasing or decreasing the size of the air bladder.) It has also been definitely established that the air bladder is an efficient hearing aid in many types of fishes. It is commonly known that the noises some fishes make are produced by the air bladder.

An essay concerning fish respiration should include the primitive lungfishes that are represented by five living species. These "living fossils" are found in Africa, South America, and Australia. The African lungfish's air bladder is purely respiratory in function; this fish cannot use its gills for breathing. If the African lungfish cannot reach the surface to gulp air, it soon drowns.

The Heart, and Blood Circulation

The circulatory system of a fish is made up of a heart, blood, and blood vessels. The function of blood is to carry to every living cell in the body the oxygen and nourishment they must have and to transport from the cells carbon dioxide and other excretory products.

The heart is a muscular organ located close behind the fish's mouth. It acts as a central pump forcing the blood through the system of pipelike blood vessels. Blood vessels are largest close to the heart and grow smaller as they recede from it until finally they terminate in a complex or network of extremely fine, thin-walled capillaries meandering through the tissues.

Fish blood, as in all vertebrates, has two parts: fluid and solid. The fluid part (plasma) transports the solid part (blood cells). As in humans, the fish's blood receives its red color from the red blood corpuscles. Hemoglobin, a substance in the blood, has the ability to attract, absorb, and carry great quantities of oxygen. Fish blood and human blood both contain white cells.

The fish circulatory system is much simpler than that of humans. In humans, the blood is pumped from the heart into the lungs, where it is oxygenated, and

CIRCULATORY SYSTEM

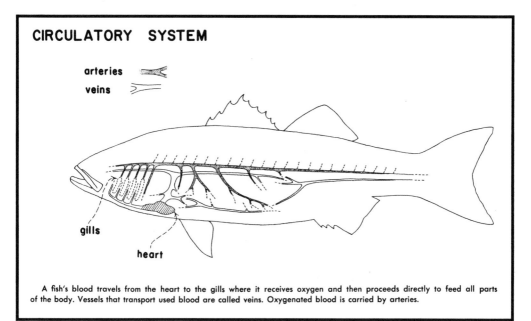

arteries

veins

gills

heart

A fish's blood travels from the heart to the gills where it receives oxygen and then proceeds directly to feed all parts of the body. Vessels that transport used blood are called veins. Oxygenated blood is carried by arteries.

then it returns to the heart where it gets a good boost for its trip throughout the rest of the body. Fish blood travels from the heart to the gills, where it is purified, and then proceeds directly to feed all parts of the body. In other words, the fish has a single circuit, while the human has a double circuit. The vessels that transport used (venous) blood are called veins. Oxygenated blood is carried by arteries.

The heart's muscular walls have the ability to contract, thereby forcing the blood through the arteries and veins. A human heart is four-chambered, two on each side—a right auricle and ventricle, and a left auricle and ventricle. The used blood (venous blood) travels through the right set, from the auricle to the ventricle to the lungs, and then returns to the left set, and thence around the body. In other words, the right side accommodates venous blood and the left side only pure or oxygenated blood. The fish heart, on the other hand, possesses only one series of chambers—auricle and ventricle. The used blood enters the base of the heart and is pumped out the forward end directly to the gills. The fish heart receives only venous or used blood.

Why are fishes called "cold-blooded," and why are they so sensitive to temperature changes in the water? Fish blood is thicker than human blood. It is pumped by a heart with only one series of chambers and consequently has low pressure. Primarily because of these two facts, the blood flow through a fish's

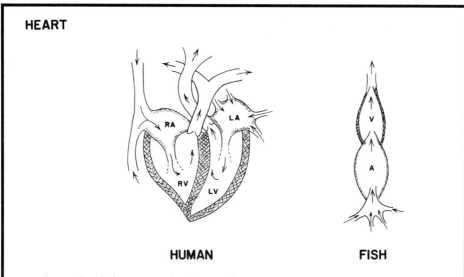

HEART

HUMAN   **FISH**

Generalized diagrams of a human heart and a fish heart (teleost or bony fish): A, auricle; V, ventricle; RA, right auricle; LA, left auricle; RV, right ventricle; LV, left ventricle.

body is slow. Because the blood flows slowly through the gills where it absorbs oxygen and because water has less oxygen than air (which humans breathe), fish blood is not as rich in oxygen as is human blood. Low oxygen means low temperature; also, fish blood cools as it flows through the gills. Actually, the term cold-blooded means that the body temperature of the fish is about the same as its surrounding medium—water. The fish cannot sustain a constant body temperature as a human does.

Senses and Nerves

SIGHT

As in other vertebrates, fishes possess sense organs and a nervous system. Besides having the obvious and most important sense—sight—they can also hear, touch, taste, and smell. Physical or chemical stimulus is received from the environment through the nerves, a spinal cord, and brain.

Although the eyes of a fish are adapted or modified for vision under water, they are not very different from human eyes. An eye may be compared to the workings of a camera, with a lens in front through which the light patterns enter to be recorded on the sensitive film or screen (retina in the fish eye). The optic nerve carries the image to the brain.

In essence, the fish eye consists of a transparent membrane called the "cornea" that covers a curved lens. The cornea and lens bend the incoming light rays so that they produce an image on the retina.

A fish has no true eyelids such as humans do. In humans, the eyelids perform an important function in preventing the eye from becoming dry and in preventing dirt from collecting on it. Since the fish's eye is constantly covered by water, it does not need a lid.

The iris—the metallic-looking ring surrounding the dark center of the fish eye—cannot move, as it does in humans. Our iris can widen or shrink. When the light is bright, only a pinpoint may be exposed in the center of the eye. On the other hand, the whole lens may be exposed when the light is poor. The fish needs no such adaptations because the light under water never attains great intensity. An important difference between the fish eye and human eye exists in the lens; it is spherical or globular in fishes and fairly flat or disklike in humans. In order to focus the eyes to varying distances, human eyes are capable of changing the curvature of the lens—flatter for long-range focusing and more curved for short-range. The fish has a rigid lens and its curvature cannot be changed, but it can be moved toward or away from the retina (similar to the focusing action of a camera). A special muscle called the "retractor lentis" is responsible for varying the distance between lens and retina; for short-range vision, the lens is moved away from the retina.

One outstanding similarity between the fish eye and the human eye intrigues scientists; it concerns the six muscles that move the eyeball. The same six muscles are controlled by the same six nerves and act the same way to move the eye on both humans and fishes. Although it may sound strange to most people, fish do move their eyes. This can be clearly seen by observing a large grouper through an aquarium window.

Many kinds of fishes have excellent vision at close range. This is made especially clear by the archerfish that feeds on insects. By squirting drops of water forcefully from its mouth into the air, it may shoot down a hovering fly or one resting on grass or weeds. As an archerfish prepares to make its shot, it approaches carefully to make certain of its aim and range. An archerfish is accurate at distances up to about three feet and is sometimes successful with even longer shots.

The four-eyed fish, one of the oddities of the fish world, lives in shallow, muddy streams in Central America. On the top of its head are bulbous eyes that are half in and half out of the water as the fish swims along near the surface. These eyes function as four eyes because of their internal structure—the lens is egg-shaped rather than spherical. When the fish looks at objects under the water, light passes through the full length of the lens and the four-eyed fish is as nearsighted as any other fish. When it looks into the air, the light rays pass through the shorter width of the lens, giving the fish good distance vision.

Fishes that live in the dusky or dimly lit regions of the sea commonly have eyes that are comparatively larger than the eyes of any other animal with backbones. Fishes that live in the perpetual darkness of caves or other subterranean waters usually have no eyes, but those that inhabit the deep sea, far below the depth to which light rays can penetrate, may or may not have eyes. The reason that most deep-sea fishes have well-developed eyes is the prevalence of bioluminescence. Deep-sea squid, shrimp, and other creatures, as well as fishes, are equipped with light-producing organs. The light they produce is used to recognize enemies or to capture prey.

Color Perception

One of the most popular questions asked by fishermen is: "Can fishes differentiate between colors?" The answer is yes. Color experimentation can be simple and yet effective. Fish can easily be trained to associate one color (say, red) with something desirable (food), and another (say, yellow) with something undesirable (a slight electric shock). Largemouth bass, for example, after being trained in that manner, will avoid yellow and swim to red even if food or the electric shock are not employed. Some scientists believed that it is the relative brightness of the various colors rather than the colors themselves that the fish distinguish. Further experimentation, however, proves that this is not so. All anglers will be interested to know that the largemouth bass (one of the most popular freshwater sport fishes) has a natural preference for red over all other colors; yellow is second.

It is not safe to generalize and say that fish in general respond best to red, because various species may differ in color responsiveness. However, scientists at a California fish hatchery have proved that trout also can distinguish color and that they preferred red color. Food pellets were colored blue, yellow, green, and red. The trout, of all sizes and ages, always chose the red ones first. To investigate further, the scientists colored corks red, blue, orange, brown, black, and white. These were presented to rainbows and brook trout in hatchery ponds in several ways. Again, a marked preference was shown for red. Another color that attracted them to a lesser degree was orange (yellow plus red). When the colored corks, with the red one withheld, were thrown on the water, the fish showed no interest. However, when a red cork was tossed in, the trout churned the water in an attempt to get at it. There was a possibility that the fish were attracted to it by a certain odor in the red color. So the colored corks were stretched across the pond by a string two to five inches above the surface. The trout not only congregated beneath the red corks, but leaped at them.

Another question that I am often asked is: "What is more important in a lure, color or action?" In my opinion, color and action are both important in underwater lures, but action is by far more important in a surface lure. Hold a colored lure, fly, plug (or any other object for that matter) against bright light and the color is lost; it appears uniformly dark or black; all one sees is a silhouette. Therefore, this is what happens with a surface lure: the fish cannot distinguish the color, and his choice to bite or not to bite depends on lure action alone. One of the deadliest lures I have used in many types of water for various species of fish has been a red-and-white spoon. The spoon wobbles from side to side, but the two bands of red sharply defined against a stripe of white between them is nicely visible because it runs deep and the light falls on it. Of course, there may be certain exceptions to the rule when refraction and position of the sun in relation to fish and lure are involved.

Sleep

Do fishes sleep? Yes they do, although it seems strange because they do not have eyelids. Sleep is a state of rest in which the body organs are recharged, so to speak. During this process, our minds are temporarily out of touch with the outside world. It is not our eyelids that cause sleep. When one considers that our ears are not shut nor is our ability to smell cut off during sleep, it is perfectly plausible that fish can sleep without a covering (that is, a lid) over their eyes. In sleep, bottom fishes or those that live near the bottom may rest on their fins, like the sea robin, or on their ventral side, like the flatfishes. Other fishes can sleep in midwater with the aid of slight and probably unconscious fin motions that balance the fish in a normal upright position.

Schooling fishes commonly separate periodically to rest. Then they become active again, and the schools reassemble. Some fishes lie on their sides when they rest; others lean against rocks or slip into crevices. Some kinds wriggle their way into the soft ooze at the bottom to take a nap, and some of the parrot fishes secrete a blanket of slime over the body at night. The preparation of this "bed" may take as long as an hour.

Hearing

Obviously, fishes do not possess outer ears as humans do, but they are capable of hearing. Our outer ears act as funnels to direct sound waves through a passage into the middle ear where the eardrum is located. The eardrum is set in vibration by sound waves. The vibrations are then transmitted to the inner ear by three little bones called "anvil," "hammer," and "stirrup." The inner ear is filled with fluid and surrounded by bone. The sound waves are then transformed into nervous impulses and carried by a nerve to the brain. Besides playing an important part in hearing, the inner ear also serves to keep us standing upright and walking in a straight line. The three semicircular canals of the inner ear are the organs of equilibrium. In other words, the human ear consists of an outer, middle, and inner ear, and functions both in hearing and in maintaining equilibrium.

The fish has only an inner ear, which is located in the bones of the skull. However, the absence of an outer and middle ear in fishes is not as disastrous to its hearing abilities as it might appear because water is a much better conductor of sound waves than is air. Some people have believed that a fish cannot hear at all because the mechanism (the spiral cochlea) that transforms sound waves into nervous impulses is not present in fishes. But experiments performed by several scientists have proved that fishes can indeed hear vibrations of varying intensities and that the inner ear is responsible for it.

The experiments were of a simple nature. The fish were anesthetized, certain nerves and portions of the inner ear were severed, and observations were made on the reactions to sound waves or vibrations set up in the water before and after the operations. The fish reacted to the sounds before the nerves and other parts were severed but showed no response after the operations. Similar experiments proved that the semicircular canals in a fish's ear play an important role in its equilibrium, as it does in humans.

Scientists have also definitely established by experimentation that the air bladder in many fishes aids them in hearing. Vibrations are transmitted to the ear from the air bladder, which acts as a sounding board. The air bladder is connected to the ear by a small bone called the "Weberian ossicle."

Why should fish possess the ability to hear? It is easy to understand why hearing is important to shallow-water fishes that live in an environment of manmade noises, splashing waves, and roaring winds. But one might wonder why the function is necessary in the deep sea. Actually, the underwater world is not a soundless one. Fishes make noises of all kinds: some croak (using the air bladder), some give off harsh sounds by grinding their flattened teeth, some even emit high squeaking sounds.

During World War II, the U.S. Navy discovered that ocean waters are much noisier than anyone had ever suspected. It is now common knowledge that the navy had trouble with a newly invented, highly sensitive submarine detector. The researchers found that the instrument picked up so many sounds that it was

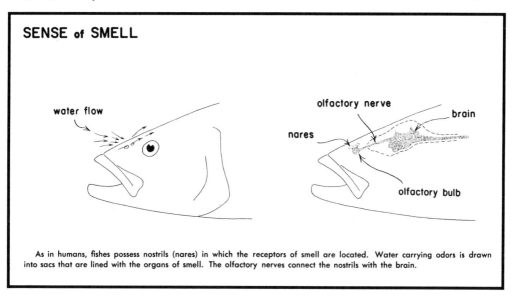

SENSE of SMELL

water flow

olfactory nerve

brain

nares

olfactory bulb

As in humans, fishes possess nostrils (nares) in which the receptors of smell are located. Water carrying odors is drawn into sacs that are lined with the organs of smell. The olfactory nerves connect the nostrils with the brain.

useless in identifying submarines. The navy eventually, however, discovered a way of screening out the sounds made by fishes and other sea animals.

Smell

As in humans, fishes possess nostrils in which the receptors of smell are located. But that is where the similarity ends. In humans, a passage connects the nostrils with the throat; but this is not so in fishes. Instead, two pairs of nostrils (openings called "nares"), one pair located on each side close to the top of the snout, open into small blind sacs immediately below the skin (one sac for each pair of nostrils, one nostril behind the other). Water carrying odors is drawn into the sacs, which are lined with the organs of smell. Either muscles or tiny, moving, hairlike cilia keep a current flowing into the front opening and out the other. The olfactory nerves connect the nostrils to the brain. Some species of fish possess an extremely keen sense of smell, especially sharks.

Taste and Touch

Fishes in general have taste organs located in the skin of the snout, lips, mouth, and throat. Although the fish's tongue is not fleshy, flexible, and muscular like the human tongue, it possesses taste buds that make it capable of tasting. The tongue is flat, rigid, and cartilaginous, and moves only when the base below it moves. (Some fishes have teeth on their tongues.) The taste buds on the tongue indicate to the fish whether to accept or discard an item taken into its mouth.

A close association exists between the senses of smell and taste in fishes as well as humans. The catfish and sturgeon, for example, are usually first drawn to food by its odor; but the food is not accepted until the whiskerlike barbels on the chin "feel and taste" it. The barbels contain taste buds. Some catfish have taste buds all over their bodies, and some can actually taste with their tails. Catfishes usually live on the bottom in dark water; their eyes are small, and nearly all their food is procured by smell and taste. Experiments with carp have proved that they are perceptive to sweet, salty, bitter, and acid tastes—the same as mammals.

Touch, the most basic sense, is possessed by all animals, including the lowest forms in the animal kingdom. The sense organs of touch in fishes are scattered over the surface of the skin (as they are in humans); they receive impressions from the outside and set up nervous impulses that travel from the taste buds or nerve endings into larger nerves to the brain. Some species of fishes, such as the previously mentioned catfishes and sturgeons, cod, haddock, pollock, and certain drums and croakers, possess barbels or feelers in varying numbers and forms located along the lower jaw. Some of the deep-sea fishes possess such feelers in extremely long or bizarre extensions.

Lateral Line

The lateral line is either conspicuous or visible in most fishes. It extends along the side of the fish's body from the gill opening to the tail. In some species it extends over the caudal fin or tail. And in most fishes, it extends on to the head and splits into several branches along the outer bones of the fish's skull, where it is not visible.

The typical lateral line is a sensory system that consists of a tube or canal under the skin. It is filled with mucus and has contact with the outside through pores in the skin, or through scales along the line or in between them. A nerve runs beneath the canal that at intervals sends out branches to it. Each branch has a sensitive end. Some fishes have several canals on each side of the body, and some possess lateral lines that are not continuous, but are broken, rather than lying in a single line.

The function of the lateral line was a subject for conjecture for many years, until scientists performed some experiments that eliminated the guesswork. We now know for sure that one of the chief functions of the lateral line system is to receive low-frequency vibrations. In this respect, it resembles a hearing organ of sensitivity greater than human ears. The lateral line may tell a fish when another is passing, may indicate the presence of prey or predator, or may be used to avoid obstacles that it cannot see in dark or silty water. The lateral line may receive sounds of oars against oarlocks, the scratch of a tackle box in a boat bottom, a footstep along a stream bank, a wobbling lure, or a sinker being dragged along the bottom. Perhaps the simplest way to describe the lateral line is to call it a sensory organ with a combined perception of touch and hearing.

The lateral line system also helps the fish to detect heat and cold. The fish does not have a constant body temperature as humans do; its body temperature is controlled by the water around it. If the fish runs into an abrupt change in temperature, an immediate reaction is noted. Fishes that can stand extreme temperature conditions when the change is gradual may die if the change is sudden. Therefore, the lateral line warns the fish of conditions such as this.

One of the most amazing facts concerning fishes is that some of them are capable of generating electricity. No other animal, to our present knowledge, possesses organs that can do this. The electric eel is well known for its ability to produce an electric current of shocking power. In a properly constructed aquarium, it can be demonstrated that the electrical current expelled by an electric eel can operate light bulbs. A lesser-known fact is that this fish's electric current not only stuns enemies and prey, but also produces harmful effects on its own eyes. Cataracts may form that eventually cause blindness. However, this handicap is overcome by its secondary output of weaker electrical discharges that acts as a sort of radar system. Sensory pits are located on the fish's head. They receive the reflections of these weak electrical currents from objects close by. Therefore, the electric eel is guided by this sensory system so that it can go about its activities as if its eyes were not blind.

The electric rays and the electric catfish also can produce electrical currents powerful enough to stun. Other fishes, such as the South African gymnotids and the African mormyrids, are also capable of producing electrical shocks, but of lesser potency. They set up an electric field around themselves; prey or predators breaking through this field warn the owner to be wary. The electric field also warns the fish of obstacles in the water that it may not see.

Pain

Do fish feel pain? That is another popular question. From the preceding sections on nervous system and sense organs, we gather that the answer must be yes. Probably, however, they feel pain merely as a warning sensation and do not suffer as we do. A fish cannot laugh or weep or scream. In other words, it cannot show its emotions or express pain. The fish brain is not highly developed. That part (the cerebral cortex) that stores impressions in higher animals is not found in a fish; in other words, the fish has little or no memory. Every angler has heard of incidents in which some fish has been caught two or three times, often within a short time. And it is not an uncommon incident for an angler to catch a fish that has a hook embedded in its jaws.

Although fishes, like other animals, may differ between individuals and between species, they are essentially creatures of reflex rather than action brought about by brain power. Therefore, an educated guess may be allowed here, and we might say that the physical sensation of pain in fishes is not very keen and that if there is any impression of pain recorded in their brain it is quickly forgotten. No one should feel that fishing is cruel.

Reproduction
SPERM AND EGG

A fish, like all other vertebrates (and most invertebrates), begins life as an egg. The egg is a single cell produced by the female. It cannot develop, however, unless a sperm produced by the male enters it. The sperm or spermatozoan is also a single cell. The union of the sperm and egg is called "fertilization." Although many thousands of spermatozoans are released by the male, only a single one is required to fertilize the egg. Fish sperm is usually referred to as "milt." The spermatozoan, tiny compared to the egg, has a type of tail by which it propels itself through the water (similar to a tadpole) in search of an egg to enter.

There are two basic ways in which the union between egg and sperm is brought about: (1) external fertilization, in which the egg is penetrated by the sperm after it leaves the female's body—the great majority of fishes use this system; and (2) internal fertilization, in which the male introduces the sperm into the female's body where it meets and fertilizes the egg. In this system, depending on the species, the egg may develop internally; that is, it is retained in the body of the female; it hatches there and finally a young fish emerges. Examples are the mako shark and the popular aquarium fishes, live-bearing tooth-carps. In other species, the egg is released and subsequently hatches outside as it does in some rockfishes of the Pacific Coast. (In some species of rockfish, the egg hatches inside the female.)

Spawning

Fish reproduction and associated activities are generally referred to as "spawning." The breeding period or spawning season is that time during which the reproductive apparatus—the eggs of the female and the sperm or milt of the male—are ripe. This condition may last only a few days, as in some warm-water species such as the largemouth bass, or extend over weeks or months in cold-water types such as the Arctic char or the whitefish. Some tropical fishes may spawn the year around. Generally, the warm-water fishes spawn during summer and cold-water species spawn during fall and winter. In areas of intermediate temperatures, fishes are generally spring spawners.

Spawning takes place in various types of environment, depending on the species of fish. Fertilized eggs, whether in the open sea, brackish, or fresh water, require certain conditions for successful development: correct amount of salt, sunlight, oxygen, and water agitation. In salt water, spawning may take place in the open ocean or closer to shore. In fresh water, spawning may take place in quiet waters where the fish makes and protects a nest, or it may take place in rapidly moving streams and rivers. Some species of fishes leave the salt water and enter rivers and streams to spawn.

The fishes of the open ocean that usually travel in schools participate in the external-fertilization-type spawning. They gather in huge groups and release their reproductive cells indiscriminately into the water. There is no effort at matching or pairing off. The eggs are at the mercy of currents, winds, temperatures, water salinities, and various other environmental factors. In this type of spawning, sometimes called "pelagic," the eggs of most species float freely. The eggs of some species of fishes, after external fertilization, sink to the bottom where they are preyed upon heavily by bottom fishes. In either case, parents show no concern for the eggs; spawning activity seems to be nothing more than relief from the pressure of overabundant sex products.

The striped bass is an example of a fish that leaves the salt water to spawn in freshwater rivers and streams; such fish are referred to as "anadromous." Its eggs are fertilized more or less freely, but a single female may be accompanied by a few to as many as fifty males. The eggs are nonadhesive, slightly heavier than water, and are rolled about by the current. The striped bass indulges in no parental care of eggs or young.

Salmon are also anadromous. Six species, one on the East Coast and five along the Pacific, enter freshwater rivers to spawn. (All Pacific salmon die after spawning. The Atlantic salmon may go back to sea and return the following year to spawn again.) Often they travel hundreds of miles before reaching the spawning site. Unlike the striped bass, they pair off and build a type of nest. These nests, called "redds," are built in clear water that is well oxygenated and runs over pebbly areas. The eggs sink in between the pebbles of the nest, where they are safe from predators. The parents, however, do not protect eggs or young. If the nest gets covered by silt, the eggs suffocate.

Bass and trout, popular sport fishes, indulge in different spawning habits. Therefore, it will be meaningful to most fisherman to summarize here each type. Largemouth bass spawning takes place in late winter and early spring in the South and from May to July in the various northern sections. Temperature is a controlling factor. The fish spawn when the water temperature reaches 64° to 73° F. in some areas, whereas in others most activity takes place when the temperature runs between 60° and 65° F. A sudden ten-degree drop in temperature under the normal conditions of the breeding season is enough to kill the eggs or the newly hatched fry. The fish usually select more or less sheltered bays in waters about two to six feet deep for spawning. The male makes a nest by excavating a depression in the sand or gravel bottom or among roots of aquatic vegetation. The nest may be two to three feet wide and six inches deep. He builds the nest by fanning the spot with his tail, and he moves small pebbles by carrying them away in his mouth.

The female may carry from about 2,000 to 26,000 eggs, depending on her size. However, counts as high as 40,000 eggs per single female have been reported. In water temperature of 66° F., about five days are required to hatch the eggs. A light deposit of silt on the eggs will cause the parents to desert their nests. This does not usually happen, because the fish fans the nest. However, if sudden heavy rain occurs over cultivated lands near the water, soil can be carried into the water to such an extent as to ruin the spawning beds. The male, with great pugnacity, guards the eggs and nest. He will immediately attack and drive off any intruder in his area. The male bass continues to protect the young fish until the school finally scatters. At this time, the fry may be about one-half inch in length. Pairs of bass may spawn about thirty feet apart, but they never nest in colonies as some of the smaller sunfishes often do.

The female trout usually digs the nest in the riffles or tail end of pools. She turns on her side and with powerful and rapid movements of the tail pushes around the pebbles, gravel, or other bottom materials, which are then carried a short distance downstream by the current. An oval or round depression is thus created. When the nest or egg pit is of the proper depth, both male and female take up a parallel position in the depression and the eggs and milt are simultaneously extruded.

Not many eggs are washed downstream, because there are no eddy currents in the nest. Actually, natural fertilization is a highly efficient process, and a high percentage (often 90 percent or better) of the eggs are fertilized. Immediately after the spawning act, the female digs another nest just upstream from the first nest, thereby covering the eggs with a layer of gravel. Several nests may be necessary and the spawning act repeated until the female has shed all her eggs.

The female is usually accompanied by one or more males during this process. The larger or more vigorous male may drive off the others.

The eggs of small fish may be covered with only an inch of gravel, while those of large trout (or salmon) may be buried in over six inches. Trout five or six inches in length may prepare nests ten or twelve inches long, whereas large females may develop an area over ten feet long before spawning is completed.

Spent fish drop down into pools where, in case of sea-run or lake inhabitants, they may wait for high water before drifting downstream and returning to the lake or ocean. Newly hatched fry remain in the gravel of the nest until the yolk sac, which provides the nourishment during this period, is absorbed. Depending on the species, the fry or fingerlings may remain in the stream for their lifetime, or they may drop down to the lake or migrate to the ocean after spending from one to a few years in the stream. (Salmon have the same type of spawning.)

Time requirements for incubation of eggs depend on the species of fish and the water temperature. For example, largemouth bass eggs hatch in about five days in water of about 66°F. The incubation period for brook trout is about forty-four days at 50°F. and about twenty-eight days at 59°F. Again, a sudden drop in temperature is usually enough to kill bass eggs or the newly hatched fry.

Attached to the typical newly hatched young fish, called a "larva," is an undigested portion of the yolk. This is usually enough food to last until the little fish has time to adjust to its aquatic world before it must begin hunting food for itself. Some kinds of fishes start to resemble their parents soon after coming from the egg and may themselves spawn within the year. Others require years of development before they mature.

Young flounders and other members of the flatfish family start life in an upright position, looking like any other little fish, but during the course of development the skull twists and one eye migrates to the other side of the head until finally both eyes are on the upper side of the fish.

Another startling example of differences in appearance between young and adult occurs in the prolific American eel (large specimens deposit 15 to 20 million eggs). The adult eels leave lakes, ponds, and streams to spawn in midwinter in the Sargasso Sea southwest of Bermuda and off the east coast of Florida. This is known as "catadromous" behavior. In its larval stage the American eel is thin, ribbonlike, and transparent. Its head is small and pointed; its mouth contains large teeth, although at this stage it apparently takes no food. The larval form lasts about a year. Then it metamorphoses to the elver, at which time the length and depth of the body shrinks but increases in thickness to a cylindrical form resembling the adult eel. The large larval teeth disappear, and the head also changes shape. The elver, however, does not take on the adult color, and it does not begin to feed until it reaches North American shores. Averaging two to three-and-one-half inches in length, the elvers appear in spring.

Carps and sturgeons are two of the big egg producers among freshwater fishes. When a female sturgeon is full of roe, the eggs may account for as much as 25 percent of her weight. The salted and processed eggs of sturgeons are prized as caviar, as is the roe of salmons, herrings, whitefishes, codfishes, and other fishes.

Bullheads and many tropical fishes lay their eggs in burrows scooped out of the soft mud at the bottom. Gouramis make a bubble nest, the males blowing bubbles that rise to the surface, stick together, and form a floating raft. After the nest is built, the female lays her eggs; the male then blows each egg up into the bubbles, where it remains until it hatches. The male stands guard under the raft to chase away intruders.

Male sea horses carry their eggs and also their young in a belly pouch. A female South American catfish carries her eggs attached to a spongy disc on her belly. Sea catfish males use their mouths as brooding pouches for their eggs; once the young are born, the pouches serve as a place of refuge until the young are large enough to fend for themselves.

Many species of fishes make nests. Some nests are elaborate, much like those made by birds. The male stickleback, for example, makes a neat nest of twigs and debris and defends it with his life. Other fishes simply sweep away the silt and debris where the eggs are to be laid and then continue to keep the nest clean and the water aerated until the eggs hatch.

Sex Determination

The sex of most species of fishes is easily determined during the spawning season. The female is usually much more potbellied than the male at this time because of the large quantity of eggs she carries. When the reproductive apparatus—milt of the male and eggs of the female—becomes ripe, a light press on the belly will cause the whitish milt or the eggs to be seen in the vent or anus. When the eggs and milt are in the advanced stages of ripeness, they can be forced out by massaging firmly and steadily along the belly from the head toward the tail. Hatcheries commonly use this method in their propagation practices. The eggs are collected in a pan and the male's milt is exuded onto the eggs. Eggs and milt are gently mixed, and thus fertilization takes place.

It is difficult to determine the sex of many fishes when they are not spawning or approaching the spawning season. Therefore, it is necessary to dissect or open the belly and search for the immature eggs or the milt sac.

As the spawning season approaches, some fishes develop outward signs that make their sex easily distinguishable. Trout and salmon males develop hook jaws, and an angular pugnacious effect is given to their head. Small horny tubercules appear on the snout and head of smelt, suckers, most species of minnows, and many other fishes, and they disappear shortly after spawning has been completed.

The males of many species have larger fins or extensions on them. Color often denotes sexual differences; the male in some species is generally brighter and his coloration is more intense than that of the female. Comparatively few fishes have permanent differences in their anatomy such as the squarish head of the male or bull dolphin and the tubelike extensions of the pelvic fins in male sharks, rays, and skates. The differences of anatomy between male and female in the various species of fishes are called "sexual dimorphism."

Migration

Migration may be defined as a mass movement of fishes or other animals along a direct route from one location to another at approximately the same time each year. Basically, migration is induced by two factors: food and spawning. Other mass movements take place for different reasons that are not to be confused with migration; sometimes fishes may move in large groups when sudden adverse conditions appear, such as pollution or sudden excessive sedimentation from unusual storms.

Oceanic game fishes may follow the abundance of bait schools for hundreds of miles or travel enormous distances between the southern spawning areas and the location of a great food supply in northern waters. Bluefin tuna, for example, after reaching northern waters, will seek and follow herring, sardines, or mackerel in the same localities year after year; but if the waters warm up or other water changes take place, and the bait schools depart from their usual haunts, the bluefins will leave the area and follow them.

Coastal fishes such as the striped bass and shad may travel short or long coastline distances before arriving in brackish stretches or freshwater rivers that fit the requirements for their spawning activities. Some species do not migate north and south, but instead travel offshore into deep water in cold weather and inshore during warm weather. Still others may combine the inshore-offshore type migration with a north-south movement.

The California grunion, a small, silvery fish, is an example of a unique and precisely timed migration. It spawns at the turn of high tide and as far up the beach as the largest waves travel. This action takes place during that period when the water reaches farthest up shore. The grunion deposits eggs and sperm in pockets in the wet sand. Two weeks or a month later, at the time of the next highest tide, when the water reaches the nests and stirs up the sand, the young are hatched and scramble out to sea before the tide recedes and prevents them from escaping.

Water temperature plays an important role in pinpointing the time of migrational departure or arrival of a certain species in a specific area. In other words, although some types of fishes may appear in an area at the same season each year, the exact dates are controlled by water temperature. For example, if spring weather is unusually cold in the Massachusetts area, the striped bass may arrive two or three weeks later than usual.

Some fishes make a practice of traveling with the tides, in to shore and out again, mostly searching for food. This habit should not be referred to as a migration but as a daily feeding habit, or "tide-running." Other fishes travel in vertical directions—from the depths to surface waters during night hours and back to the depths when daylight appears. Other species may travel offshore and onshore or upstream and downstream during daylight and darkness.

Stream-dwelling trout, suckers, lampreys, and carps usually travel upstream for spawning. Lake dwellers, such as lake trout, certain whitefishes, and landlocked populations of walleye, move to shoal waters for spawning. Lake-dwelling brook trout, brown trout, and landlocked salmon seek streams in which to spawn. If there is none, they may spawn in shallow areas where the water is moved by wind action.

Salmon are anadromous, as previously mentioned, and all have the same general life pattern. They are hatched in shallow streams, spend their early lives in fresh water, grow to maturity in the ocean, and then return to the stream of their birth to spawn. Among the species, and among populations of the same species, there is variation regarding the length of time spent in the freshwater and saltwater habitats. All Pacific salmon die after their first spawning. The Atlantic salmon drops back to salt water and may return to spawn again.

During the spawning migration into freshwater rivers, salmon travel at a rapid pace, and some cover thousands of miles. The Chinook, for example, is found spawning in the headwaters of the Yukon River. Chum and pink salmon usually spawn within a few miles of the salt water and often within reach of the tides. Dams, waterfalls, and other obstructions often block the path of migratory salmon.

What factor directs the extensive migration that causes salmon to return to their home rivers to spawn? Although the travels of salmon have been studied with increasing intensity for over eighty years, the mechanics of this phenomenon are not fully understood. Available data indicate that a high percentage of salmon return as adults to the stream in which they were born. The distinctive runs in various streams, the recapture of marked salmon, and the return of salmon that have been introduced into new streams prove this point. Young salmon, artificially propagated in hatcheries, return to the stream in which they were liberated, not to the stream to which their parents returned or in which they were hatched. Working experiments have shown little deviation.

One trend of thought, the "Zone of Influence Theory," does not credit the salmon with undertaking purposeful migrations. This theory maintains that salmon tend to stay in the water from their parent river as it forms a more or less recognizable zone in the sea. In other words, the fish simply follow, by scent, the traces of the river in the sea. Strong evidence indicates that salmon are passively transported in the sea, even to great distances. It is argued that the ascent or descent of a river by a salmon is not due to some ability to achieve a purposeful migration, but upon its existing physiological condition and upon its surroundings.

A set of interesting studies was conducted by scientist Hasler at the University of Wisconsin on the theories of migration; it was determined that the sense of smell may be a factor in the homing of migratory fishes. Experiments proved that water carries a distinctive odor, which, through discrimination and memory, may serve as a guide to the fishes in directing them toward their original habitat. It was also shown that fishes could distinguish between chemical differences in creeks.

The theory that a true homing instinct does not exist, and that fishes return to their birthplace only if they are near the influence of the fresh water from that stream, is weakened by facts concerning conditions of some California streams. The mouths of most of the salmonid streams (which salmon enter) are closed by sandbars during the entire summer. In some instances, the lower reaches are entirely dry—no fresh water reaches the ocean, yet the fish return to these rivers to spawn. The mechanics guiding the fish in its return to the parent stream are an intriguing problem that remains a subject for conjecture.

The habits of the eel present similar challenges to the scientist. For centuries, it was known that young eels (elvers) run up into fresh water in the spring, and adults migrate downstream in the autumn, but the life history of the eel was not known for many years. The breeding grounds of the American and European eels were discovered and the history of their larvae traced, mostly by the long researches of the Danish scientist Johannes Schmidt. Spawning takes place in midwinter off the east coast of Florida and southwest of Bermuda, in the depths of the Sargasso Sea. The zone of reproduction, apparently, is located between latitudes 20° and 30° N., and between longitudes 60° and 78° W. (The spawning grounds of the European eel are located to the eastward of this area, but portions of the spawning areas of the two species overlap.)

Most of the eels caught in fresh water are females, although some of them remain in salt marshes and harbors. Most males, after reaching the continental shores, stay in brackish waters or travel a relatively short way into a freshwater stream. The females migrate long distances and often travel thousands of miles from salt water. The females may spend about five to twenty years in ponds and lakes before returning to the sea to breed. In the course of migrating, eels may clamber over falls, dams, and other obstructions. They are also capable of squirming over rocks, wet grass, and through underground waterways. This answers one popular question: How do eels get into landlocked ponds and lakes? An Italian scientist proved, in his experiments with European eels marked for recognition, that they traveled thirty-one miles along underground waterways.

After spending several years in a lake or stream, the female stops feeding, becomes nearly black, and her eyes begin to enlarge as she commences the long journey to the Sargasso Sea. En route to the breeding grounds, the males join the females. The males at this time also become nearly black and their eyes become enlarged. The males have only grown to about a foot or so in length. These eels, as they approach sexual maturity, cease to feed in their travels downstream, which occurs mostly at night in the autumn. The American eels require one to two months to migrate from the coast to the spawning grounds. The eels disappear once they leave the shore. Not until the females move out to sea do the ovaries fully mature. No perfectly ripe female eel has ever been seen. Eels die after their first spawning. This fact seems evident, because no spent (spawned out) eel has ever been collected, and large eels have never been observed to run upstream again.

3

The Most Commonly Caught Game Fishes

Marine Game Fishes

Of the more than 20,000 species of fishes that inhabit our world, approximately 14,000 are marine. The International Game Fish Association currently accepts about 250 in its published list of saltwater game fishes. Obviously, it is not possible to give a full treatment of all species in this volume. Rather, the objective is to give the angler an overview of the more popular families of marine game fishes. For an inclusive guide to overall identification and distribution of all types of marine fishes, the two volumes in the Peterson Field Guide series mentioned in Chapter 1 are highly recommended. Chapter 1 also presents the vagaries of the technical classification of fishes.

The kingdom of fishes, as divided into two principal categories—(1) cartilaginous fishes, which include sharks, rays, and skates (with skeletons of cartilage, not true bone); and (2) the bony fishes—is accepted by fishery scientists as a natural separation. But aside from this major split, any further attempts at classification are controversial. This is especially true of any attempt to categorize in a popular way the individual marine game fishes. For example, they can be grouped in many ways: cold-water and warm-water types, reef fishes, rock fishes, migratory and nonmigratory, bottom fishes, surface fishes, big-game fishes, commercial kinds, light-tackle and heavy-tackle types, and so on. But regardless of the care used in placing each species in a particular niche, the results would not be satisfactory to all anglers and fishery scientists. Therefore, the list of marine sport fishes included in this chapter has been separated into two groups: (1) open-ocean fishes and (2) coastal and inshore fishes.

The family summaries to follow include only the more popular or better-known saltwater sport fishes found off the coasts of the continental United States, Canada, and Mexico. The family names, both common and scientific, are those recommended by the American Fisheries Society.

Marine Game Fish Families

Open-ocean Fish Families

Sailfishes, Marlins
Swordfish
Dolphins
Mackerels (tunas, bonitos, mackerels, wahoo)
Sharks

Coastal and Inshore Fish Families

Barracudas
Bluefish
Bonefish
Cods
Cobia
Croakers, Drums
Flatfishes
Greenlings, Lingcod
Grunts
Jacks

Tarpons
Sea Basses
Temperate Basses
Porgies
Scorpion fishes, Rockfishes
Surfperches
Snappers
Snook
Tripletail
Wrasses

Open-Ocean Fishes

SAILFISHES AND MARLINS: *Istiophoridae*

Fishery scientists generally agree that there are eight distinct forms in the billfish family *Istiophoridae:* Atlantic sailfish, Pacific sailfish, blue marlin, white marlin, striped marlin, black marlin, shortbill spearfish, and longbill spearfish (spearfishes are rare). They are spectacular, oceanic game fishes noted by the extension of the upper jaw into a weapon commonly referred to as a bill or spear.

The range of the Istiophorids seems to be restricted by definite barriers of water temperature. Both above and below the equator, these fishes are seldom found where surface temperatures fall below 59°F. For example, on the west coast of the United States, under normal conditions, the 59° line occurs off southern California; in South America, off southern Chile. In between these two temperature lines, billfishes are found. If 59° is a confining factor, then it seems likely that these fishes are restricted also to the upper layers of the water whose temperatures range above 59°.

Inhabiting tropical and subtropical seas of the world, sailfishes are the most abundant members of the billfish clan to be found off our coasts in the Atlantic and the Gulf of Mexico. Everyone recognizes them immediately because they carry huge saillike dorsal fins on their backs.

A prime favorite with a multitude of fishermen, the sailfish is the easiest to catch and usually the first large fish taken by most budding big-game anglers. On the other hand, the fish's leaping, skittering acrobatics when hooked are spectacular enough to excite the most experienced sportsman. The Atlantic sailfish, also found in the Gulf of Mexico, reaches a weight of about 128 pounds; its Pacific cousin may weigh about 100 pounds heavier. In the United States the flesh is not

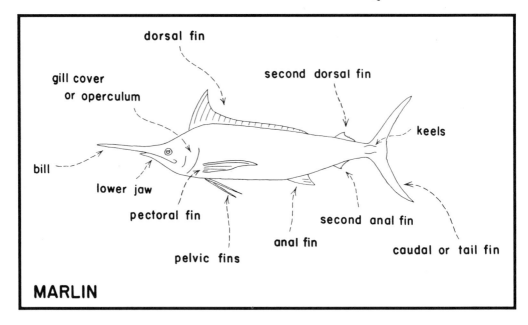

MARLIN

considered excellent as food. When smoked, however, it is delicious and growing in popularity.

As a group, marlins are considered the elite of big-game fishes. These blue-back gamesters are extremely fast, with an estimated speed of thirty to sixty miles an hour. Marlin prefer the warmer blue-water currents of the open seas. They are famous for their acrobatics—twenty, thirty, or even forty jumps displayed by a hooked fish are not rare.

Angling techniques employed in capturing the billfish are based upon its feeding habits. The usual method is to troll a bait from the outrigger; the bait skips and dances on the surface; the billfish is attracted and hits the bait; the line comes down from the outrigger, allowing slack line; the slack-line interval permits the bait to appear stunned; the fish grabs it and the angler sets the hook. But this does not always happen in such a cut-and-dried manner. Sometimes the fish, after hitting the bait, will wait a bit before taking it. Often, the billfish will crash-strike the bait without tapping it first.

Many stories revolve around the ferociousness of billfishes and their prowess in attacking vessels. Some of the tales are without foundation, but many are backed by evidence. It is not unusual for a marlin to strike and damage a vessel, especially when the fish is hooked or harpooned.

SWORDFISH: *Xiphiidae*

The swordfish, also known as "broadbill swordfish," derives its name from its upper swordlike, prolonged, and flattened upper jaw; within its family there exists only one species. It is a famous sport fish, important commercially, and is found around the world in tropical, and primarily temperate, oceanic waters.

Generally speaking, it prefers warm waters and is usually most plentiful in areas where the temperature is higher than 60°F. However, facts show that the swordfish tolerates colder waters than do the marlins. For example, swordfish have been caught on halibut lines set at depths of 200 fathoms. It is not unusual for swordfish, taken on the offshore banks of the Gulf of Maine, to contain in their stomachs different types of deep-sea fishes that live outside the continental shelves, mostly below 150 fathoms. It is evident, therefore, that the swordfish do some foraging at great depths far out to sea. These instances may substantiate the belief that their very large eyes indicate deep-water habits. Also, the broadbill is found on the Newfoundland banks, which proves that they can tolerate waters as low as 50° to 55°F. Evidence indicates that swordfish frequent the depths during nightfall and surface in daylight.

DOLPHINS: *Coryphaenidae*

Dolphins (not to be confused with the porpoise) are beautiful and exceedingly fast inhabitants of the open seas. They spend much time near the water's surface and

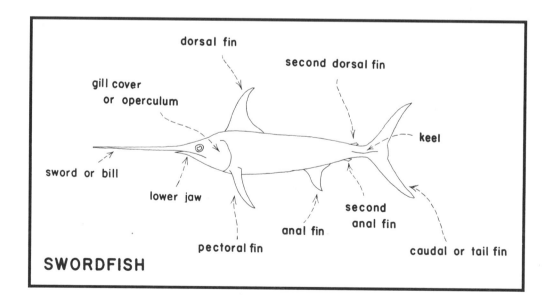

SWORDFISH

rate highly as food and game fishes. The usual method of fishing for them is by trolling. Although gregarious and fairly common, nowhere do they appear in quantities large enough to induce a commercial fishery. They are distributed widely throughout the oceans of the world in warm waters (preferably not below 70°F.).

The other member of this family is the much smaller pompano dolphin. Both are easily recognized by the long-based, continuous dorsal fin, extending almost from head to tail.

MACKERELS: *Scombridae*

Tunas, bonitos, mackerels, and wahoo form one of the most important groups of fishes in the sea, for they supply a great amount of the world's protein food. They are often referred to as tunalike or mackerellike fishes, or scombrids. The annual commercial and sporting catch runs to many millions of pounds. Their thick bodies are sold in the market, steaked, filleted, or canned, but because of their rich blood supply the meat can spoil rapidly in the tropics and cause "scombroid" food poisoning. About thirty-nine species are currently recognized.

All members of this group possess finlets; these are small fins situated on the dorsal surface between the second dorsal fin and tail fin and on the ventral side between the anal fin and tail.

The family *scombridae* provides both sport and commercial fishing in all oceans. They constitute an international resource; home to them is no particular country. Nearly all spend their lives and reproduce their young outside the territorial limits of any nation. All are swift, predacious, oceanic, schooling fishes distributed in greater or lesser abundance throughout the world's great bodies of water. These powerfully muscled, streamlined fishes generally do not jump or perform acrobatics when hooked. Instead, they zoom off like torpedoes; and every member of the clan is capable of sustaining an amazing amount of resistance when worked with rod and reel of proper size in relation to the fish. Typically, the fight of a scombrid is a long, fast run followed by a series of smaller runs, with a tendency to circle when approaching the gaff or landing net.

TUNAS In the oceans and seas of the world, the tunas are the giants of the scombrids. All are superior game fishes, and some are ranked among the world's best. The tunas all have robust, streamlined, bullet-shaped bodies that immediately separate them from the slender mackerels. Any tuna can be distinguished from the bonitos, skipjacks, or wahoo at a glance. Tunas have dark backs and silvery sides minus stripes, bars, dark spots, or any other pronounced markings that the other scombrids possess. The rod and reel world record for the largest of the tribe, the bluefin tuna, is 1496 pounds, taken off Nova Scotia.

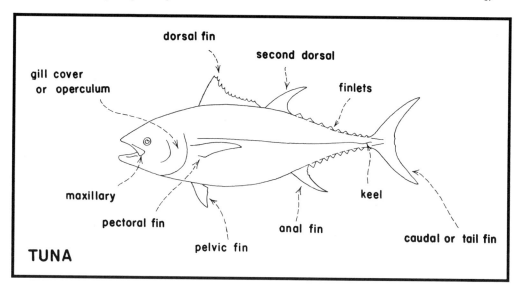

TUNA

BONITOS The bonitolike fishes—Atlantic bonito, Pacific bonito, skipjack tuna, little tuny, bullet mackerel, and frigate mackerel—are close cousins of the tunas. They are migratory, fast swimmers that travel in large schools in the open oceans. Like their larger relatives, they possess strong, streamlined, bullet-shaped bodies that contain strength and endurance. To sportsmen, this group is one of the most distinguished and bewildering of all game fishes. Although mackerels are easily distinguished from tunas, anglers have difficulty in identifying some members of the mackerel family. And that is not surprising because, with the extensive distribution of these fishes and the multiple use of names, fishery scientists also have problems with the popular use of names and technical identification of these widely traveled scombrids.

MACKERELS Close relatives of the tunas and bonitos, the mackerel tribe is one of the most important and most popular groups of scombrids plying the Atlantic and Pacific oceans. Commercially, mackerel are valued for there table qualities; and sportsmen rate these fishes highly for their fighting ability. They range the open sea and coastal waters in large, fast-swimming schools while searching for masses of bait fish to feed on. The mackerels' bodies are more slender than those of the tunas and bonitos.

WAHOO The wahoo is an oceanic fish found in the warmer portions of the great oceans. They are streamlined, cigar-shaped, and renowned for their speed when hooked. Not much scientific work has been done on the life history of this fish. It is not known whether or not there is a single species with worldwide distribution.

There is a question regarding some mackerellike fishes found along the western Pacific as to whether they are a species of mackerel or young wahoo.

SHARKS

Sharks, most commonly accepted by the general public as the predators of the seas, are not all dangerous. Many are small and inoffensive, especially those found in deep waters. The number of species accepted by ichthyologists is about 300. About twenty-five species are known to attack man, with the white shark having the greatest reputation as "the man eater." As an indication of its maximum size, the rod and reel record for this shark is 2664 pounds caught off South Australia. The majority of sharks are of moderate size, but some are huge—the basking shark reaches about forty-five feet in length and the whale shark over sixty feet. Although these two are the largest of the shark tribe they are not predators; they feed on tiny plankton strained from the water.

Many different types of sharks abound in all seas, but they are in greatest profusion in tropical and subtropical waters. Some cruise the high seas, but most of them inhabit relatively shallow water along the coasts. Some live predominantly near the surface; others live at or near the bottom; and still others inhabit the great depths. Some sharks swim constantly, others may rest on the bottom or in caves. Few types enter large rivers and travel far enough upstream to enter fresh water.

The typical sharks, as opposed to the rays and skates, have a shark shape, and

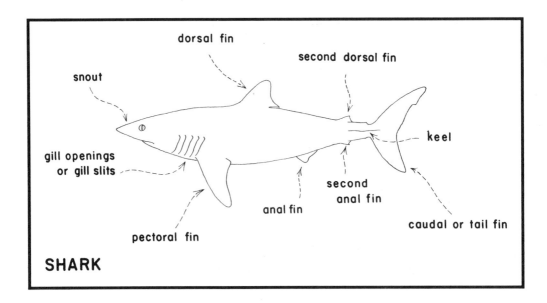

SHARK

a large mouth usually on the underside of the head. The majority have five gill slits on each side of the head in front of the pectoral fins; some have six or seven. Nearly all have several rows of sharply pointed teeth, one or more rows being functional. When the functional teeth break off or are worn down they are replaced by the teeth from the next row. The number and shape of the teeth, especially those in the upper jaw, aid in identification. Shark teeth resist deterioration and are often found on beaches. Great numbers of teeth, polished by wave action and sand, are washed ashore and collected for sale as fossils in curio shops.

The attitude toward sharks as food fishes has changed dramatically during the past few years. Formerly only the mako was considered fit to eat, and only a few anglers enjoyed it occasionally on the table. But today mako meat is considered as good as swordfish and brings high prices at the fish market. The taste for other species of shark has also increased generally; in addition, the demand for shark fins in Asiatic countries and the absence of the predators where long-liners have worked has created a concern among conservationists because sharks have a slow growth rate and do not produce many young. There is a present feeling that sharks are being overexploited and that some restrictions should be placed on their harvest.

Although the IGFA's annual record book lists about twenty-five species of shark, it could be debated that all of them are true game fishes. Be that as it may, charter boats that specialize in rod and reel shark fishing are rapidly increasing; otherwise, most sharks are caught as incidental to fishing for other types of game fishes.

Whether or not certain kinds of sharks should be accepted as game fishes can be questioned. But one fact, in my estimation, remains clear: from my experiences in fishing many seas and catching different kinds of sharks, the mako is by far on top of the list as a sport fish.

Anyone who has witnessed the graceful leaps of a mako as its blue and silvery body reflected the sunlight, will agree that when alive it is a handsome fish. Most sharks are dull brownish or grayish in color, but the mako is a beauty. When alive, its dorsal surface is a deep cobalt blue that meets the silvery sides in a sharp line of demarcation. The entire ventral surface is white. The mako has wicked-looking teeth which are sharply pointed; most of them curve inward. They are smooth-edged without lateral denticals, and the first two in each jaw are much the largest. The teeth that follow toward the rear are broader and more bladelike.

The mako is mostly a fish eater and is often seen pursuing mackerel and other fishes; that is why this speedster will often take a fast-trolled bait on the surface intended for marlin or sailfish. It does not hesitate to attack and feed on larger fishes. On record, a 730-pound mako taken off Bimini in the Bahamas was found to have a 120-pound swordfish in its stomach. Another specimen of about 800 pounds harpooned off Montauk, New York, had been seen attacking a swordfish. When opened the mako contained about 150 pounds of its victim.

When hooked, this shark not only jumps clear of the surface in a spectacular manner but it also makes strong runs. Much of the action is near the surface, and its dogged resistance to rod and reel makes the mako a first-class big-game fish. The largest mako captured by an angler to date in the north Atlantic occurred off Montauk, New York; it weighed 1,080 pounds.

And as an additional note: the flesh of a mako is tender, juicy, and delicious, and comes closest in taste to young swordfish. For best culinary results I suggest skinning the shark as soon as possible and placing the meat on ice or in a cooler for a day or two before eating or freezing for future use.

For the identification of the sharks of the Atlantic and Pacific coasts of North America I recommend the *Peterson Field Guides* listed in chapter 1.

Coastal and Inshore Fishes

BARRACUDAS: *Sphyraenidae*

There are close to two dozen kinds of barracudas inhabiting the oceans of the world. Along our shores, five are recognized: four in the Atlantic and one in the Pacific. Because of its large size and ferocious appearance, the great barracuda of the Atlantic receives most attention from anglers. Barracudas have injured people; but these are cases of mistaken identity, sometimes in turbid water. Flashy light of wristbands, face masks, camera lenses, and so on, will attract barracuda and sometimes cause them to strike. A wounded barracuda may turn and strike a spear fisherman. The Pacific barracuda does not grow as large as the great barracuda but is much more numerous; many are taken by sportsmen and commercial fishermen. The other three are small species. All are warm-water fishes that prefer shallow, inshore reef areas and are quite similar in appearance. The characteristic long, pikelike body and outstanding dentition separate them easily from all other saltwater fishes.

The great barracuda may reach a length of six feet and a weight of eighty-three pounds. They are good eating, but occasionally cause food poisoning because some of them may contain ciguatera toxin.

BLUEFISH: *Pomatomidae*

The bluefish, generally considered the only member of its family, is an important food and game fish; it is voracious and travels about swiftly in large schools. It is exceptionally strong and renowned for its sporting qualities when taken on rod and reel. On the table it is excellent. Much publicity is given the bluefish "attacking" bathers; such injuries from bites are accidental when bluefish chase schools of small fishes into shallow water.

BONEFISH: *Albulidae*

Unquestionably, the silvery, bottom-living bonefish ranks with the best of the world's game fishes, especially when taken on a fly rod and artificial fly. It is found in the clear, warm waters of tropical and subtropical seas and often feeds on mollusks, crustaceans, and worms in shallow areas where sometimes schools are located in water only a few inches deep. When they grub for food on the bottom their tails may break the water surface as they feed. *Albula vulpes* (white fox) is well named because it is usually one of the most wary of fishes.

CODS: *Gadidae*

The cod group—cod, pollock, haddock, and tomcod—are characterized by lack of fin spines. They are bottom dwellers important commercially and in sportfishing. All are delectable on the table. They occur in arctic and cold-temperate shelf and slope waters. Many retreat into deep water during the winter.

COBIA: *Rachycentridae*

The cobia is the only species in its family. Although it has a sluggish appearance, it is excellent both as a table delicacy and as a sport fish. More names commonly are attributed to this fish than any other popular saltwater rod and reel species.

CROAKERS AND DRUMS: *Sciaenidae*

This family, comprising a group of diversified fishes—weakfishes, croakers, drums—are distributed in warm-temperate and tropical seas mostly in muddy bays, estuaries, and shallow waters. Some are inhabitants of reefs whereas others are almost entirely oceanic; a few species are found in fresh water. Of the many species that make up the clan, a comparatively few are of interest to anglers. They range from small reef fishes to types that migrate fairly long distances and grow to large sizes. All are fine table fishes, and many are of considerable economic importance. Several representatives of this group rank with the elite of our smaller game fishes, especially in the opinion of surf casters and pier fishermen.

Along the Atlantic shores of the United States, the weakfish, spotted sea trout, black drum, and red drum (channel bass) rank high with sportfishermen. The spot, a pan-size drum, is a popular food and sport fish with bridge and pier anglers. In the waters of the eastern Pacific, from southern California to Peru, at least fifteen different species of the genus *Cynoscion* are found. They closely resemble and possess characteristics of their Atlantic relatives.

Along the coast of southern California, the white sea bass is a large croaker growing to about five feet in length and ninety pounds in weight; it is a fine game fish. Most of the other members of this group are found in greatest abundance in Mexican waters and southward.

Many fishes in the croaker clan possess common names that include in part the words "drum" or "croaker." The common names are a matter of choice in different areas. Croakers have large calcareous "ear stones" in their inner ear canals, considered good-luck pieces by early Europeans and used by American Indians in jewelry and other ornaments.

FLATFISHES: *Bothidae, Pleuronectidae, Soleidae*

The flatfishes comprise a large group of commercially important fishes. This tribe includes the halibuts, flukes, flounders, turbots, and soles. It is hardly necessary to state that the outstanding characteristic of this group is the flat body, that is, compressed from side to side; but perhaps many anglers do not realize that the different species swim either on one side or the other, being right-sided or left-sided flatfishes. When young, they look much like other fish larvae; but during the course of development, the skull twists and one eye migrates to the other side of the head so that finally both eyes are on one side. The entire underside of the body is usually white or light gray, while the top side is colored, usually in dull brown like the bottom on which they are found. The very long dorsal and anal fins, which run along the edges of the body, are also characteristic of this group.

The flatfishes are an unusually large tribe with more than three hundred species known worldwide. They range in size from a few inches in length to enormous fish (halibut) of hundreds of pounds. Nearly all spend most of their lives on or close to the bottom, feeding predominantly on invertebrate life, although some species are very active and voracious attackers of small fishes. Most are inhabitants of salt water; a few types may be found occasionally in brackish and fresh water.

Although they contribute greatly to man's food supply, not many are known as sporting fishes. Only a few kinds are of interest to sportsmen or are taken consistently by rod and reel.

The American Fisheries Society separates the group into three sections: *Bothidae*, left-eyed flounders; *Pleuronectidae*, right-eyed flounders; and *Soleidae*, soles (eyes and color also on the right side).

GREENLINGS AND LINGCOD: *Hexagrammidae*

This fairly small family of fishes, related to the rockfishes and sculpins, has a limited distribution along the North Pacific shores. Of the group, two species stand out as food and sport fishes—the kelp greenling and the lingcod; the former is commonly found on kelp beds and sand bottoms. It is caught by shore and skiff fishermen and speared by divers. The lingcod is a valuable commercial species as well as being an important sport fish. The adult lingcod loves rocky areas, inshore and out in deep water. Spear fishermen consider it a prize to capture because a large specimen may measure to five feet in length and sixty pounds in weight. Because of its size and wide distribution along the Pacific coast it is the best-known member of the *Hexagrammidae*.

GRUNTS: *Haemulidae*

Grunts are medium-sized, perchlike species living in tropical and subtropical waters around the world. They feed mostly at night on small fishes, crustaceans, and other small invertebrates, but come into sheltered areas—reefs, harbors, and under piers and docks—during the day where, because of their abundance and excellent pan-fried qualities, they are avidly sought by fishermen.

Haemulids closely resemble the snappers, but do not have teeth in the roof of the mouth. The genus *Haemulon* contains many species. The name "grunt" is derived from the grunting sound these fishes are capable of producing. The sound is made when the upper pharyngeal (throat) teeth grate against the lower teeth. The swim bladder also acts as a sound-making device. Yellow color is found in various degrees in most of the species, and many have splashes of red on the inside of the mouth. When young, some of the species have two or more horizontal dark lines along the sides.

JACKS: *Carangidae*

The family *Carangidae* includes jacks, amberjacks, pompanos, and scads. They are medium to large swift-swimming fishes that inhabit warm waters around the world and number between 140 and 200 species, depending on where the information comes from. Twenty-seven dwell along the Atlantic coast of North America and twelve, along our Pacific coast.

Most jacks are silvery bright on the sides that shade darker above, but they lack bright colors. Although mostly regarded as sport fishes in the United States, they are fished for commercially in the Indian Ocean and South Pacific. Some species (definitely the great amberjack) are known to contain ciguatera toxin, which can cause a type of severe food poisoning.

Most of the carangids have a series of sharp scutes along each side of the caudal peduncle (just anterior to the tail fin) that may inflict a nasty wound to the careless angler. They usually rove in closely packed schools and are located easily when chasing small fish because they create a commotion on the surface of the water that can be seen from a long distance. They seldom jump but produce a dogged resistance characterized by short but powerful runs that delight the angler.

TARPONS: *Elopidae*

"The silver king, greatest of game fishes" is a phrase often used to describe the tarpon. Whether it rates as the greatest is debatable. However, it certainly is the most available of our big-game fishes; and because of its exciting jumping after being hooked, it surely is one of the most spectacular of the larger gamesters. It also holds the distinction of being the only one of our highly respected game fishes that is almost completely ignored as a food fish.

The ladyfish, a member of the same family, is a well-known, silvery coastwise fish that often travels in schools and is found in warm seas. It resembles a small tarpon.

SEA BASSES: *Serranidae*

The sea basses consist of a worldwide group of small to giant fishes, mostly of tropical coastal waters, but with many species that occur along temperate seas. The serranids are related to the popular freshwater family of basses, *Centrarchidae*. The marine and freshwater families closely resemble one another in body form, fin arrangement, and other anatomical features. However, technical characteristics distinguish the groups into separate families. Generally, the carnivorous assemblage of saltwater basses is divided into the following categories: sea basses, giant sea basses, groupers, and rock basses. Although the great majority are inhabitants of warm, tropical seas, a few species range into cold waters as far north as Nova Scotia and the St. Lawrence River.

There is no other large group of fishes where the individual species resemble one another so closely as in the bass fishes. The general appearance of the members of this family is usually accepted as the most typical or the most fishlike of fishes. They all have large mouths containing teeth, and the maxillaries (upper lips) are prominent. There is a great diversity of coloration among them, and with individuals the color changes are astounding. The basic color, spots, stripes, bands, and other markings may appear in different degrees of vividness or may disappear—all depending on the changing emotions of the individual fish.

Rock bass is a good name for any of the serranids because they prefer rocky areas and reefs and are more or less sedentary in habit. They usually inhabit an area that is not affected by tidal flow or rips, but they may take part in some offshore-onshore movement. Most of their time is spent close to the bottom; and among their items of diet will be found fishes, shrimps, and crabs.

The sea basses are important to anglers, spear fishermen, and commercial fishermen. They are also prized by marine aquarists. All are excellent food fishes, although the meat of a few of the large, fish-eating types is known to cause ciguatera, a fish poisoning.

TEMPERATE BASSES: *Percichthyidae*

Previously grouped with the family *Serranidae*, the striped bass, one of the most popular sport fish with surf casters along the Atlantic coast (introduced to California waters in 1879 and 1882), is now classified by researchers as a member of the *Percichthyidae*. Taxonomists use anatomical features to separate them from the true marine basses. The striped bass migrates along the coast and moves into rivers to spawn in fresh water. It has declined drastically in numbers in recent years mostly because of pollution in its spawning waters. Some populations are landlocked.

The white perch is another popular sport and pan fish along Atlantic coastal waters, mostly along mouths of rivers and in brackish and fresh waters.

PORGIES: *Sparidae*

Although the porgies are small to medium in size, they are important as food and sport fishes and are found in warm-temperate and tropical coastal waters. They number about 120 worldwide species and are most common in bays, banks, and coral reefs.

The porgies are deep bodied, compressed, and energetic. Rowboat anglers take special delight in catching them. When taken on light tackle, porgies demonstrate a surprisingly strong resistance to rod and reel and are easy to catch on almost any kind of cut bait or worms. When the porgies are hitting there is not much waiting between bites.

SCORPION FISHES AND ROCKFISHES: *Scorpaenidae*

This is the largest family along the Pacific coast of North America, with about sixty-five species; about twenty-five species occur off the eastern coast of the United States. Along the California and Oregon coasts, rockfishes are common in clean bays, along shore, in kelp beds, and offshore to great depths. Rockfishes look very much alike in general appearance and are often difficult to distinguish as to separate species.

Some anglers do not consider the members of this clan to be game fishes. However, in recent years, rod and reel fishing for rockfishes has increased greatly. Now they are generally considered one of the more important groups recognized by sportsmen. The fin spines are associated with venomous tissue in most species and can cause huge discomfort to any angler pricked by them. Some Pacific and Indian Ocean species (stonefishes) are very dangerous when handled, or when stepped on in shallow water; they have caused painful fatalities.

SURFPERCHES: *Embiotocidae*

Surfperches are found only in the North Pacific. Along the California coast occur about twenty species. They are well-known, small, pan-size fishes that prefer shallow inshore waters, usually in the surf, along rocky areas or sandy shores. Many species are great favorites with surf, skiff, and pier fishermen because they are easily taken on baited, small hooks and are a delicacy on the table. Commercially, they are harvested in fairly good numbers. Most species are silvery; a few are brightly colored. The members of this family are of unusual interest because the females bear young alive. (Nearly all other bony fishes spawn eggs that are fertilized externally.)

SNAPPERS: *Lutjanidae*

The snappers comprise a large, worldwide family of predacious warm-water fishes found in tropical and subtropical regions. Although of mainly shore waters, some species are wide ranging and oceanic. Valued for both their commercial and sporting qualities, they prefer to live close to the bottom most of the time, along shore and offshore rocky areas, around islands and rocks, in sloughs, mangrove locales, and sometimes close to shore along surf and sandy beaches. It appears that most of the species do not migrate lengthy distances and seem to be present the year round in the areas they inhabit. Snappers from deep, rocky slopes are usually red. Reef types are tan and yellow, often with some red.

Members of this clan all have, more or less, the same feeding habits and will take small fishes, crawfish, crabs, and marine worms. They appear to be voracious but cautious. Often, the angler cannot coax them to take any type of bait or lure. Usually chumming with ground bait will attract and induce them to strike.

All snappers caught on rod and reel, regardless of their size, put up a fine scrap. Often they will make a strong run or two and then attempt to head for the rocks. They are not only fun to catch; they rate as one of the best of food fishes. The flesh of the dog snapper and the cubera snapper is sometimes toxic when eaten and may cause ciguatera.

SNOOK: *Centropomidae*

The snook is an excellent and unusual food and game fish widely distributed in Central America, northern South America, throughout the West Indies, and north to Texas and South Carolina. It is available to the most diversified group of anglers and appreciated by all, from the fly-rod purist to the cane-pole fisherman sitting on a canal bank.

The snook is a coastal fish that has made its best reputation along the shores of Florida and the Gulf of Mexico. It hugs the shore and prefers brackish areas. Occasionally, it strays into nearby fresh waters. Many are taken by anglers far up rivers and in drainage canals such as abound in southern Florida. It also frequents inlets, channel banks, under mangrove banks, and around bridge and pier pilings. Rocky areas, sandy shores, and jetties of stone and rock are also spots where the snook can be found. In other words, there are large populations spread in different types of locales throughout its range.

When hooked, the snook cannot be "horsed," for the hook tears out of the soft mouth fairly easily. Often, it will jump a couple of times when first hooked; and many are lost at this point. Most of the resistance to the angler's efforts is dogged and strong. The edges of the operculum (cheek plates) are sharp, and the fisherman should take notice when handling a flopping fish.

TRIPLETAIL: *Lobotidae*

The tripletail, well known along the shores of northeast Florida as chobie, is a close relative of the snapper but is placed in a separate family, *Lobotidae*. Similar in general mode of life and choice of warm waters to most of the marine basses, it also takes a baited hook readily.

The common name is derived from the unusual placement of the second dorsal and anal fins, which are located posteriorly on the body close to the tail. When these fins are folded back, they produce a superficial appearance of three tail lobes, hence, tripletail.

The tripletail seems to be a fish that inhabits different types of waters; it may be found in the shallows and it may enter river mouths. Often, it frequents waters as deep as twenty-five fathoms, and sometimes it schools and feeds along surf areas and beaches. It likes rocky areas and may be found around submerged wrecks and pilings. The tripletail may occur solitary, in a small group, or in schools. It is primarily a bottom fish with a choice of food in shrimp, crustaceans, and small fishes. Compared with other basslike fishes, the tripletail is not often hooked by anglers; but when taken on light tackle, it is a scrapper. It may take an artificial lure, but baits are by far the best producers. Most authors state that this fish is edible. I have eaten several and found them to be excellent.

WRASSES: *Labridae*

Wrasses, found worldwide mostly in the tropics with a few occurring in warm temperate waters, constitute one of the largest families of fishes in existence—between 400 and 500 species. Many are brightly colored. Most wrasses have protruding tusklike teeth that help in picking food off rocks and reefs. In some species sex reversal is known, that is, an individual fish first functions as a female, but changes to a male in later life. Even though there is a great profusion of species, very few are pursued with rod and reel. Two of the most popular taken by sportsmen along United States shores are the tautog in the Atlantic, where it is an avidly sought sport fish along the northeast coast, and the California sheepshead, which has declined because of fishing pressure, including spearfishing, and reduction of kelp beds.

Freshwater Game Fishes

The true freshwater game fishes are closely bound to land masses. About 6,000 species, found throughout the world, are mostly confined to their own watersheds or drainage systems. North America has a varied assortment of types that number approximately 600 species within twenty-one families. Here, however, we are concerned with game fishes, those most commonly caught by rod and reel. The International Game Fish Association lists about 110 freshwater fishes in their annual publication, *World Record Game Fishes*. And since it is beyond the objectives of this volume to treat all of them individually, the following overviews of families include only the freshwater sport fishes of North America. A few of the families have representatives found in both fresh water and salt water: some are marine fishes that enter fresh water only to spawn; but they all can be taken by rod and reel in either freshwater ponds, lakes, streams, or rivers.

Inquisitive anglers seeking more detailed information concerning specific species of freshwater game fishes may consult the related reading listed at the back of the book.

The family names, both common and scientific, are those recommended by the American Fisheries Society.

Freshwater Game Fish Families

Sturgeons
Paddlefish
Gars
Bowfin
Herrings
Whitefishes, Grayling, Trouts, Salmons
Smelt
Mooneyes
Pikes (pickerel, pike, muskellunge)
Minnows, Carps
Suckers
Catfishes
Eels
Codfishes
Temperate Basses
Sunfishes
Cichlids
Perches
Drums

The first and most primitive group of freshwater fishes is made up of four North American families generally categorized as "living fossils"; the group includes sturgeons, paddlefish, bowfin, and gars. These fishes are referred to by scientists as the "primitive ray-fins," because they have not changed much in form from their ancestors of millions of years ago. In other words, this group has survived through the centuries, while many relatives have long since become extinct. Fossil remains of the ancestors of these fishes are found in Europe and the United States.

STURGEONS: *Acipenseridae*

The sturgeons are ancient fishes distributed widely in Europe, Asia, and North America. They tolerate a wide range in water temperatures and in types of water, from the salty ocean and silty rivers to clear, cool lakes and streams.

All sturgeons possess long snouts. A fleshy, protrusible, suckerlike mouth situated on the underside of the head is an adaptation for sucking food off the bottom. Four sensory barbels or "feelers" in front of the mouth aid in locating food. Seven species, of which the white sturgeon is the largest, inhabit the waters of North America. Specimens of over 1,000 pounds have been captured.

Sturgeon meat has been appreciated by man for centuries, especially for its roe (caviar). When taken on rod and reel, they prove to be sporting, particularly the white sturgeon in the rivers of Oregon and Idaho.

PADDLEFISH: *Polyodontidae*

This family has only one living representative, the paddlefish. It is also known as spoonbill, spoonbill cat, boneless cat, shovelnose cat, flatbill, and spoonbill sturgeon. Although it may be found in some lakes, it is essentially an inhabitant of the open waters of large, silty rivers, especially in the Missouri and Ohio rivers and their main tributaries. It is a long-lived, slow-growing, slow-maturing fish, and one that cannot stand extensive harvest.

It feeds on small and microscopic organisms called "plankton" that float or swim feebly and are carried by currents. Generally, it will not take a bait, but it can be "snagged" with treble hooks at the end of a rod and line. It is also a market fish. Sixty and seventy pounders are taken occasionally.

GARS: *Lepisosteidae*

The gars, often called garfish or garpike, were widely distributed around the world during early geological periods. At present, the majority of living species of gars are confined to eastern North America, where they range from southeastern Canada southward to Cuba and Central America. All gars are capable of existing under conditions that other kinds of fishes cannot tolerate. They feed on animal matter, dead or alive. The alligator gar is the largest of the group; specimens of two hundred pounds are taken occasionally, and giants of over 300 pounds have been reliably reported.

Although gars have gills, they also possess an auxiliary breathing apparatus with an air bladder that partially serves as a lung. They are capable of gulping or sucking air at water surface, enabling them to survive in drying pools and muddy waters depleted in oxygen. If kept moist, they can live out of water a surprisingly long time—twenty-four hours or more.

Scientists apparently disagree on the number of species of gars found in North America; some believe that there are up to ten. The American Fisheries Society and the International Game Fish Association list five species.

BOWFIN: *Amiidae*

The bowfin is the single representative of the family *Amiidae* and the fourth and final member of the clan (sturgeon, paddlefish, gar, bowfin) of the so-called prehistoric fishes found in North America today. Also commonly called the grindle, grinnel, dogfish, spot-tail, and mudfish, the bowfin prefers to live in quiet waters.

Similar to the gar, it has a vascularized air bladder that acts as a lung or auxiliary breathing apparatus. Therefore, it is able to live in stagnant waters where other types of fishes could not possibly survive. Frequently, the bowfin comes to the surface to gulp air. Because it takes in and expels air, it is possible to locate the fish by "signs" in calm shallow waters.

It is primarily carnivorous and feeds mostly upon other fishes, but it also takes frogs, crayfish, leeches, and aquatic insects. It puts up a good fight when hooked.

HERRINGS: *Clupeidae*

The clupeids or herringlike fishes form a large group, abundant in the ocean. Although most of them are marine, some types run up freshwater rivers to spawn. A few species spend their entire lives in lakes or streams far from salt water. They are commercially important.

Nearly all are plankton eaters and take their food at either the middle or upper layers of water. The gizzard shad, a small species, differs in that it strains the mud of the bottom. The skipjack herring (fresh water) and the hickory shad (salt water) also do not conform in food habits with the tribal majority, for they are more or less predacious and largely feed on small fishes.

Three fairly good-sized members of this family, the American shad, the hickory shad, and the skipjack herring, readily take artificial lures and produce notable resistance to rod and reel when hooked.

WHITEFISHES, GRAYLING, TROUTS, AND SALMONS: *Salmonidae*

Some scientists prefer to separate this group into three families: whitefishes, *Coregonidae;* grayling, *Thymallidae;* trouts and salmons, *Salmonidae.* The American Fisheries Society "bunches" the four clans into the single family *Salmonidae.*

WHITEFISHES: *Salmonidae*

Whitefishes, closely related to the trouts, salmons, and grayling, are essentially cold-water fishes, distributed in the northern portions of Eurasia and North America. Some of the whitefishes are of great commercial value and rate as highly as the best of North American food fishes; they are especially appreciated as smoked fish.

They are all silvery fishes with large, smooth scales, forked tails, and soft-rayed fins. In common with grayling, trouts, and salmons, they possess an adipose fin and a gristlelike process in the angle of the pelvic fins. Any whitefish can easily be distinguished from a trout or salmon by its large scales.

The representatives of the whitefish group are small to medium-sized fishes. The inconnu or sheefish, a fish of the far north, is the largest species; specimens of ten to twenty pounds are not uncommon; the rod and reel record is fifty-three pounds, taken in Alaska.

Some inhabit rivers, and some may run into the sea in Arctic areas where the water salinity is low. The majority, however, are found in the deep lakes of North America, especially those of Canada. The majority of whitefishes prefer deep water. Some ciscos or chubs inhabit depths of over 700 feet, but in most cases the various lake species do not go deeper than 180 feet.

Four members of the whitefish group rank high as sport fishes. They are the lake whitefish, cisco or lake herring, mountain whitefish, and the inconnu.

GRAYLING: *Salmonidae*

The grayling, closely related to the whitefishes and trouts, is one of the rarest of North American sport fishes. It is confined to areas of cold, clear water that have not been befouled by civilization. Its decline continues as man progressively tears down the wilderness. Aside from Alaska, the grayling is sustained in the United States only by heavy stocking of certain areas.

The Arctic grayling, *Thymallus arcticus,* apparently is the only grayling found in North America. A form known as Michigan grayling is now considered extinct. Attempts to introduce or restock Michigan streams with Montana grayling have been unsuccessful.

Because of its beauty and scarcity, sportsmen show keen interest in the Arctic grayling. It is the only fish found in Arctic regions that will consistently take a dry fly.

TROUTS: *Salmonidae*

Trouts are primarily northern fishes that survive only in cold, clear, pure waters. Although some are lake dwellers, most species of trout inhabit rivers and streams. Sometimes, stream trout do very well in lakes with tributary streams, or in landlocked lakes into which they have been introduced. Some may spend most of their lives in salt water but return to fresh water to spawn.

They are rarely found thriving in temperatures much above 65° to 70°F. Among the clan, the brown trout has the most tolerance for warm water—up to 75° to 85°F.

Trouts are Arctic and north-temperate species that have been widely transplanted on an enormous scale around the continent and from one country to another. They are natives of the Northern Hemisphere; those found in the Southern Hemisphere were established through artificial transplantation.

Some trouts take part in extensive migrations to and from saltwater; others travel from lake to stream. There are species, however, that take only short migrations—from deep water to shallow water. Most of the migratory activity is associated with spawning.

Most trouts spawn in streams over a gravel bottom. A few types spawn in lakes in shallow water along the shore or over reef areas.

The lake trout grows the largest of the group; specimens around 100 pounds have been netted. The rainbow trout, when hooked, is the best jumper. The brown trout can withstand pollution to a greater degree than can its relatives. The brook trout is the easiest of all to catch.

To the majority of freshwater anglers, trout fishing signifies the very essence of sportfishing. And more has been written about trout than about any other fish. Trouts are important market fishes. Many hatcheries around the United States grow them specifically for sale to the public.

Taxonomists usually divide the trout contingent into two principal groups: trouts and chars. The trouts are members of the genus *Salmo,* and the chars are of the genus *Salvelinus.* The differences between chars and trouts are definite, that is, they are well marked. Chars have smaller scales and rounder bodies. The bone in the center of the roof of the mouth, known as the "vomer," has a few teeth, and

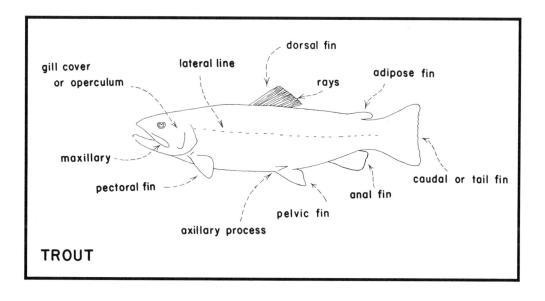

TROUT

only on its front end. The vomer of trouts is much longer and runs almost halfway to the gill arches and has teeth all along it.

The trout clan that are generally accepted as being inhabitants of North America are: Arctic char, *Salvelinus alpinus;* brook trout, *S. fontinalis;* bull trout, *S. confluentus;* Dolly Varden, *S. malma;* lake trout, *S. namaycush;* brown trout, *Salmo trutta;* Ohrid trout, *S. letnica;* Apache trout, *Oncorhynchus apache;* cutthroat trout, *O. clarki;* Gila trout, *O. gilae;* golden trout, *O. aquabonita;* rainbow trout, *O. mykiss.*

Some authors include the following as distinct species; others recognize them as a form of Arctic char: sunapee trout, *Salvelinus aureolus;* Quebec red trout, *S. marstoni;* blueback trout, *S. oquassa.*

Hatchery experiments on trout hybrids have produced some interesting results: brook trout, brown trout, rainbow trout, and lake trout have been involved with successfully producing reciprocal crosses, back crosses, and three-way crosses. For example, the tiger trout is a cross between a brook trout and a brown trout; the splake is a hybrid produced by a lake trout and a brook trout. Just like mules, these mixed breeds cannot reproduce naturally.*

SALMONS: *Salmonidae*

The salmons that inhabit our coasts, rivers, lakes, and streams include some of the world's most widely known and most highly sought food and game fishes. Despite the circumstances that have caused a gradual and serious decline in the supply, salmons continue to provide a fishery with a combined recreational and commercial value in North America termed in the hundreds of millions of dollars annually. Salmons take part in mysterious migrations to and from the sea. Practically nothing is known of their life in the ocean depths, but in freshwater streams they can be observed in shallow water. After they leave the sea to spawn in freshwater rivers, their brilliant silvery appearance changes; each species takes on characteristic markings and coloration that include bright reds, greens, and blacks, as well as a variety of somber colors. Salmons have inspired some of our best authors to produce the finest of angling literature. Because of their tremendous value, more scientific work has been done on this group than on any other fishes. Violent controversies about salmons have involved commercial fisheries, dam builders, conservationists, and sportsmen. Salmons are strong, well-shaped,

*Recent scientific investigation has been found that the skeletal structure of the Pacific trouts more closely resembles the anatomy of the Pacific salmons than that of the Atlantic salmon. Consequently, The American Fisheries Society, through its "Names Committee," has recommended that the Pacific trouts be taken out of the genus *Salmo* and placed in the genus *Oncorhynchus.* Thus, rainbow trout, *Oncorhynchus mykiss;* cutthroat trout, *Oncorhynchus clarki;* golden trout, *Oncorhynchus aquabonita.*

beautiful fishes, excellent when smoked or canned; and a fresh, sea-run fish, smoked properly, is superb. The sporting qualities of some members of the clan are rated among the finest of the finned tribe.

The representatives of the clan that figure most prominently in the world of angling are Atlantic, Chinook, and silver salmons. The kokanee, a landlocked form of the sockeye, and the landlocked salmon, a lake form of the Atlantic species, also rate very highly as sport fishes. The sockeye is the most important commercially. The chum, pink, and sockeye are practically insignificant as sport fishes.

The North American salmons include seven species—six along the Pacific Northwest and one, the Atlantic salmon, *Salmo salar,* in the Northeast. The Pacific salmons are: Chinook, *Oncorhynchus tshawytscha;* coho, *O. kisutch;* sockeye, *O. nerka;* chum, *O. keta;* pink, *O. gorbuscha;* and the steelhead, *O. mykiss,* classified as a trout until recently.

All Pacific salmons die after their first spawning. The Atlantic salmon drops back to its marine environment after spawning. Not many fish, however, survive the hazards of the sea to return for a second spawning, or a third. An additional species is found in northern Japan and Russia that is not present along the North American coast.

SMELTS: *Osmeridae*

The smelts, distant cousins of the trout and whitefishes, are small, slender, silvery fishes found in North America and Europe. They are primarily a marine family with some representatives that run into fresh water to spawn. Some types, however, live permanently in fresh water. Three kinds of true smelt spawn in the saltwater surf. Fewer than several dozen species make up this group, all of which are Arctic or north temperate.

Smelts are extremely valuable fishes from a commercial and recreational viewpoint. Also, they are important food for large sport fishes. Most North American smelts are found on the western side of the continent; but the American smelt, an eastern species, is one best known to sportsmen. Most of the smelt catch is made with various types of nets, depending on the locality and regulations.

MOONEYES: *Hiodontidae*

The mooneye family is found only in North America; it is composed of two species, the goldeye and the mooneye. The former is a fine sport fish and an excellent food fish when smoked. In contrast, the mooneye is seldom eaten and is caught by sportsmen only by accident.

PIKES: *Esocidae*

All members of the pike family, pickerel, pike, and muskellunge (musky), are predacious. The adults are almost exclusively fish eaters. Their preferred habitat is quiet waters where weeds abound, especially in coves and bays where submerged brush and logs offer cover. However, they are sometimes found in open water or deep channels. The *Esocidae* are characterized by long cylindrical bodies and prominent jaws shaped like the bill of a duck. Their mouths are large and contain many teeth.

They have a reputation for being solitary, aggressive, and voracious. The pickerel, pike, and musky clan are appreciated as fine sport fishes by freshwater anglers. Characteristically, any one of the pike family, after being hooked, may jump clear of the surface several times and produce strong resistance to the fisherman's efforts to haul it in. Trolling and casting are the sportsman's favorite methods of angling for these fishes.

The family is composed of five species. All are fishes of northern waters. The northern pike also occurs in Eurasia; in Manchuria, there is another species, the Amur River pike. The *Esocidae* have a wide variety of common names. The grass pickerel and redfin pickerel are the smallest members of the pike family, seldom reaching a foot in length.

MINNOWS AND CARPS: *Cyprinidae*

The minnows are by far the largest group of freshwater fishes in North America, both in species and in numbers. Although anglers tend to refer to the young of all species as minnows, the *Cyprinidae* constitute a well-defined family of fishes. They inhabit all types of aquatic environments—lakes, ponds, streams, quiet water, swift water, cold water, and warm water. They are found at sea level and at high altitudes in mountain streams. The great majority of species are small fishes, averaging two to four inches in length, although several kinds reach beyond 1½ feet, while some western types (squawfishes) commonly attain a length of about three feet.

As a group, minnows are highly important to sport fishing. They are competitive, inhabiting the same space and feeding upon the same organisms on which the young of the more important sport fishes depend. In turn, the minnows provide an important source of food for the large sport or game fishes.

Minnows are beneficial to man, consuming larvae of mosquitoes and other pests. Fish-eating birds, such as herons, kingfishers, terns, and cormorants, depend largely on minnows for food. The *Cyprinidae* are economically important because enormous numbers are purchased for bait by sport fishermen. They are bony but delicious when fried crisp. About a dozen species, which attain a length of eight inches or more, are taken on rod and reel.

The carps are the largest of the minnow family; a specimen of seventy-five pounds, eleven ounces was captured on rod and reel in France.

SUCKERS: *Catostomidae*

The suckers are medium-sized fishes, numerous in number and species, and almost entirely North American. About 100 kinds range widely over our continent; one species is found as far south as Guatemala; a few are found in Siberia and China. The different types that make up the family *Catostomidae* are known as suckers, carpsuckers, quillbacks, chubsuckers, hog suckers, buffalos, jumprocks, and redhorses. Suckers are closely related to minnows, and several are just as difficult to identify as are some of the minnows. All are bottom-dwellers of ponds, lakes, and streams.

The majority of species are medium-sized fishes about eighteen inches long. Some types, such as the chubsucker, may reach only ten inches or less. However, some of the buffalos and redhorses commonly reach two and three feet in length. The bigmouth buffalo (rarely taken on hook and line) grows up to thirty pounds in a few of the larger lakes in the Mississippi River or drainage. A specimen of over eighty pounds was reported taken from Spirit Lake, Iowa.

Commercially, the large types of suckers are important in the Mississippi River system, Great Lakes, and the St. Lawrence River. During the cooler seasons of the year, suckers are specifically sought by anglers.

The American Fisheries Society lists about sixty-five species in the *Catostomidae* in the United States and Canada; however, the great majority are never taken on rod and reel. Yet, a few, which are important in providing recreation and food for sportsmen, should rate as sport fishes. Attitudes and sportfishing efforts concerning the suckers differ widely around the country and between specific localities within areas.

Although they are bony, suckers are tasty, especially during the colder months of the year when their flesh is firm.

CATFISHES: *Ictaluridae*

Although the fishes in the catfish tribe are important commercially, they are the most controversial freshwater sport fishes in the United States. They are appreciated by relatively few northeastern anglers, but southerners and midwesterners do rightfully approve of them. Catfishes now play an important role in California's sportfishing. Many thousands of anglers fish for them, and millions are caught annually. A wide variety of methods are employed in capturing members

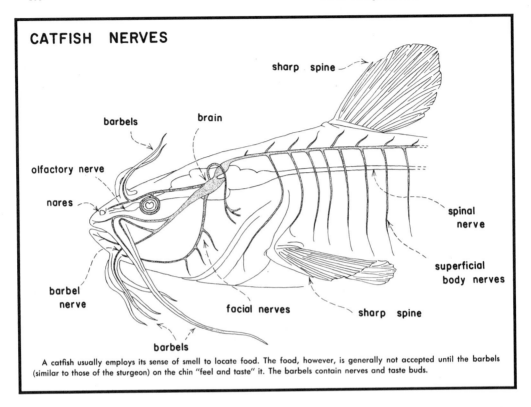

CATFISH NERVES

A catfish usually employs its sense of smell to locate food. The food, however, is generally not accepted until the barbels (similar to those of the sturgeon) on the chin "feel and taste" it. The barbels contain nerves and taste buds.

of this bewhiskered family, and all species are excellent on the table.

The catfishes constitute a large group that is distributed throughout the world. They live mainly in fresh water, and the numerous species range from the smallest of freshwater fishes to the largest. Freshwater catfishes range from Canada to Guatemala. No species were in the Pacific drainage of the United States until introduced in the 1800s. They have spread widely since then.

There are two families of catfishes in North America. The freshwater catfishes, *Ictaluridae,* consisting of twenty-four species listed by the American Fisheries Society, and the saltwater family, *Ariidae,* with only two species. The sea catfishes may be found occasionally in brackish water. The freshwater family may be partitioned into three groups: (1) catfishes; the largest species are found in this category, some exceeding 100 pounds in weight; (2) bullheads; they are commonly called "horned pout" and are popular with anglers who fish small ponds and lakes; (3) madtoms; these are secretive fishes, not more than a few inches long.

EELS: *Anguillidae*

All of the family *Anguillidae* spawn in the sea but live and grow most of their lives in fresh and brackish waters. The American eel, *Anguilla rostrata*, is found throughout eastern North America, to southern South America, including the Bahamas and other large islands.

There are many families of eels, such as the marine conger eels and snake eels, around the world. Most are in tropical and subtropical areas; some are in temperate regions. In the freshwater family of eels, there are about sixteen species, most of which occur in the Indo-Pacific. There is not a single member of this family in the eastern Pacific; therefore, it is not found along our western coast. The three most important freshwater eels are the American eel, the European eel, and the Japanese eel.

The female eels are larger than the males and average twenty-four to forty-two inches in length. Any eel over eighteen inches is probably a female; a specimen over twenty-four inches is definitely female. They may reach four to five feet in length and weigh about sixteen pounds, although the present rod and reel record is seven pounds, seven ounces.

The American eel is taken in great numbers by fishermen using hook and line and other varied methods. And it is economically important; thousands of tons are sold as food. Also, it makes an excellent bait or lure in fishing for some of our finest sport fishes. *Anguilla rostrata* has one of the most intriguing life histories of all creatures (see *"Migration"* in Chapter 2).

CODFISHES: *Gadidae*

The codfish family is a fairly large group of well-known marine fishes. The clan includes the cod, tomcod, haddock, pollock, and hake. Only one member of the family is a strictly freshwater inhabitant, and that is the burbot, *Lota lota,* a highly controversial fish in regard to its value, both as a sport fish and a food fish. The Atlantic tomcod, *Microgadus tomcod,* an inshore marine species, runs into freshwater rivers during winter, and quantities are taken on hook and line. It is landlocked in some Canadian lakes.

The burbot is an extremely voracious cold-water species, existing predominantly on a fish diet. It is known by a variety of names: freshwater cod, cusk, ling, eel-pout, lawyer, and maria loche.

TEMPERATE BASSES: *Percichthyidae*

The temperate basses, formerly known as the sea bass family, are a worldwide group of fishes found predominantly in tropical and subtropical waters. There are hundreds of saltwater types, but only a few species are found in fresh water. The white bass and the yellow bass can be termed strictly freshwater fishes. The white perch and the striped bass live in salt water and brackish water but enter freshwater streams to spawn. However, there are landlocked populations of both striped bass and white perch that live and produce successfully entirely in fresh water.

The largemouth bass, smallmouth bass, and other basslike species are members of the sunfish family *Centrarchidae* and should not be confused with the *Percichthyidae* or *Serranidae*.

Members of the *Percichthyidae* found in fresh water—white bass, yellow bass, white perch, and striped bass—are avidly sought by fishermen. They are fine sport fishes, important commercially, and excellent on the table. The natural reproduction of stripers, after introduction in large freshwater impoundments in southeastern United States, has attracted worldwide attention.

SUNFISHES: *Centrarchidae*

As a group of sport fishes, the sunfish family is the most popular in North America. A surprisingly vast number of anglers pursue the catfishes, and trout receive an incredible concentration of angling effort in certain sections of the continent. But the greatest number of freshwater fishermen, by far, confine their

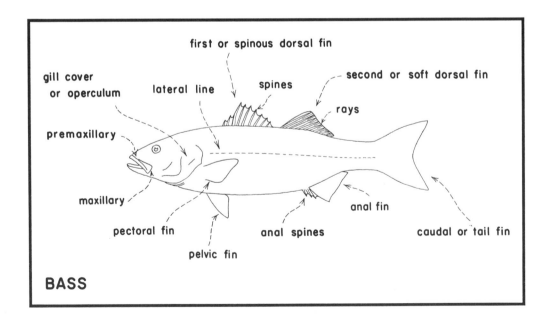

efforts primarily to the sunfishes. Appropriately, these warm-water fishes, which provide so many thousands of American men, women, and children with recreation and food, are native only to our continent.

The family includes the freshwater basses, the true sunfishes (bluegill, pumpkinseed, and so on), rock bass, Sacramento perch, and the crappies. There are thirty species listed in the family. Nearly all types are large enough to be of importance. The largemouth and smallmouth basses rank among the top freshwater game fishes; the smaller sunfishes, especially the bluegill, are also appreciated as first-class rod and reel fishes.

The so-called true sunfishes, the rock bass and the crappies, do not receive as much attention from the "expert" freshwater anglers as do their larger relatives, the basses of the same family *Centrarchidae*. However, the overall fishing effort that is placed on the smaller pan-sized types by the general run of fishermen is phenomenal. Some members of the true sunfish clan are appreciated for their "scrappy" actions when caught on light tackle, besides being a delight in the frying pan.

CICHLIDS: *Cichlidae*

The cichlids constitute a family of attractive tropical fishes, well-known to aquarium enthusiasts. Its members are found in Syria, Palestine, southern India, Madagascar, Africa, the West Indies, and South and Central America. The velvet cichlid and the Rio Grande perch are the only species in the family that enter the United States; but only the latter is known to anglers, and that only to a limited extent. Throughout a good portion of their range, cichlids are important commercially, and interest in them as pond fishes continues to grow.

The highly colored peacock bass is one of the most widely distributed cichlids found in the fresh waters of tropical South America. It may reach weights of over twenty-five pounds and average five to six pounds in some Venezuelan streams. Introduction and management programs are being tried in Florida and Texas.

PERCHES: *Percidae*

The perches constitute a large group of fishes found in Europe and North America. Close to a hundred species are listed for the United States and Canada. The family includes only four species of interest to the angler: walleye, blue pike, sauger, and yellow perch; the rest are darters. Except for the logperch, which may reach a length of six inches, the darters are tiny fishes that seldom exceed 2½ or three inches and are of no value to the angler. However, the four species mentioned rate among the most valuable sport fishes on the continent. They are important commercially and unexcelled on the table.

DRUMS: *Sciaenidae*

The family *Sciaenidae* is composed of a great number of marine species, many of which are well known. They are important food and game fishes. A few kinds, on occasion, may run into brackish and fresh water. However, only one representative of this group, the freshwater drum *Aplodinotus grunniens,* is a permanent inhabitant of fresh water. All members of the family, at times, make a "purring" or "drumming" sound that can be surprisingly loud when the fish is removed from the water; but the noise can also be heard as it is emitted from the fish underwater. Apparently, the sound is produced by workings of the air bladder, or the pharyngeal teeth, or both.

Related Reading

Herald, Earl S. 1972. *Fishes of North America.* New York: Doubleday & Co.

International Game Fish Association. 1988. *World Record Game Fishes.* Fort Lauderdale, Florida.

McClane, A. J. 1978. *McClane's Field Guide to the Freshwater Fishes of North America.* New York: Holt, Rinehart and Winston.

Migdalski, Edward C. 1962. *Freshwater Sport Fishes of North America.* New York: Ronald Press Company.

Scott, W. B., and E. J. Crassman. 1974. *Freshwater Fishes of Canada.* Ottawa: Fisheries Research Board of Canada.

Smith, Phillip W. 1979. *The Fishes of Illinois.* Champaign: University of Illinois Press.

4

Marine Factors Related to Fishing

Just as limnology, the study of lakes and rivers, is important to the inquisitive freshwater angler, so too, should oceanography be of interest to the intelligent saltwater fisherman. The sciences that encompass the study of oceans are many, varied, and too technical to delve into here in detail. Nevertheless, the overview of oceanic factors and their relationship to fishes and sportfishing is presented herewith for the benefit of the inquisitive angler-ichthyologist.

Game fishes are found in all the world's great bodies of water referred to as oceans and seas. Generally speaking, the tropical and subtropical waters contain a greater number and a more varied assortment of game fishes than do the colder waters of more northern latitudes.

The composition of seawater contains in solution gases and solids that can be recovered by evaporation. Over three quarters of the dissolved material is common salt; the remainder is made up of small quantities of almost every known chemical element (including gold and silver), the greater part consisting of sodium, magnesium, and calcium.

Salinity, or the actual quantity of salt dissolved in water, is one of the controlling factors in the distribution of fishes. The amount of salt per given quantity of water varies in the different seas and oceans of the world and from time to time in any specific area. Open-ocean water varies little in its salinity, being almost always between thirty-four and thirty-six parts of salt to 1,000 parts of water by weight. Close to land in some areas, the amount of dissolved salt is less because of the fresh water that flows off the land. A good example is Long Island Sound, where the salt content is twenty-five to twenty-eight parts per 1,000. All oceans derive their salt from the earth. Fresh water drains the land in the form of rivers and brings with it salt and other substances. The salt, now so noticeable in seawater, has been washed from the soil in minute quantities over countless centuries.

The salinity of seawater in warm latitudes may be considerably higher than that in the open ocean because of the constant evaporation of water at the surface and the resulting concentration of salts left behind. The highest salinities in the world for open waters are found in the Red Sea—forty parts per 1,000. The eastern Mediterranean contains more salt than the open Atlantic; in this ocean the highest salinities occur in the Sargasso Sea. The polar regions contain the lowest salinities because rain and snow dilute the surface waters.

Phosphates and nitrates, present in minute quantities, are the most important elements found in seawater. These are substances that have a great nutrient value and are responsible for development of plankton, which is the start of the food chain for fishes.

Oxygen is one of the gases dissolved in water. Without it animals cannot live. It appears that there is no area in the open sea where oxygen is not present in solution in sufficient quantity to support a large number of fishes. However, there are unique instances where this element is not present; in some areas in the Black Sea there is no oxygen below about 100 fathoms. Therefore, no fish or other animals can live there. But in the open ocean life is still possible in the greatest depth where oxygen is present because of the circulation of water in the enormous ocean currents.

Sea temperature is another important factor in reproduction and distribution of fishes. Surface temperatures vary generally from about 80°F. near the equator to about 30°F. near the poles. Actually, the highest sea temperatures occur in the Persian Gulf, where the water is 96°; the coldest is 28°, in the polar regions. Between these two extremes all temperatures are to be found. Temperature drops with depth and varies with the change in seasons. Approximately one-half mile down, the temperature is about 40°F., and readings on the ocean bottom are about 35°F. The effect of the sun's rays is not felt to a depth greater than 300 fathoms; the heat rays are rapidly absorbed by the upper few inches of water; any warmth developed in the deeper waters is carried there by a mixture of warmer surface waters.

Water requires a great amount of heat energy for it to rise in temperature; then it retains the heat well and is slow to give it up. This is why, in some areas, the fishing may continue to be good well into the fall even though the weather may be uncomfortably cold for the angler. Water temperatures (in oceanography) are given in degrees centigrade rather than degrees Fahrenheit, which may confuse the sportsman who is accustomed to the latter. Centigrade thermometer space between freezing and boiling is divided into 100 equal parts: 0° (freezing) to 100° (boiling). The space on the Fahrenheit thermometer, between freezing and boiling, is divided into 180 equal parts: 32° (freezing) to 212° (boiling). Here is a simple conversion formula that is easy to work and accurate enough to satisfy the angler: $(°C \times \%) + 32 = °F$.

The average depth of the ocean is about 2½ miles; the greatest depth is approximately six miles. Specific areas of unusually deep waters (below 18,000 feet) are known as deeps or trenches. For example, the Philippine Trench is 35,400 feet deep, and the Puerto Rican Deep is 28,707 feet in depth. There are fifty-seven deeps—thirty-two in the Pacific, five in the Indian Ocean, nineteen in the Atlantic, and one that lies partly in the Indian Ocean and partly in the Atlantic. The fathom, used in water measurements, is equal to six feet.

The density of seawater is about 1.03 times that of fresh water; therefore, salt water exerts a greater buoyant force on bodies immersed in it (swimming is easier in salt water). Because water is incompressible, the increase in density with depth is extremely small. In other words, the great pressure in the depths of the ocean has but slight effect on the density of the water. The actual weight or specific gravity of seawater depends upon its temperature and salinity; warm water is lighter than cool water, fresh water lighter than salt water; higher salinities make for heavier water. The pressure in the sea varies with depth. Approximately every thirty-three feet of depth the pressure is increased by fourteen pounds to the square inch. Therefore, pressures in the depths of the ocean are tremendous—as much as three tons to the square inch.

Light plays an important part in sea life; without it no plants could survive, and all fishes are ultimately dependent upon plant life for food. Therefore, ocean areas rich in nutrients and with abundance of sunlight (some areas, like Peru, have practically no rainfall) produce great quantities of plankton, which attracts fishes. The penetration of light in any part of the sea depends upon the strength and altitude of the sun, weather conditions, and the amount of sediment and turbidity in the water.

Coastal fishes are found in waters along the continental shelf, which is an extension of the continental mass into the ocean. The material forming this shelf was worked down from the land by running water and deposited in the ocean. Then the waves and currents over the centuries spread out the deposits and formed a gently sloping floor that extends outward from ten to about 100 miles.

The oceans and seas of the world are not merely great masses of water; they are composed of huge currents that circulate and move the water from place to place. Ocean currents are made up mostly of the "blue water," which is a common term to big-game fishermen. The forces that set these gigantic bodies of water in motion are varied; some of the important ones are the rotation of the earth, winds, heat from the sun, and polar ice. To illustrate some of the phenomena involved in the movement of ocean waters, let us consider the Gulf Stream, which sees more sport fishing than any other oceanic current in the world. This gigantic river of warm blue water, fifty miles wide and 350 fathoms deep, originates in the Gulf of Mexico. Actually, this current is part of a system of currents of continuous circulation in the Atlantic and really cannot be said to start or end anywhere. In brief, this is what happens:

1. The surface water just north of the equator is heated by the tropical sun, and salinity is raised by constant evaporation.

2. Continual winds from the northeast (Northeast Trade Winds) blow across this warm saline water and help move it (known as the North Equatorial Drift) toward the north coast of South America and then into the Caribbean Sea and the Gulf of Mexico.

3. The waters become piled up at a level higher than that outside the islands of the West Indies.

4. Because these forced waters must flow somewhere in order to keep equilibrium, they push through the Straits of Florida; hence the birth of the Gulf Stream, which continues at a rate of approximately four knots.

5. As it moves northward this stream is deflected to the right, or eastward, because of the rotation of the earth; when it reaches the latitude 40° north, the current is flowing across the Atlantic due east.

6. Approaching cooler climates, it has lost a certain amount of its warmth, lost some of its speed, and has widened a good deal.

7. Ice drifting down from the polar seas on cold Labrador currents meets the Gulf Stream and cools it.

8. Cool water is heavier than warm water; therefore it sinks and is replaced by more warm water near the surface; this action causes a downward current of water.

9. The process continues while the ice melts, so that in a way the ice attracts the warm water.

10. The enormous masses of ice exert great power and cause part of the Gulf Stream, which is flowing east, to split off from the current and head north. The remainder of the east-going stream continues across the Atlantic and, because of the earth's rotation, continues right until it returns to equatorial waters where it originated.

Two types of water movement are distinguished in the great bodies of oceanic circulating water: the currents, which are definite bodies of flowing water, and drifts, which are horizontal movements of water brought about by wind action and which travel more or less in the same direction the wind is blowing.

The movements of bodies of water in a vertical direction are of two types known as upwelling and sinking. When the density of surface water increases by cooling, it travels downward or sinks. Upwelling occurs when a deep current meets the shelving bottom or submerged bank in coastal regions. Persistent offshore winds can also bring about upwelling by blowing the surface waters outward. This movement of vertical water to the surface is of great importance because the bottom waters, which are rich in nutrient salts, phosphates, and nitrates, are brought to the surface. That is why in regions of upwelling there is a great abundance of sea life.

Tides are periodic water movements familiar to all marine fishermen. This rise and fall of ocean water is caused by the gravitative pull of the moon and the sun. A rising tide is said to flow, and a tide that is receding is said to ebb. To put it briefly, the workings of the tide happen this way: the water is drawn or attracted by the moon from all around the earth to a point beneath the moon so that it is accumulated there. High tide takes place where this bulge of water occurs. At the same time, exactly similar forces act on the hemisphere of the earth opposite the moon, causing high tide there too. Therefore, there are two high tides simultaneously on the earth—one on the side of the earth facing the moon, and the other on the side of the earth away from the moon. These two high tides are responsible for the water between them being pulled away. In other words, the two regions lying on either side of the earth, midway between the two high tide areas, at the same time will be at low water. Two high tides and two low tides take place every twenty-four hours. Because the moon moves around the earth in an elliptical orbit, the interval between one high tide and the next is not exactly twelve hours. There is a progressive change; the time of high water is not the same every day. High tide of one morning will be close to an hour later than that of the previous morning.

With the change in tides there is also a change in the range of tides. These periods are known as spring tides (a better name would be big tides because "spring" has no association with the season of the year) and neap tides. During the spring tides the high-water mark reaches its highest and the low-water mark its lowest—in other words, the range between the tide marks is greatest. On the other hand, during the neap tides the tide comes in and out at a short distance. Spring tides are in effect when the moon and sun are exerting their pulls in the same direction and the force is at its greatest (shortly after both the new and full moons). When the sun and moon are on the same side of the earth (new moon), the range of tides is at its maximum; at full moon the spring tides are less because the sun and moon are opposite each other. When the forces of the moon and sun are at right angles to each other (half moon), the range of tides is least or neap tides.

Currents and Fishing

An ocean current may carry some types of fishes almost passively, while other kinds are seen always swimming against it. Warm-water fishes may go beyond their usual northerly limits when ocean currents temporarily change their course slightly, or the fishes may appear closer to shore because of natural fluctuations of the currents. Good fishing may be had fairly close to the coast in some areas, while, at a nearby shore, fishes are not present within hundreds of miles because the ocean current shoots off from the coast. This situation usually exists where an abrupt and deep depression takes place in the continental outline. Underwater ridges and canyons affect, to some extent, the directional flow of currents, which in turn influence the distribution of fishes.

In coastal areas, underwater ridges and canyons create rips and races during incoming and outgoing fast-flowing tides. Bait fishes are drawn to areas of such conditions because the turbulent waters produce small organisms on which they feed. In turn, game fishes are attracted to the same areas because of the abundance of small fishes on which they prey.

An excellent example of an unusually productive race is located at the head of Long Island Sound where, during the proper seasons, the fishing for bluefish and striped bass is spectacular, for the reasons cited.

Soldiers Rip, ten miles south of Wedgeport, Nova Scotia, at one time the world's most famous giant bluefin tuna fishing area, is another example of a productive rip or race. The rip is a tidal stream with a six-knot current, about a mile wide, near Bald Tusket Island. This underwater canyon is seventeen fathoms deep and, years ago, harbored enormous schools of herring and mackerel. That is why the bluefins were there.

In schooling fishes such as the tunas, a double strike is not uncommon. In big-game angling, one fish has to be cut off or both will be lost. Lines will criss-cross, and the angler can handle only one fish while in the fighting chair. *Photo credit: Nova Scotia Information Centre.*

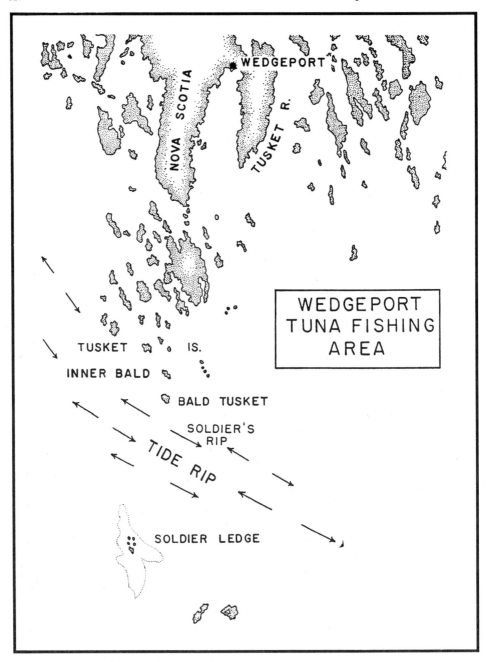

Soldiers Rip, at one time the world's most famous angling grounds for giant
bluefin tuna, is ten miles south of Wedgeport, Nova Scotia. It is a tidal
stream with a six-knot current, about a mile wide near Bald Tusket Island.
This underwater canyon, seventeen fathoms deep, once harbored enormous
schools of herring and mackerel. It is hoped that someday the herring and
mackerel will return, drawing the bluefins with them.

A giant bluefin tuna of seven hundred pounds or more hits a herring bait on the surface. Such spectacular strikes require no second effort by the angler in setting the hook. The hook is usually well embedded in the upper jaw. *Photo credit: Nova Scotia Information Centre.*

The so-called "daisy chain"—a string of seven or eight herring tied by the tips of their upper and lower jaws to a wire leader—is lowered into the Tusket River enroute to the once-famous Soldiers Rip off Wedgeport, Nova Scotia. When trolled, the turbulent chain simulates a school of herring evading the pursuit of a bluefin tuna. *Photo by author.*

Water Temperature in Relation to Sportfishing

In the marine environment, water temperature is one of the most important factors in controlling the well-being and behavior patterns of both coastal and pelagic, or open-ocean, fishes. Certain game fishes can tolerate only certain temperatures of water. For example, in the eastern Pacific the cold temperature toleration of the sailfish and marlins is approximately 59°F. In other words, billfishes, under ordinary conditions, usually do not travel farther north than Point Conception, California, nor farther south than Valparaiso, Chile, because beyond these points the water usually drops below 59°F.

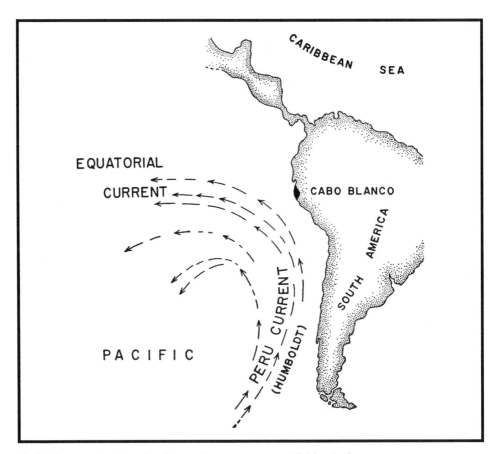

A classic example of marine factors that promote good fishing is the upwelling and well-defined food cycle that occurs off the coast of Peru.

The depth limits of the sailfish and marlins may also be controlled by the 59° temperature factor. An excellent example of a fairly abrupt line of demarcation formed by a temperature difference takes place off the coast of North America where the cold Labrador Current meets the warm water of the Gulf Stream. Although the water masses are close to each other, the differences in the water temperatures of the warm and cold currents act like a wall that discourages penetration by fishes inhabiting the two zones.

Seasonal variations in the temperature of the sea also influence the distribution of fishes. For example, the Atlantic mackerel, which prefers warm waters, remains in the open sea or in deep-water areas during the winter; when the inshore waters become warmer in summer, it frequents coastal areas. Another example is the occurrence of white marlin and blue marlin in waters off the Massachusetts islands in summer; when the water temperature drops, the fishes leave. The seasonal occurrence of bluefish along our Atlantic coast can be followed progressively—farther north as the warm season progresses and the water temperatures go higher.

Water temperature also plays a key role in pinpointing the time of migrational departure or arrival of a certain species in a specific area. In other words, although some types of fishes may appear in an area at the same season annually, the exact dates are controlled by water temperature. For example, if spring weather is unusually cold in the Massachusetts area, the striped bass may arrive two or three weeks later than usual.

Specific Temperature Tolerances of Fishes

Any attempt to focalize the best and specific water temperatures at which game fishes will more readily take a bait or lure is dangerous because so many other factors are involved—proximity to spawning season, climatic conditions, water depth, current flow, salinity, upwelling, and swimming depth of bait fishes. Nevertheless, it cannot be disputed that the following examples confirm the fact that fishes of specific environments will tolerate a certain high and low range of water temperatures.

Cod, haddock, halibut, and pollock, four of our most important food and game fishes found in deep, cold, northern waters, are close-to-bottom feeders where water temperatures may range from 32° to 60°F. (Pollock are often taken on lures trolled close to the surface where temperatures are higher than along the depths.)

Flounders inhabit inshore waters, often in shallow bays and estuaries where water temperatures vary seasonably: winter flounder, 35° to 60°F.; summer flounder (fluke), 69° to 80°F.

Sheepshead and tautog (blackfish) prefer reef and rocky areas along coastal zones and may be found in 60° to 78°F. waters.

Dolphin and wahoo rank high with sportfishermen. They prefer blue waters of the open seas and are usually taken in warm waters, close to the surface, in temperatures about 68° to 85°F.

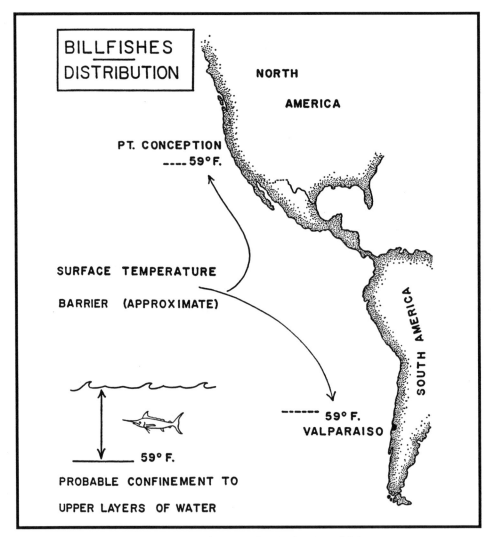

Sea temperature is another important factor in the distribution of fishes. Successful angling occurs within the temperature barriers of specific gamefish.

Bonefish, seatrout, snook, and tarpon are well known and highly prized as game fishes in shallow, warm waters. Snook and tarpon are often found in narrow canals and rivers far up from the sea. This group will accept temperatures from 65° to 90°F.

Barracuda, Atlantic and barracuda, Pacific are excellent examples of closely related species whose water temperature tolerances differ because of environment. The Atlantic species loves reef areas of 65° to 90°F; its Pacific cousin, of more open waters about 55° to 70°F.

Striped bass is a migratory species that travels along coastal marine waters, but enters brackish and freshwater rivers to spawn; its water temperature tolerance is a wide 40° to 80°F.

Bluefish, one of the most popular of sport fishes available to coastal fishermen, including surf casters along Atlantic New England shores, will take water of 50° to 80°F.

Sailfishes and marlins (billfishes) are most often found in temperate and warm oceanic waters. Their temperature tolerance may vary within a range of about 15°F., depending on the particular ocean they are swimming in at the time. Generally, black marlin, blue marlin, and sailfishes will be found in 77° to 88°F. temperatures, while the striped marlin and white marlin will comfortably occupy slightly cooler zones of 60° to 85°F.

The swordfish, often grouped with the "billfishes," is another open-ocean fish, but with more variety in its eating habits at greater depths with associated colder water of 50° to 78°F.

Bluefin tuna, like the swordfish, is a highly migratory, transoceanic swimmer capable of one of the widest ranges in temperature tolerances of all fishes, 50° to 82°F., with the most comfortable range being in the lower half of the 60°sF.

Upwelling and the Food Cycle

Throughout the seas of the world the upwelling of waters may be created by different phenomena such as currents colliding with obstructions in their path; by underwater islands, canyons, ridges, or reefs; or by surface waters blown away from the coast through wind action and replaced by upcoming waters from down deep. Whatever the reason for an upwelling, the area of such a displacement or interchange of marine waters provides good fishing because predatory fishes at the apex of the food chain or food cycle are attracted there.

It was during a Yale University expedition to study big-game fishes off the coast of Peru, South America, that I witnessed a classic example of upwelling and

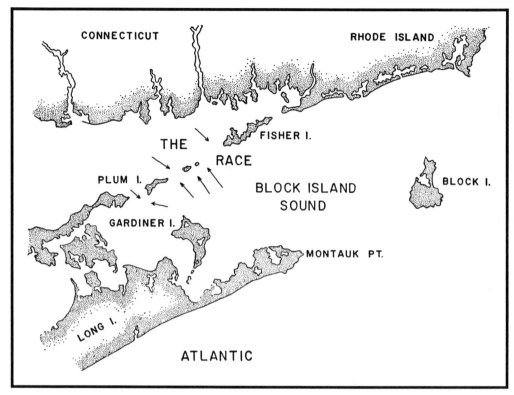

In coastal areas, underwater ridges and canyons create rips and races during
incoming and outgoing fast-flowing tides. Baitfish are drawn to such areas
because the turbulent waters produce small organisms on which they feed.
In turn, gamefish are attracted to the same areas because of the abundance
of small fish on which they prey.

a well-defined food cycle that provided us with excellent marlin fishing at its apex.
Because similar situations occur in other marine environments that cause upwelling, I here relate the story of the Peru upwelling because I have experienced it and
because it is the best way to demonstrate the phenomenon.

The most graphic way to explain the sequence of events constituting "upwelling" and "food cycle" is to analyze the situation: marlins, swordfish, bigeye tuna,
and a profusion of other fishes are found in the Peru Current, which approaches
Chile somewhere near Valparaiso, flows northward along the coast of Chile and
Peru, turns westward off Cabo Blanco, and loses its identity in the South Equatorial Current. Although the Peru Current flows close to the equator, its waters
are cool. For example, surface temperature off Cabo Blanco is about 71°F., while

Ultimately, angler success is directly associated with nature's food cycle. Phytoplankton are eaten by zooplankton, which in turn are taken by the smallest fishes. Small fish are preyed upon by larger fish, ad infinitum. Any organisms that escape being eaten eventually die and sink to the bottom, where they are consumed by such scavengers as worms and crabs. Finally, by bacterial action, the nutrients are returned to the water in soluble inorganic form. To complete the cycle, the phytoplankton benefit from the development of nutrients.

at the same latitude out to sea the surface water temperature is approximately five or six degrees higher.

The theory or reason for the cooler water that is accepted by most scientists today is that the prevailing winds blow along the coast and literally turn the water over; that is, the surface waters are driven away from the coast, and cold bottom water rises from a depth of 600 to 1,000 fathoms to replace it. This phenomenon, called upwelling, brings up water very rich in nutrients, and this is basically the cause of the abundance there of big-game fishes. To elaborate: let us consider the food cycle of the sea. Sea plants contain chlorophyll just as land plants do. The microscopic kind, called floating phytoplankton, are eaten by minute sea animals (zooplankton), which in turn are taken by the smallest fishes. Small fish are preyed upon by larger fish, ad infinitum. Any organisms that escape being eaten eventually die and sink to the bottom, where they are consumed by scavengers such as worms and crabs. Finally, by bacterial action, the nutrients are returned to the water in a soluble inorganic form. When the upwelling brings the rich bottom waters (nutrients) to the surface, phytoplankton benefit and grow fast, and in turn the larger animals are attracted. We can put it in a nutshell by saying that the big-game fishes and all the others abound in this area because of the vast food supply caused by the upwelling.

Celsius—Centigrade

In centigrade thermometer readings of marine waters, Celsius is often used instead of centigrade. Celsius is the name of the Swedish scientist who invented the centigrade system, that is, freezing point is 0 and boiling point is 100 (as opposed to the more familiar Fahrenheit freezing point at 32 above its zero and the boiling point at 212).

Fathom

The fathom is a unit of measurement used in water-depth calculations; it measures six feet.

Seawater—Freezing

Seawater has more resistance to freezing than fresh water because it is almost constantly and rapidly moving and because the salt in its composition is an obstruction against freezing. When frozen, the ice is made of fresh water; the salt, separated from the fresh water by the process of ice formation, dissolves in the remaining water below, thereby raising its salinity.

Knot

A knot is a measure of speed equal to one nautical mile, or 6,080.20 feet per hour.

5

Limnology in Angling

Limnology is the science or study of lakes, and, by inclusion or extension, of all inland waters; its involvements are primarily concerned with the biology of waters, but also include the grounds in which they are held or over which they flow.

Although limnology is a specific science different from ichthyology, they intertwine, that is, they are closely related. Today's sophisticated approaches to the study of fishes include limnological references to habitat and water conditions.

Aside from the necessary fishing tackle, two of the most valuable tools that a freshwater angler may possess is a contour map of the lake he or she intends to fish, and a water thermometer.

Charts and maps are usually obtainable at nominal cost from state fish and game departments or environmental protective agencies. Often, a map of a large impoundment may be purchased at local bait and tackle shops in the vicinity of a particularly popular lake. In most cases, a contour map denoting depths at regular intervals is of more practical value than an electronic depth finder because it shows the overall structure of the lake.

The contour maps sponsored by state agencies in booklet form not only give the location of deep holes and shallow areas, so important to fishing success, but usually provide information concerning water-surface area, access directions, parking capacity, a briefing on bag limits, powerboat use, boat rentals, and the type of fishes that inhabit the water.

A water thermometer is an important piece of equipment that should be carried in the tackle box of the inquisitive angler. During the summer months nearly all lakes are stratified. A thermometer can inform the angler where fish may be found because of temperature tolerances. Thermometers especially designed for water use by fishermen are available in some bait and tackle shops, or may be purchased through fishing-tackle catalogs.

Because limnological factors have a profound effect on sportfishing, the following definitions and treatment of these elements are presented.

Simnological Factors in Sportfishing

Abyssal Depth, *in Lakes*

That depth at which the water remains uniform in temperature or is stagnant; it is mostly lacking in oxygen and fish life. In other words, an angler would be wasting time to troll a bait or lure in such an area.

Acidity, *in Water Chemistry*

Acidity is usually expressed as low pH (hydrogen-ion concentration). A pH below 7 is considered acid and is detrimental to fish life. Fishes can sustain life in water having a pH range from about 6 to 9 or 10. At a pH around 5.5 fish develop a hypersensitivity to bacterial parasites, and usually die quickly if the pH is 4.5 or lower.

On the other hand, very hard waters can be toxic to fishes (an upper pH range of 10 or more) when maximum alkalinity is attained and plants use up all the free carbon dioxide in the water. An accumulation of organic matter in older ponds and lakes acts as a buffering agent against high pH.

The hydrogen-ion concentration of a solution may be determined in various ways, but all are essentially either electrometric or colorimetric.

Acre foot, *of Water*

An acre foot is considered to be an acre of surface water to a depth of one foot. In pond, lake, or reservoir, an acre foot of stored water will produce a flow of one-half cubic foot of water per second for twenty-four hours. One acre foot equals 43,560 cubic feet, or 325,851 gallons. In fisheries management, the term may be used as a unit of measurement in formulating the carrying capacity of fishes in a given body of water.

Affluent, *of a Lake*

Brooks and streams receiving the runoff from a watershed and flowing into a lake make up its affluent; in other words, it is a tributary or feeder stream. Because of the affluents, with cooler, well-oxygenated water and the conveyance of food organisms, fishes will concentrate at an affluent and be more accessible to the angler.

Aging, *of a Lake*

The enrichment of water through prolific growth of aquatic vegetation accelerates filling and aging, thereby shortening the life of the lake, but in early stages it promotes good fishing for warm-water fishes such as largemouth bass, pickerel, pike, and perch.

Algae

Algae are vascular plants that encompass a huge number of genera and species both microscopic and large in size. They are mostly aquatic and present in both salt water and fresh water. In ponds and lakes, when in mass, it is usually referred to as "pond scum" or "bloom." Different types have a characteristic color: green, yellow-green, blue-green, brown, and red.

Alkalinity

In ponds and lakes alkalinity is usually expressed in a pH above 7. Usually, waters in the pH range 7.6 to 9 are in the alkaline class (see pH).

Alluvium

The formal term for sediments or detrital matter of lakes transported by inflowing streams and deposited on lake bottoms is "alluvium." Fishes will generally avoid areas of heavy alluvium.

Alpine Lakes

Alpine lakes are associated with snow, ice, and a cold climate where lakes are in high mountain regions. The sport fishes surviving such environments are a certain species of trout.

Anchor Ice

Anchor ice is attached or frozen to the pond or lake bottom. It is also referred to as bottom ice, depth ice, and ground ice (see winterkill).

Aphytal Zone

The plantless zone of a lake bottom is an aphytal region.

Aquatic Plants

The aquatic plants of standing-water bodies are the type whose seeds germinate in the lake bottom soil. They grow in water and are grouped as floating, submerged, and emergent. If overabundant, fishing will be affected adversely.

Artificial Lakes and Ponds

Artificial lakes and ponds are formed by grounds being excavated or dammed by man into basins and filled with water by natural runoff, by pumping, or by redirection of natural bodies of water. Some of the best fishing is provided by such controlled impoundments: warm-water ponds (especially farm ponds) for bass, bluegills, and catfish; cold-water ponds for trout.

Backwash

The flow of water from the upper shore after the uprush of waves is referred to as *backwash;* it is dangerous to fishermen wading in big waters along windy shores.

Bacteria, Lake

In all natural lakes and ponds bacteria are found in association with bottom muds and the digestive tracts of animals. In water, pathogenetic bacteria (affecting humans) can be found especially where sewage and sewage outflow is present.

Basin

"Basin" is another word for an impoundment of water or the bottom and sides that contain it. The word is interchangeable with reservoir, pond, and lake. Impoundment is also called a storage basin.

Bathymetric Map

This is a chart that includes depth measurements; it is a contour map of the submerged part of a lake basin and a handy tool to the angler-ichthyologist or inquisitive angler who notes the depth and physical aspects of the area in which fishes will take a bait or trolled lure.

Beaver Pond

This is a body of backwater created by a dam built by beavers. At times, surprisingly large brook trout can be taken out of such water entrapments.

Carrying Capacity, Fisheries

This refers to the number of fishes in a body of water that can be healthfully supported depending on the amount of food available or naturally produced.

Coliform Bacillus

In order to determine the presence of fecal coli entering through discharge or seepage into a lake, a test for coliform bacteria is used. A positive test is an indicator of gross fecal pollution. The remote possibility that coliform bacteria may develop has been used as an excuse by some bureaucrats to prevent public fishing in certain reservoirs.

Color, Lake Water

Color of water in both lakes and rivers may have a direct bearing on fishing. Heavy rainfall, for example, will turn a river brown or gray through land runoff and ruin the fishing until it clears. Generally, however, color is an effect of light penetration, radiation absorption, and reflection. Color is also related to degree of transparency, depth of water, type of lake bottom, and matter held in solution or suspension, or floating.

Current Canal, Through Weed Beds

A continuous flow of water by an inlet or an outlet stream may retard or eliminate the growth of aquatic plants and establish canallike openings through weed beds. The knowledgeable angler who fishes such openings or pothole-type areas in lakes formed by upward movements of underground springs will catch fish, whereas an angler who is ignorant of these ecological conditions will not experience a hook-up. The reason the fishes are there is that the moving canal waters and spring-fed potholes provide cooler water, more oxygen, and an abundance of nymphs and other aquatic insects on which they feed.

Currents

Currents are present in all bodies of water, even those that are landlocked and have no visible inlets or outlets. The movement of water is set in motion by the effects of winds and waves, by differences in temperature and density, and even by gravity.

Deeps, in Lakes

Deep holes, trenches, or other defined depressions in the bottoms of lakes are usually nonproductive because of lack of oxygen. A deep hole, however, may be a "hot spot" for fishing if a cold, underground, oxygen-laden stream feeds into it.

Destratification

Destratification is the mixing or circulating of water artificially by compressed air forcing the cold, stagnant, bottom water (hypolimnion) up through the top layer, thereby mixing it with the warmer, oxygenated water (epilimnion). Destratification is a tool used in fisheries management.

Diatoms

Diatoms are microscopic plants that appear as floating forms in plankton. When in abundance they produce a water "bloom" tinted yellowish or brownish that discourages anglers.

Dissolved Oxygen

Dissolved oxygen in water is measured in parts per million. Available oxygen in water is critical to fish life.

Drawdown

The decrease of water from a reservoir or other impoundment by controlled opening of a dam is called a "drawdown" by engineers. A drawdown is important to fishermen. For example, a sudden drawdown, when fishes such as bass and bluegills are spawning, will wipe out the new crop.

Also important: an angler wading the river miles below the dam, if caught unexpectedly by the heavy rush of high water may have a nasty experience, or even drown.

Drop-off

The drop-off occurs where the gentle or gradual slope from shore drops suddenly into deep water. It is sometimes referred to as "step-off."

Trolling along the steep side of the drop-off line usually produces good results. Toward evening, especially in warm weather, the larger predacious types such as bass, walleyes, and northern pike will cruise the drop-off zone waiting for the shore waters to cool in the evening before invading the shallows in search of minnows, frogs, sunfish, and the young of any species.

Dugout Pond

A dugout pond is a comparatively small body of water created by excavation, in opposition, by definition, to one made by the construction of a dam.

I have such a fish pond, dug out by a bulldozer, a short distance from my home. It is fed by natural runoff and underground springs. The pond is viewed from our living room window and has been, for many years, a source of untold pleasure during all seasons.

Effluent, Lake

The effluent of a lake is an outlet stream, that is, a surface stream that flows out of a lake. It is usually called "the outlet."

Enriched Lake

A lake that receives an infusion of nitrates, phosphates, and other nutrients causes the increase of algae and other aquatic plants. Although enrichment often results from the inflow of sewage effluent, fertilization may be the result of domestic animal wastes and commercial agricultural fertilizer brought into the lake by runoff as the result of rain falling on the surrounding terrain.

For fishing, the aquatic plants will stimulate the growth and increase the abundance of warm-water fishes such as bass, pickerel, northern pike, perch, and bluegills. The plant life, however, if not contained, may overwhelm a body of water and make fishing difficult or impossible.

Epilimnion

In a lake that is thermally stratified the epilimnion is the top, active layer of water that extends from the surface to the middle layer or thermocline.

In a stratified lake the epilimnion will contain most fishes because of a good supply of oxygen. The third or bottom layer (hypolimnion) is unsuitable to fish life because of oxygen deficiency.

Fishkill

A "fishkill," that is, an abrupt annihilation of a mass of fishes, usually refers to a winterkill; it is the destruction of fishes in lakes and ponds caused by prolonged ice and snow cover and resulting oxygen deficiency. Fishkill also comes when a shallow body of water freezes down to the bottom.

In summer a thorough fishkill may occur as a result of oxygen deficiency caused by unusually high amounts of organic matter (algae blooms) in suspension, but a summer kill may also happen because of temperature change, or a supersaturation of oxygen in dense stands of submerged vegetation.

A not uncommon fishkill occurs drastically when chemical pollutants are discharged by industry into rivers and streams.

Glacial Flow

This is a term applied to the milky-gray-colored runoff of melting glacier snows. Larry Sheerin and I experienced such a phenomenon of a glacial flow causing a sharp line of demarcation along brown shore waters on Alaska's Naknek River. We trolled a three-inch, red and white spoon along the edge of the brown water that adjoined the milky flow; it produced spectacular Chinook salmon fishing, resulting in several fish over thirty pounds being boated and one of fifty-two pounds being landed on shore.

Hatch (Matching the Hatch in Fly-fishing)

Every fly-fisherman knows what a "hatch" is; it refers to aquatic insects that under proper conditions of time and water temperature go through a meta-morphosis from egg to adult. Some species undergo a change of four stages: egg, larva, pupa, and adult. In others, the cycle includes three progressions from egg to larva (nymph) to adult. The nymphs rise from the bottom of the river, pond, or lake, swim to the surface and change into winged adults; the larvae of some types crawl from under rocks and debris onto the bank where they shed their nymphal skins and emerge as adults.

The adults have a short life. After mating and extrusion of eggs by the female the insects die and fall to the water surface where they are eagerly awaited by hungry trout that continue to feed greedily, even after their stomachs are crammed to capacity. It is at such times that the dry-fly fisherman will have best results, that is, if he uses an artificial floating fly resembling in size, shape, and color the natural insect—hence, "matching the hatch."

Hypolimnion

To fish the hypolimnion in a stratified lake is a waste of time; it is water below the thermocline (middle layer of the stratification) that extends to the bottom of the lake and lacks suitable oxygen to hold fishes.

Ichthyotoxin

In fisheries management it is a term frequently used when applying a substance that kills in order to eliminate unwanted fishes or to reduce overstocked or stunted populations of pan fishes.

A natural derivative of the South American derris root rotenone has been used throughout the world as an ichthyotoxin, but today there are many synthetic materials used.

The angler should never use ichthyotoxins even for collecting bait fish; it requires professional, technical knowledge and a permit of approval from the state environmental protection agency in order to use it legally.

Inlet

An inlet is the surface river or stream that enters a lake; it is always a good place to fish, and one reason is, game fishes gather there because the inflowing waters are cooler, well oxygenated, and carry food organisms.

At times, fishes will concentrate at the inlet while waiting for proper conditions for them to enter the stream to spawn. At other times, certain species—land-locked salmon, for example—will pursue prey (smelt) that are en route upriver to spawn. Under such conditions, the salmon are available to both the fly-fisherman, who uses a streamer-fly imitating a smelt, and to the spin-caster using a narrow, flashing spoon.

Offshore Wind

Offshore winds blow from the land toward the lake and usually produce a lee along the shore where casting is easier and fishing with bobbers and bait can be employed to best advantage.

Onshore Wind

Onshore winds blow from the lake toward the shore. Often moderate onshore winds will create good boat fishing along the breezy shore because the waves and turbulence increase oxygen and cool the water (in warm weather), thereby attracting fishes to a more comfortable environment.

Oxygen (and Carbon Dioxide)

Everyone knows that fishes, as well as humans, require oxygen to sustain life. Humans receive oxygen from the air they breathe; fishes absorb it through their gills from the water they live in. Much is written about the necessity of fishes to have an adequate supply of oxygen in order to function healthily, but anglers generally do not recognize the fact that too much oxygen can be as harmful to fishes as not enough of a supply.

At times, both oxygen and carbon dioxide occur in water in excessive or subnormal amounts with resulting detrimental effects on fishes. In warm weather and bright sunshine, abnormally high oxygen supersaturation may happen within dense stands of submerged vegetation; and in the other direction, unusually high carbon dioxide saturation may occur where rapid decay of organic substances takes place on the bottom of a lake or pond. In either case, if the fishes cannot escape, that is, move off to another more healthful environment, a "fishkill" will take place (see Fishkill).

Although the angler will generally find the best fishing (all other factors being equal) where water has a good supply of oxygen, at times a reduced amount or inadequate amount will help in subduing a fish after it is hooked. For example, an Atlantic salmon that takes a fly in fast water along an undercut bank will tire quickly if it can be reeled into quiet water that holds less oxygen and is warmer. When the fish is exerting itself and is forced into less oxygenated water the rate of breathing will be faster and it will pant, so to speak, like a track athlete after running a race.

From personal experience of seven trips to Iceland's Grimsa River fishing for Atlantic salmon, where the angler wades the water rather than fishing from a canoe, I have proved the above theory many times.

Pond or Lake?

In literature, when is a body of water referred to correctly as a pond and when is it called a lake? I believe that a sharp distinction cannot be made to everyone's satisfaction. Some will say that a lake is a large body of water, whereas a pond is a small one. The imperfection in that definition becomes immediately apparent when the measurements of "large" and "small" are called for.

According to the specialists, any impoundment thermally stratified through most of the year should be called a lake. Such a definition is illogical when a huge body of, say, 3500 acres of shallow water is called a pond because it seldom shows thermal stratification.

Some fisheries scientists in individual states have adopted a size classification; one state accepts ten acres as representing the separation of pond and lake; another sets it at four acres, and still another at five acres.

Sediments

Sediments is the term applied to the depositing of all types of detrital matter on the lake bottom. In the singular, "sediment" usually is taken to mean detrital matter held in suspension, as in silting.

Silting

Silting is a major concern in the longevity of a body of water, especially in reservoirs whose waters are retained by dams. Inflowing rivers carrying silt cause a buildup of sediments on the lake bottom, eventually overwhelming the impoundment's productivity.

Silting, after a heavy rain from runoff, is a serious detriment to trout and salmon fishing until it settles.

Stratified Lakes and Fall Overturn

During the warm summer months, most of the lakes in the United States are thermally stratified, that is, the water occurs in three layers that show differences in temperature. The upper layer is known as the epilimnion; the stratum below it is called thermocline, and the bottom layer is the hypolimnion.

During the period of summer stratification, most impoundments contain no oxygen in the hypolimnion. In the early season, once the lake has been stratified, there may be oxygen in the lower waters, but the oxygen demand from the decay and the respiration of bacteria, plankton, and fishes soon use up all available oxygen.

Anglers take note: fishes will avoid areas of inadequate oxygen.

In stratified lakes, the fishing may vastly improve in the fall. The thermal stratification is broken up by wind action, and the epilimnion cools to a temperature approaching that of the hypolimnion. Gradually the entire lake starts to circulate because the winds across the surface develop water currents and compensating currents develop across the lake bottom. Consequently, the summer bottom water comes into contact with the surface layers, where free and dissolved carbon dioxide has a chance to be released, and the dissolved oxygen supply is replenished.

In the fall, when the majority of anglers put away their tackle for other pursuits, the fishing is best because the fishes have gained maximum weight for the year and, because of fall overturn, they become more active and more receptive to taking the bait or the lure.

Temperature—Water

Along with pH and oxygen, water temperature is one of the most important factors influencing freshwater fishes and their behavior. Each species has a certain preference or tolerance of temperature and they can only survive within a given high-low range, or bracket, of temperature.

In a general way, freshwater fishes can be separated into two groups, warm-water and cold-water species; for example, trout and salmon are representative of cold-water types, thriving in water with a maximum summer temperature of 70°F. Warm-water representatives such as the largemouth bass, bluegill crappie, and catfishes in ponds and lakes are almost never killed by high temperatures alone.

The fishery biologist is attentive to water temperature because it influences rate of metabolism and resulting growth rate in fishes.

The inquisitive angler may find it fruitful to carry a thermometer (attached to a line) in his tackle box in order to note water temperature as associated with depth and angling success.

Some thermometers have readings in *centigrade* and others are marked off in *Fahrenheit*. The centigrade thermometer is segmented into 100 equal parts: 0°

(freezing) to 100° (boiling). The space on the Fahrenheit thermometer, between freezing and boiling, is separated into 180 equal parts: 32° (freezing) to 212° (boiling). Here is a simple conversion formula that is easy to work and accurate enough to satisfy the angler who is using a centigrade thermometer, but would like to know what the corresponding Fahrenheit reading is established: (°C × ⅑) + 35 = °F. (Water temperature thermometers are partially encased in a metal frame and have a ring at the head end to which the cord or line can be attached).

Temperature Tolerance (Freshwater Fishes)

Freshwater sport fishes are popularly separated into cold-water and warm-water types—trouts and salmons in cold water, and such as the largemouth bass, perch, pike, panfishes, and catfishes in warm water.

Lake trout inhabit deep, cold-water lakes in northern areas and generally prefer the coldest water temperatures, 45° to 55°F.

Brook trout prefer 55° to 65°F. and will seldom survive above 65° to 70°F.

Rainbow trout, is the same category as the "brookie," but will accept colder temperatures when migrating out to sea and returning to freshwater rivers as steelhead, to spawn.

Brown trout are the hardiest of the trout clan; they are able to survive more readily in polluted waters where other trout will not, and they can also tolerate higher temperatures, from 75° to 85°F.

Salmons; the Atlantic, and all five species inhabiting our northwestern coasts, are highly migratory and only comfortable in cold river and ocean temperatures of 52° to 60°F.

Musky, yellow perch, walleye, and rock bass, inhabiting, more or less, the same type of environment, are mostly comfortable in temperatures from 60° to 70°F. The various smaller panfishes can take warmer water, about 5°F. higher.

Largemouth bass and smallmouth bass are excellent examples of closely related species that tolerate slightly different water temperatures because of environmental preferences. The largemouth survives best where there is plenty of vegetation in calm waters at about 70° to 75°F., whereas the smallmouth is more often found in running water or rocky and sandy bottom areas of lakes at 65° to 70°F.

Turbidity

Turbidity and consequent change of color in river water due to heavy winds or rain storms is caused by land runoff, resulting in suspended silt in water (see silting).

Turbid waters may also occur when carp, suckers, and sturgeon feed along the bottom of rivers and lakes. Their mode of feeding involves digging, sucking, and uprooting of vegetation, resulting in water discoloration. Such silt-laden water drives away the more desirable fishes.

Undercut Bank

An undercut bank in rivers is formed by current flow excavating its base, leaving an overhang in front. Such a bank will harbor fishes when other parts of the river will not because the flow under the bank is cooler, usually holds more oxygen, and affords shelter, and the passage of food organisms is greater. The angler should always fish such a spot.

Wetlands

Environmentalists list a wide group of wet habitats within the scope of wetlands. It includes areas that are permanently wet or intermittent in water coverage— swamps, marshy meadows, bogs, muskeg, potholes.

Not too many years ago, the term "wetlands" was familiar mostly to wildlife specialists, especially where waterfowl and other aquatic-bird life was concerned. "Wetlands" has now become a familiar term to the general public because the excessive draining of wetlands for housing and industrial development is common. Not only is the disappearance of groundwater detrimental to fish and wildlife, but water that is used for public consumption is adversely affected; the water table drops suddenly, and, when water becomes unavailable, everyone concerned goes into a panic.

Winterkill

See "Fishkill".

6

Anatomy Relative to Fishing

Anatomical Advantages and Restrictions

Much can be learned from simple observation of a fish's anatomy—facts that can be applied to enhance successful fishing. The degree of speed and maneuverability of a fish's body has a direct bearing on the way a fish will take a bait, live or artificial. The key to relative speeds that fishes attain is in direct relationship to the size, shape, flexibility, or rigidness of its caudal fin (tail). For example, sharks are not fast swimmers; tails are soft in action and flexible, as are their cartilaginous internal supports (not a true-bone skeleton). Sharks' teeth are not the cutting, slicing, scissorlike type. Their recurved dentition is ideal for grasping and holding, aided by vigorous convulsions of the body in tearing away the flesh in mouthfuls.

Sharks will take slow-moving or drifting bait, often swimming around it in ever

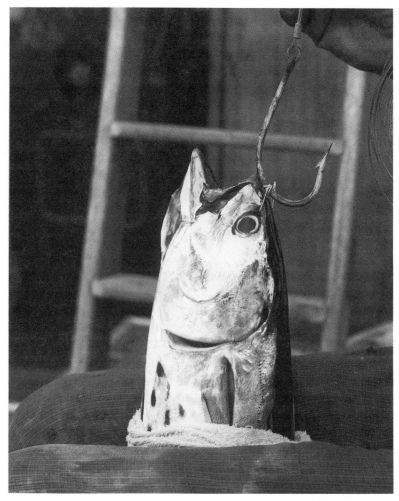

Knowledge of fish anatomy is important in many aspects of angling, as
indicated by one of the most unique and highly effective methods of rigging
live bait for big-game fishing employed in waters off Panama. The hook is
not directly embedded in the baitfish, in this case a bonito, but is connected
to it by needle and thread passed through the anterior portion of the eye
socket. The fish's brain is located posterior to the eye (see illustration) and
is not affected. The operation is done quickly. The bonito is held firmly
encased in a towel between the mate's knees; it is returned to the water
virtually unharmed. When the bonito, trolled close to the surface by the
outrigger, frantically zig-zags in an attempt to evade a pursuing marlin,
cleaving the blue water with its dorsal fin extended, it produces one of the
most exquisitely exciting moments of big-game fishing. *Photo by author.*

decreasing circles because they hunt mostly by use of their powerful olfactory nerves. As usual, there is an exception to the rule. The mako shark, the best shark performer against rod and reel, with its pointed nose and more streamlined body form, will overtake a surface bait trolled fast in a straight line.

The freshwater largemouth bass and the groupers of marine reefs have similar anatomical features with the same type of mobility and comparable speed. They have large fanlike tails adapted for short bursts of speed and agile turning and twisting in and around rocks, aquatic vegetation, and other underwater growth. Consequently, the groupers, basses, and other similar forms will seldom be attracted to a rapidly moving bait or lure, especially if it is traveling in a straight line. The angler's presentation should resemble the fish's preference—a slow-moving offering with erratic motion and an occasional pause in movement.

Trout and salmon tails are also flexible, but not to the extent of the bass. Add to that fact a more elongated form and it produces a body capable of sudden, swift movement and a flash of speed for a short distance. To contradict that statement I must admit that I have had salmon on the terminal end of my fly line that moved like lightning for a great distance downstream!

In contrast to the slow and occasional pause retrieve of lures that will draw the interest of bass, members of the popular freshwater pike family—pickerel, northern pike, and musky—will grab a lure in fast retrieve. Because of their comparatively rigid, long, cylindrical body form and camouflaged coloration they are well suited for short, darting, fast attacks in a straight line from out of a weed bed. It is true that all three of these well-toothed gamesters are mostly attracted to and taken on wobbling spoons and rotating spinners, but it must be remembered that the lures have to be retrieved in a fast, straight line to make them work.

The really consistent speedsters of the underwater world have tails that are specialized and highly developed. Tuna, marlin, swordfish, bonito, wahoo, king-fish, and others possess rigid tails—thick, rugged, and set in position; they are also lunate or forked in shape.

Having hooked, played, and boated many bluefin tuna, including eleven that weighed over 500 pounds each, I can attest to the incredible, sustained speed of giant bluefins when hooked. As a basis for comparison: I have been fortunate in having the opportunities to play and successfully boat all species of the fast big-game fishes in different oceans and seas of the world. Therefore, in my estimation, the bluefin is the fastest big-game fish that swims, at least at the terminal end of my rod, reel, and line.

The propulsion that provides locomotion for the speediest of big-game fishes comes from the tail being "waved" from side to side, resulting mostly from body undulations. But the bluefin's body has practically no flexibility in its rigid,

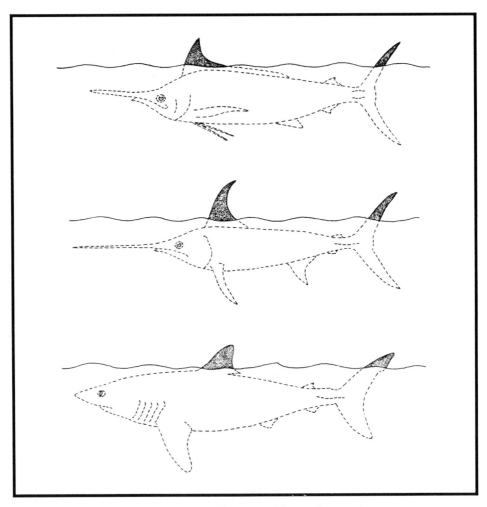

Marlin, swordfish, and sharks, when basking or cruising at the water's
surface, can be distinguished, one from another, by the characteristics
of the exposed portions of their dorsal and tail fins.

   Top: marlin—rigid, pointed tail; dorsal fin usually folded down into a
groove and not extended unless excited (same for sailfish).

   Middle: swordfish—sickle-shaped dorsal fin, rigid and cannot be folded;
tail fin also rigid.

   Bottom: shark—dorsal fin fixed in upright position; tail not rigid, flexible,
and wallows in movement.

   Often, at a distance, the upward-curved tips of a basking, manta's
wings—ends of the pectoral fins—above water are mistaken for gamefish.

football-shaped (fusiform) body; it derives its impressive swimming speed solely from its tail, which beats in a short arc at an incredible ten or twenty times per second. From taking these observations into consideration it can be easily understood why the tunalike fishes prefer a fast-moving lure, preferably in a straight line. I am also sure that some bluefin tuna angler will be quick to point out to me that bluefins will take a slowly drifted bait below the surface after following a chum slick to point of origin and baited hook, suspended practically without motion. One must remember, however, that such a situation is an artificial creation.

The behaviorisms, due to anatomical structure, exemplified in the preceding paragraphs are but a few samples portrayed on the subject. Nevertheless, they should spark a sense of inquiry, or at least curiosity, in anglers regarding the pros and cons of presenting lures or baits to the sport fishes they seek, because the same principals involved are applicable to every fish that swims.

Releasing for Survival

Today's sportfisherman, more than ever, is exhorted by fisheries biologists and conservation agencies, as well as by his peers, to release the fishes he catches, or at least cut down on his take. The reason for such inducement may be to maintain sound conservation measures, to preserve dwindling populations of certain species, or to be a good sportsman, participating in "catch and release" events such as in "fly-fishing only" programs in trout waters or bass-release in lakes. Such practices are worthwhile, especially in tournaments, fishing for marlin and sailfish in marine waters.

Whatever the reason for the release, certain precautions in handling must be employed so that the fish will have the best possible chance for survival after release.

Releasing freshwater fishes with the least possibility of injury, after the trauma of resisting rod and reel, is much easier than freeing bigger and tougher marine types. In trout and salmon angling the fish may be kept in the water in the net and the hook removed with a pair of long-nose hemostat-type pliers. The same system is just as easily executed from a boat when removing a hook from the mouth of a largemouth bass. It can be held immobile by grasping its lower jaw with thumb and forefinger. In the "old days," anglers were advised to wet their hands when holding a fish so that the protective mucus covering the fish would not be worn off by a dry hand. More harm than good was done because the fish had to be held tightly with consequent injury to its abdominal organs and connective tissues.

Fish that are not fought until "belly-up" will slowly swim away after hook removal. If the fish is unable to regain its natural position and swim away, it often helps to hold it gently upright in the water until it regains its equilibrium.

Fishes intended for release should never be grasped through the operculum (gill cover) and throat, because the delicate gill filaments responsible for drawing oxygen from the water through them into the circulatory (blood) system will be injured and chances of survival will be greatly reduced. One of the most effective ways of holding a fish, one that I use if the catch is planned for the table, is to grasp it tightly overhead by the neck, with thumb on one side and second finger on the other. I advise *not* to use this method when the intention is to release because the pressure necessary to subdue the fish usually injures the gill structure. Also, care must be taken with fishes that have sharply pointed spines in their first dorsal fin, and some fish have extremely sharp gill cover edges capable of lacerating a hand.

When releasing medium-sized and big-game marine fishes, the process is more difficult because the waters are deeper, the specimens more troublesome to handle, the fight is longer, the boat's gunwales are high, and the fish should not be gaffed.

When species such as grouper and snapper are brought up from the depths they often reach the surface with gas bladder (air bladder) protruding from mouth. This is caused by gas coming out of the solution in the blood. (It is commonly referred to as "the bends" when human divers come up too fast from deep water to the surface. If a bubble forms in the circulatory system and travels to the brain or other organ it is called an "embolism" and may kill.)

Many years ago, as an ichthyologist at Yale, I was assisting Lou Mowbray, then director of the Bermuda Aquarium, to collect reef fishes intended for tank display. Many of the specimens, taken on hook and line, came up with their air bladders drawn out into their mouths and exposed, or expanded but held partially within the abdominal cavity. When placed in the live well these fishes floated, belly-up, until Lou punctured them with a long, pointed, hollow needle-tube. Specimens whose air bladders were expanded because of gas accumulation, as indicated by the swollen belly, but not exposed, were also "degassed." Lou inserted the needle through the skin, under a scale, high up the side of the abdominal cavity into the air sac, and the gas was released. Immediately after the operation the fishes swam naturally, to the bottom of the tank.

Because of the composition of salt water, external body injuries to marine fishes are less apt to become infected than is the case with freshwater inhabitants. A fish that can be hefted to photograph before release, for example, may be safely handled without serious injury to the fish by grabbing it underneath the jaw on both sides of the throat away from the gills. In some cases, a gaff inserted through the skin and lower mandible (jaw) will not prove fatal to the fish.

Big fishes, if intended for release, should never be hoisted up a gin pole (pole and rope pulley aboard the boat) vertically because their weight out of the water can rip the blood vessels from their origins or insertions and also damage the viscera by stretching.

The best method for release of big-game fishes is to cut the leader as close as possible to the hook. The hook may or may not work free eventually, but if it doesn't it will become covered by scar tissue and made harmless. Many instances have been documented of healthy fishes being caught that had hooks already embedded in their jaws, and in some cases found in their abdomens when opened up.

If possible, a fish to be released should never be played to total exhaustion because in that helpless state it may become easy victim to sharks, or it may not recover from lactic acid buildup in the muscles to a point of toxicity.

Lactic Acid

When a fish swims at a sustained rate of speed (one may call it a cruising speed), it energizes its muscles and removes the waste from them through the circulatory system, that is, via its bloodstream, at a balanced rate, continuously. During sudden explosions of high speed such as experienced when strenuously resisting rod and reel, lactic acid grows rapidly in the muscles. If the hooked fish is fought excessively to exhaustion the lactic acid can build up and kill the fish by slow internal poisoning a short time after extensive exertion. Obviously, if the angler intends to release the fish it should not be played until it "bellies up," for even if it slowly swims away after hook removal it may die later from lactic acid poisoning.

The fish's natural ability to save energy by controlling its output, thereby eliminating complete muscle fatigue and lactic acid buildup, has been demonstrated to me over the past six seasons of fly-fishing for Atlantic salmon in Iceland. There the fish must negotiate an unusual number of difficult falls and rapids enroute to their ancestral spawning grounds. Unless the previous winter's ice has drastically gouged or realigned the river's banks or bottom, the salmon are to be found annually in the same, certain pools, usually the first pools that meet the requirement of safe and well-oxygenated waters, where the fish can rest and recoup after the great exertion of swimming against the tremendous pressures of the falls and rapids of violently rushing water. Salmon will "lie" in such pools conducive to rest until they are ready to move on. Their departure from a pool to travel farther upstream may be induced by factors such as rainfall, water temperature, and development of gonads (reproductive organs), but they never move until their unconscious metabolism signals that their muscles have recouped and are again ready for travel. The salmon angler who recognizes this phenomenon, and knows the pool, may be lucky if his artificial fly is presented properly at the time a salmon decides to take it. (One way of looking at it is, if the angler knows where the salmon lie, he will not waste time working parts of the river where the fish don't stop; and still another way of looking at it is to hire a good guide and follow his advice.)

Resistance to Rod and Reel

During many years of experience as a lecturer in ichthyology and sportfishing, two of the questions most often asked of me were, "What is your favorite type of fishing?" and "What is the best fighting fish?" The first query was, and is, easy to answer: "Wherever I happened to be fishing." The second is impossible to answer with unequivocal assurance.

The best fighting fish in fisherman's language refers to a hooked fish's ability to resist rod and reel. One of the best-known expressions used by writers who laud the magnificence of their favorite sport fish is, "Inch for inch and pound for pound, the gamest fish that swims." Many years ago, John Henshall, in his book on the smallmouth bass, made that overzealous interpretation of the sporting qualities of that bass. Since then, Henshall's words have been imitated, overworked, and applied to other species described in numerous books, reports, and articles. To compare the fighting qualities of one type to another demands imagination and speculation—even if the author takes into consideration the weight and age of the fish, temperature and strength of water flow, time of year, development stage of the reproductive organs, type of tackle used, and—not least—the capabilities of the angler.

In my estimation, generally speaking, the degree of resistance produced by a hooked fish, regardless of species, depends mostly on the location of the lodged hook in the fish's anatomy. A fish can fight at its best when the hook is embedded forward in the upper jaw, allowing breathing to take place without too much difficulty. If the hook is gripped in the lower jaw there will be a definite impairment to the rhythmic opening and closing of the jaws necessary for the water to be pushed over the gills, which provide life-supporting oxygen. When the hook is

The fighting qualities—that is, the strength and endurance of a fish's resistance to rod and reel—depend greatly upon the anatomical lodgment of the hook.

This striped marlin was taken by the author in the Humboldt Current off the coast of Cabo Blanco, Peru; it crash-striked a strip bait and was hooked in the upper jaw. If the marlin had been hooked in the outer, lower jaw or in its throat, the fight would have been much shorter in time and less spectacular in action.

When a billfish such as the marlin hits the bait with its bill, the angler usually free-spools the reel, allowing the bait to appear stunned. The billfish then may swallow the bait, directly affecting its ability to resist (note remora attached to marlin's belly). *Yale Expedition Photo.*

taken deeply into the throat, wounding the gills, or even deeper into the esophagus, the fighting qualities will be reduced dramatically, and the chances for survival are minimal if the fish is to be released. The heart is located far forward of the abdominal cavity under the esophagus; if the heart cavity is punctured by the hook the fish will bleed and the fight will terminate quickly.

This striped marlin is foul-hooked. The hook is embedded in the base of the left pectoral fin and the leader has cut across the dorsal fin. Because the unobstructed mouth allows water to flow regularly over the gills, thereby producing oxygen naturally, the fish can give more than usual resistance to the efforts of the angler. *Photo by Foster Bam.*

Foul-hooked Fishes

The degree of difficulty in subduing a foul-hooked fish also depends on where in the fish's anatomy the hook is fixed, or the leader wrapped. If the restraining hook or leader takes place in the caudal peduncle, that is, in the tail-end, the victim may quit suddenly because its main force for propulsion has been seriously hindered, and it will suffocate because the pull of the line will cause water to travel backward through the gill cover openings. When the hook is stuck in the body, dorsal fin, or ventral fin, the mouth is not obstructed, so the fish may breathe freely, and its speed will not be affected because the tail will not be restricted in movement. Such a fish, therefore, is capable of demonstrating resistance to the angler's efforts far beyond that of a specimen of equal size hooked naturally in the jaw.

For me, the best example of a miscalculation in size of a big-game fish due to a foul-up occurred off the shores of Nova Scotia. During an International Tuna Cup Match in which I was chairman of the Fishing Committee, and as an observer, I boarded one of the boats representing a segment of the U.S. team participating in the competition. The team member, who was to do the fishing, was a friend of mine, Jack Anderson, of Detroit, Michigan. Jack is vice-president of the International Game Fish Association, and a big-game fisherman of note with worldwide experience, including the taking of a black marlin of over 1000 pounds in Australian waters. He was in the fighting chair when a bluefin tuna grabbed the herring-baited hook. After more than two hours of give and take between angler and fish, excitement was growing in the committee room at the Grand Hotel in Yarmouth, where the description of the action was being received by radio from the judge's boat at the scene of the battle. Because of Jack's fame as a big-game angler, my assistance in turning the chair, and the best of tuna guides running the boat, the overly long fight was conveying to the committee members the impression that Jack was onto a world-record tuna.

A dozen times or more during the fight, Jack had most of the line retrieved on the reel with no sight of the stubborn fish down deep. When the fish was rod-pumped up close it appeared to gather momentum directly under the stern of the boat, or so it seemed, causing me to hand signal frantically to the captain at the wheel to go full speed ahead, or the propeller would cut the line. After much more rod-pumping and arm-killing reeling, the tuna suddenly bellied up to the surface, and to the dismay and embarrassment of everyone aboard, especially to the angler, the fish looked to be about 200 pounds. Usually, Jack handles a fish of that size in about ten minutes.

When the lip-hooked tuna took the bait it must have turned a couple of times, causing the leader to wrap around the midsection of its body. The mouth was under no disadvantage for breathing, and the awesome strength of the tuna's tail was free for sudden, fast spurts of speed. But the most effective cause for resistance was sustained because the fish's body acted like a plate, broadside to the line, and under the unusual influence of the tide-flowing waters. This was especially marked when the tuna's body scaled down directly under the boat.

It was tough for all of us aboard to face the crowd at the dock at St. Mary's Cove. They had been expecting to witness the weighing of a possible world-record giant bluefin tuna!

The most dramatic occurrences of foul-hooked fishes that I have witnessed happened with big-game, but I have also experienced many instances while fly-fishing in fast-flowing rivers when trout and salmon were foul-hooked or leader-wrapped. An outstanding example of misinterpreting the approximate weight of a fish being played in a river took place in the wilds of Labrador.

During a two-week camping and fishing trip to the primitive area of the Hunt River in the company of Charlie Gage, Larry Shields, Bob Mays, and two native camp assistants—Joe, a Mountainais Indian and Chesley Flowers, of Scottish-Eskimo strain—we caught and released a considerable number of gorgeously colored brook trout weighing up to eight pounds.

Although I had fished for salmon in Nova Scotia, Newfoundland, New Brunswick, Quebec, and Iceland, the jaunt to Labrador was unusually interesting and exciting because, without guides, we explored practically unfished waters. Our two native helpers knew nothing of sport fishing.

We flew "commercial" from Montreal to Goose Bay. From there we chartered a plane to travel northward to Hopedale. At Hopedale our transport continued by plane with a bush pilot at the controls and two canoes lashed to the pontoons. We dropped down to slide on a river festooned with above-the-surface rocks and boulders at the outlet of a nameless lake where we were to set up camp.

As soon as the canoes, tents, and supplies were deposited ashore, the pilot, with a sign of "thumbs up," took off. He had been instructed to pick us up two weeks later at a predesignated spot several miles downriver. We were to be completely out of touch with the civilized world during that time.

After having enjoyed the trout fishing of a lifetime, we portaged and paddled about ten miles downstream to a part of the river where, Chesley assured us, salmon appeared at that time of year. Toward evening, while camp was being set up in the new spot, Charlie Gage, my longtime friend and treasurer of Yale, suggested that he and I take a canoe and try for salmon at the confluence of waters around a small island. I paddled us across the river and beached the canoe. We had plenty of room to wade and cast in separate pools. Charlie hooked a good fish that immediately started downriver to strip out line off the reel at an alarming rate. I thrashed over the rocky bottom as fast as I could to the canoe and pushed it to where Charlie was standing in knee-deep water with the rod held high over his head. When he came aboard, the remaining backing of his line on the reel was about to sing good-bye. I paddled furiously to keep up with the fish as we crashed into the white water of the rapids. As we went zooming by the campsite our friends ashore cheered. The salmon never jumped. Every time the line was retrieved to safe proportions on the reel, the fish, under the influence of the strong current, pulled out line faster than I could manipulate the canoe.

Charlie Gage was a fly-fisherman of wide experience who had fought and landed many salmon, some in the twenty-five- to thirty-pound range. He believed me when I said, "You'd better not rush it because that fish should go thirty pounds." After another long stretch of rapids we suddenly arrived at a large area of flat, calm, clear water over a sandy bottom. Abruptly, the rod straightened; the resistance was gone. I thought we had lost the fish. But there it was, still on the line, motionless, with its brilliant silver side easily seen in the shallow water. It was dead. We came ashore, dragged in the salmon and discovered that the leader was wrapped several times around the midsection of the fish's body. Now it became obvious that for most of the time Charlie had been fighting a dead fish, broadside to the swift currents and bouncing along the undulations of the rocky bottom.

Chesley and Joe arrived in the other canoe to help us struggle back upriver to camp. The fish weighed twelve pounds. Charlie and I were greatly disappointed and slightly embarrassed, but our Indian associate was all smiles because he spent most of his time in camp whittling, and smoking fish to take home to his village. Charlie's salmon was a welcome addition to his collection!

Indian Joe whittled away every moment when sitting by his improvised smoker constructed with three limbs and a raincoat, under which the filleted fish were hanging over smoky, moss-covered coals. I would ask him, "Joe, what are you whittling?" He would answer, "I don't know, but it may come in handy."

7

Especially for
the Inquisitive Angler

Acid Rain

When sulfur and nitrogen oxides are released from industrial smokestacks they cling to water molecules and form acid that falls in rain. Nitrogen oxides, emitted from the burning of fossil fuels, are connected to nitric acid, a prime component of acid rain. Nitrogen oxides eventually become nitrates, a potent fertilizer. When nitrates fall on coastal waters that may be already polluted and heated up by hot spells they may set off algal bloom (see Algae, in Chapter 5, p. 133), which deprive seawater of oxygen and light, thereby murdering the fishes and further polluting the water.

Acid rain kills fishes in ponds, lakes, and streams. Although it is generally conceded that soot, smoke, and sulfur dioxide are blown from point of origin to areas hundreds of miles away, some officials representing the Environmental

Protection Agency (EPA) claim that there is insufficient evidence to prove that pollution in the northeast of the United States and Canada originates hundreds of miles away.

Examples:

Recent acid sensitivity studies of St. Mary's River, a high-quality trout stream in Virginia, have identified the water as one of the most acid-sensitive. The pH (see pH) has declined from 6.8 in 1983 to 5.2 in 1988. In 1976, fish population data showed a healthy fish distribution, with good numbers of rainbow trout, brook trout, and associated fish species. The 1986–1988 data showed a sharp reduction in rainbow trout and a drastic decline in the population of acid-sensitive fish species.

In a study released by the New York State Department of Environmental Conservation it was reported that 25 percent of the lakes and ponds in the Adirondacks are too acidic from acid rain to support fishes.

Dwight Webster, one of the fisheries professors under whom I studied at Cornell University, was one of the early investigators of acid rain in the Adirondacks. He experimented with the application of lime to the water in order to neutralize the acid, but soon found that the procedure, to be effective, was too costly. His findings indicated that acid rain first affects the lakes, reclining at the highest altitudes and progressively affecting the lakes in successively lower altitudes.

Twenty-five years after scientists found the first evidence of acid rain, the country is still struggling to solve and to rectify the matter.

After many years of warnings by reputable scientists in both the United States and Canada, stating that acid rain is one of the most pressing environmental problems facing both countries today, an official, positive attitude has finally and just recently been announced by George Bush, the President of the United States.

Aquaculture

Aquaculture, the production and management of fishes under artificial or programmed conditions, has long been practiced in some parts of Europe and Asia. In more recent times in the United States, the growing of trout in cold-water hatcheries and catfish in warm-water ponds has developed into an exact science, with many highly successful commercial projects in operation. Also, on the Pacific coast, experimentation with privately owned stocks of salmon is showing encouraging possibilities for successful commercial application.

To me, however, the most dramatic aquaculture project occurs in the inshore area off the coast of Nova Scotia, where I have fished for the giant bluefin tuna for many seasons. I have witnessed the following procedure several times and photographed it. The giants are trapped alive, some of them weighing more than 1,000 pounds, in mackerel net traps of local fishermen. The fish are transferred to holding pens (formed by nets); they are actually open-water corrals with the tops of the pens marked by buoys. The tuna, trapped anytime between June and October, are each fed fifty pounds of mackerel or herring daily. They grow fat for fall harvest and sale to the Japanese market, where the tuna with the highest fat content bring the best prices. The bluefins are killed in the pens, butchered, boxed in ice, and exported to Tokyo for a waiting market.

Artificial Reefs

Freshwater anglers who pursue bass, crappie, perch, bluegills, and other pan-fishes know that some of the best results can be had by fishing over and around submerged tree stumps, fallen trees, brush piles, boulders, and other underwater objects. The reason for angling success in such spots is quite simple: microscopic organisms attach themselves to these underwater hook-and-line hazards; other aquatic animals (zooplankton) find sustenance on the tiny aquatic vegetation (phytoplankton). Bait fishes and the young of other species feed on the zoo-plankton, and they also can hide in the branches, sheltered from the larger predatory fishes. The end result—game fishes patrol such spots, constantly searching to attack the small fishes concentrated there. And finally, the angler is drawn to these locations, where the game fishes he seeks are more apt to be localized.

Fisheries managers have greatly improved fishing in many flat-bottom, smooth-shore waters by artificially erecting bottom outgrowths. In ponds and lakes, for example, small trees and brush piles are weighed down with concrete blocks, boated out, and dropped overboard to sink to the bottom. In the larger bodies of water in the north country, where lakes freeze over, artificial cover is dragged out on the ice by snowmobile. When the spring thaw arrives and the ice melts, the discarded auto bodies, piles of concrete blocks, tires cabled together, refrigerators, and other kinds of worthless junk sink to the bottom. In effect, an artificial reef is created.

Anglers who fish in warm oceanic waters for grouper, snapper, yellowtail, sheepshead, amberjack, barracuda, and a host of other species, know that the best fishing is found over and along the sides and edges of coral reefs.

On the other hand, in some offshore seas there are miles of clear, flat-bottom, sandy areas with no irregularities to attract any life. Consequently, no fishes of interest to the angler are there. The many opportunities to improve or establish fish populations in such barren areas are not so available to scientists as they are in freshwater environments, where management tools can be employed—stream improvements, hatcheries, fish ladders at dams, water drawdowns, seasons, size and bag limits, fish population balances, and the like. The marine ecosystems are too enormous and complex for any such management attempts.

Along the coastlines of the United States there is growing concern to protect our estuaries and saltwater and brackish marshes because, among other reasons, they serve as nurseries for young fishes and remain a vital link in the production of some of our most popular coastal game fishes. But the case in offshore waters is different. Just to attempt to standardize size and bag limits or initiate seasonal restrictions requires a great deal of political involvement with bureaucrats between and among states; and for the highly migratory, transoceanic species such as tuna and marlin, international agreements are required. Nevertheless, one tool, the artificial reef, employed to introduce or enhance sportfishing in barren grounds, has proved highly successful, even spectacular, in some places such as off the coasts of South Carolina and Alabama, where the coastal waters flow over unobstructed bottoms.

I had my first practical experience of successful artificial-reef fishing off the coast of South Carolina during an Intercollegiate Fishing Tournament directed by Professor Don Millus of the faculty of the University of South Carolina. Don, a former Yale Fishing Team member, carries out the tradition of the Yale Intercollegiate Fishing Match and Seminars that were held annually in Wedgeport, Nova Scotia, for twenty years. The five-day event was sponsored by the Nova Scotia government and directed by Yale University until the giant bluefin tuna and other game fishes became scarce. Five universities from the United States, five from Canada, plus a six-man team from Japan and another from Mexico, participated.

The students in the South Carolina tournament fished for king mackerel from private boats in areas close enough to shore to be reached by outboard-powered skiffs during good weather. At other times, all the collegians were on an oceangoing "head boat," and they fished successfully over artificial reefs where the boat captain easily pinpointed the "hot spot" by the use of the vessel's electronic devices.

A choice setting for artificial reefs in coastal waters, easily available to boat anglers, ranges in depth from about thirty to eighty feet. Again, the principals involved regarding these reefs are similar to those occurring in freshwater settings. In marine waters the junk materials situated on the sea floor induce the attachment and growth of marine life: phytoplankton, zooplankton, sponges, barnacles, and seaweed. Bait fishes are drawn to the reefs for food, where they try to hide from the large predators sought by anglers. As previously mentioned, the reefs are easily located by boat captains using marked charts and electronic equipment. The closer-to-shore reefs are also marked by buoys, and their locations are a matter of public knowledge secured at the nearest bait shop or boat marina.

Unquestionably, the installation of artificial reefs, especially in barren sea areas, has proved to be highly successful in attracting fishes to focal points, thereby making them accessible to the angler. The good news, however, is not without its problems. Conflicts between commercial and recreational fisherman over the use of artificial reefs is on the increase. Sport divers have also become involved with recreational fishermen regarding the use of artificial reefs.

Another problem looming on the horizon is the more than likely possibility of the reefs being overfished. North Carolina and Washington State have regulations that allow for the closure of reefs in case of overfishing, but no other state has incorporated such management options. To further confuse the issue, states have no official management jurisdiction over artificial reefs in federal waters. Reefs in federal waters come under the control of the National Marine Fisheries Service (NMFS).

With some foresight, the Sport Fishing Institute's Artificial Reef Development Center (ARDC) made a study and produced a report, "Artificial Reefs and Fishery Conflicts: Problems and Opportunities for the Sport Fishing Industry." (Anglers, take note. This study was funded by the American Fishing Tackle Association.)

The ARDC serves as a national clearing house of artificial-reef information. More details may be obtained from the director of ARDC, 1010 Massachusetts Ave. N.W., Suite 100, Washington, DC 20001.

Although artificial-reef projects are presently gaining much attention in the coastal waters of the United States, the recognition of the importance of building such structures to attract fishes is not a recent invention. Richard B. Stone, chief of the Artificial Reef Task Group of the National Marine Fisheries Service, mentioned that in a book on fishing in the Carolinas in 1860 a reference was made concerning a group of local fishermen who built oak- or pine-floored enclosures, five to six feet high, floated them out, and sank them with stones at inlets to attract the return of sheepshead, which had disappeared when large fallen trees were removed from the inlets.

Another bit of research by Stone reveals that a successful reef-building venture took place in 1916, initiated by the Boatmen's Association of Great South Bay,

New York. Butter tubs were half-filled with cement and sunk near Fire Island Inlet. For about thirty years the tubs attracted fishes, until they had to be replaced.

In 1935 the Cape May Wildwood Party Boat Association sank four vessels and tons of other material in the New Jersey Fishing Preserve, ten miles southeast of Cape May Inlet. It proved highly successful.

Others followed: the Atlantic City Chamber of Commerce financed an artificial reef constructed ten miles southeast of Atlantic City Inlet; the Briell Chamber of Commerce produced a reef off Manasquan Inlet; in the 1950s the McAllister Grounds off Long Beach, New York, were built from demolished Manhattan buildings; the "Beer Case Reef" in Fire Island Inlet was made of 14,000 concrete-filled Schaefer beer cases. In 1954 the Alabama Department of Conservation, and local fishing groups, produced one of the first reef projects sponsored by a state; it was a series of artificial snapper banks. Six months later, after 250 automobile bodies were dumped offshore, the reef produced substantial catches of grouper, sea bass, red snapper, spadefish, and shark.

Another example of recycling waste into a productive force: off the Florida Keys, five new reefs are being constructed with broken concrete from old bridges that are being replaced.

About the time the United States was trying reef building sporadically, the Japanese government, through its Ministry of Agriculture and Forestry, took a more serious view and embarked on a plan to enrich its coastal areas for commercial fishing. In 1974 Japan adapted a seven-year plan for construction of artificial reefs. Today Japan is spending several hundred million dollars to develop fishing reefs.

Following Japan's success, Taiwan developed its own program and now boasts of fourteen major reefs set off its coasts. In 1960 the Japanese ideas spread to Europe. France built a reef on its Mediterranean coast. Australia followed suit, starting in 1965 in Port Phillip Bay, Victoria. Six years later, twenty-one reefs had been built.

In the United States, petroleum platforms are drawing attention for possible recycling as artificial-reef material when they have outlived their usefulness. In California waters, twenty to fifty times more fish have been in evidence under in-use platforms than over nearby areas of comparable size and character.

Texas, through its Coastal and Marine Council, is another state interested in making use of the obsolete platforms for recycling as artificial reefs.

Around 37,000 of the platform structures exist in the Gulf of Mexico alone; about forty of them become obsolete each year. Consequently, major oil companies are taking an interest in performing a useful service with the defunct platforms, for mutual benefit. Example: Exxon presented a 2,200-ton obsolete platform to the state of Florida; it was taken from its location in the Gulf waters of Louisiana and towed 300 miles to a spot thirty-five miles off the coast of Apalachicola, Florida, and deposited in 110 feet of water. Exxon footed the bill for everything until the reef was in place.

In 1972 the United States government demonstrated its confidence in artificial-reef principles when it initiated the Liberty Ship reef project. Congress passed a law making World War II ships from the National Defense Reserve Fleet available to states for reef building. Alabama, Florida, Georgia, Mississippi, and Texas have taken advantage of this program.

Coral Reefs

Coral reefs evolved in the sea where no previous land existed; they are rocky mounds, ridges, and platforms built up from the shallow sea bottom and made up of coral skeletons and the remains of other marine life. Corals that are reef builders grow only in warm, saline water that is clear and free of silt. As every angler who fishes warm marine waters knows, coral reefs are inhabited by a great variety of colorful fishes.

Not all coral reefs are of the same type. Fringing reefs extend out from the slating shores of some islands and continents, making platforms that may extend as much as a mile offshore and can be seen above water at low tide. Barrier reefs are coral outgrowths separated from shore by a channel, or lagoon. The most famous example of this type of reef, well known to anglers interested in big-game fishing, is the Great Barrier Reef; it runs parallel to the coast of Australia for about 1,200 miles. An atoll is a roughly shaped reef enclosing a lagoon.

Drift Nets

Drift nets, also known as drift gill nets, or entanglement nets, are made from synthetic materials and are used in both marine and fresh waters. Drift nets are, in effect, a barricade of netting stretching through the water for several miles; they kill or entangle, indiscriminately, any animal that comes into contact with it, whether it be fish, mammal, or water bird.

Practically invisible, these nets are a destructive and wasteful way of fishing because they are set and then left to drift with the current for hours, mostly unattended, before they are retrieved. Nets or sections of nets are often lost, cut by other vessels or torn away when snagged on submerged objects. Like lobster pots without buoys, the neglected and forgotten portions of net continue to fish unseen indefinitely.

Because of its indiscriminate and highly effective killing of great numbers of sport fishes, the use of gill nets has been, for the past twenty-five years, the source of bitter controversy between recreational anglers, divers, and environmentalists on one side and the commercial interests on the other. The most notable and most recent confrontation dividing the factious groups occurs in the fisheries of the south Atlantic and the Gulf of Mexico, southern California, and the salmon fisheries of Alaska.

Action is increasing nationwide to control or eliminate the use of gill nets in order to conserve and wisely maintain depleting stocks of game fishes. Through the efforts of ESLO (Empire State Lake Ontario) fishing advisory council, a bill has been passed to end gill nets in the New York State waters of Lake Ontario; no licenses have been issued since July 1, 1988. Unquestionably, the passage of this bill is an important step to protect the salmon, walleye, and other sport fishes.

In California, similar efforts have been made by ARM (Alliance for Resource Management) based in Sacramento. ARM is a society of freshwater and marine anglers, scuba diving clubs, boatmen, and members of the recreational fishing industry.

As an example of the worldwide devastation being caused by drifting gill nets, in international waters north of Hawaii there is a rapidly increasing fleet of more than 1,000 Japanese, Taiwanese, and Korean vessels setting drift nets at least forty feet deep and up to fifteen miles in length. Supposedly, these nets are intended to capture squid, but they indiscriminately kill every living body they entangle, including marlin, swordfish, porpoises, whales, seabirds, seals, and turtles.

In the south Pacific, the size of the nets has expanded beyond belief. The drift nets range between twenty and twenty-five miles in length and double the depth of the squid nets in the north Pacific.

The set gill net is similar to the drift net in construction; because it is made of synthetic materials invisible to the fishes it is highly effective in entrapping its victims. The net is not set adrift; one end of it is secured to the shore while the other end extends out, anchored in the river at a right angle. The fishes that swim along the shoreline swim into the net and cannot escape because their gill covers are entangled in the mesh. Such nets are especially effective in Alaskan and

Canadian fisheries where salmon, migrating in great numbers, follow the coastline enroute to the rivers where they spawn.

A great antagonism has always existed between commercial netting interests and sportfishermen. Poachers also set gill nets. The deadly gill nets, if not controlled by law, are capable of decimating a river's population of salmon to the point of extinction.

Estuaries

To put it simply, an estuary is an aquatic environment where rivers mix with shallow salt water of coastal bays and inlets; but the not so simple fact is that the effects of the human population explosion in recent years around the shorelines are dealing a death blow to our valuable sport and commercial fisheries. The U.S. Census Bureau predicts that 75 percent of the U.S. population will live within fifty miles of a coastline within a few years. With this enormous migration to our coasts comes a demand to obliterate our wetlands and estuaries by landfill and construction projects. And with the "developement" of our shorelines the modern-day society brings pollution that pours into our once-pure waters at such an alarming rate that our nation's estuaries are becoming gigantic cesspools.

It is finally being recognized that estuaries are a national resource base equal in importance to prime agricultural land in the midwest, or national parks in various areas around the nation. Healthy estuaries provide a bountiful environment that is a necessary breeding or feeding ground for about 70 percent of the seafood catch in U.S. waters, with a value of over $5 billion to the nation's economy.

Anglers should note that estuaries and near-coastal waters generate $7.5 billion annually through the sportfishing industry. These statistics are produced by the National Oceanic and Atmospheric Administration (NOAA), the federal agency that overlooks estuarine environments.

Through digitized satellite photographs and direct sampling, the NOAA has been busy securing information that points the finger on the sources of pollution on estuaries nationwide; it has established a data base containing detailed information on the extent of chemical pollution in estuaries. The scientists monitor more than fifty organic chemicals, including the well-known DDT, PCBs, and polycyclic aromatic hydrocarbons—plus seventeen heavy metals. In addition, samplings of bottom-feeding fishes, shellfish, and sediments have been collected from about 150 sites around the country in order to study the degree of toxic contamination.

The outpouring of agricultural, industrial, and household waste has had a disastrous effect on aquatic life in numerous bays and tidal ranges; one of the most devastating phenomena, the red tide, causes a tremendous kill of fishes and other aquatic life.

Farm Ponds

In recent years, farm ponds have greatly influenced the expansion of freshwater fishing in America; they now number in the millions and average about one acre in surface area. Farm pond is a general term usually applied to any pond, large or small, constructed where no water was previously present. The creation of these ponds in astounding numbers throughout the United States is a serious attempt to develop more fishing areas. A great many ponds, previously used only as a water supply by farmers, are now stocked with fish, adding a valuable source of recreation and fresh fish for the table.

Although the majority of these ponds are privately owned, the state fish and game departments are interested in their development because the ponds do alleviate, to some extent, fishing pressure from public waters. One of the most important attributes of these artificially constructed water impoundments is the initiation of fishing interest in many thousands of persons who would otherwise not have received such a blessing!

The big farm-pond movement started in the south about 1934, and interest quickly spread throughout the country. The general "rule of thumb" stocking of warm-water ponds is a bass-bluegill combination, but successful ratios of one species to the other change in different parts of the country. The principle is that bluegills feed on tiny organisms and insect life, while the bass feed on the bluegills.

Schools offering studies in fishery science introduced courses in farm-pond management, and specialists in the subject began to appear. Various combinations of fishes were tried. Trout were successful in northern ponds, and catfish were a great success in other areas. Results were increasingly successful—a new fishery science was born. Now, every state fish and game department has a qualified person to guide or lead the prospective pond developer to sources of information on the subject. Many states have a fishery biologist on their staff, formally trained in farm-pond management. They assist any person who wishes to build a pond and stock it with fish.

Literature on the subject is available in both scientific and popular publications. Many pamphlets may be obtained free of charge or at a nominal fee from various institutions, federal agencies, and the like. However, I would suggest to anyone interested in a pond project to first secure help from their state fish and game department. The state biologists are competent and will advise as to the best plans and procedures for the particular area.

International Game Fish Association (IGFA)

The IGFA was founded in 1939 by a group of farsighted angler-ichthyologists who used a room in New York's American Museum of Natural History for its meetings and storing of records pertaining to world-record-catch data. Today the IGFA is a world-renowned organization with impressive headquarters in Fort Lauderdale, Florida, where it houses an ever-expanding library of books, films, tapes, scientific and popular publications, and other materials of interest to the fishery scientist as well as to anglers and anyone in the general public who may seek information pertaining to sport fishes and fishing.

IGFA's objectives are founded on the belief that game fish species, related food fish, and their habitats are economic, social, recreational, and aesthetic assets that must be maintained, wisely used, and perpetuated; and that the sport of angling is an important recreational, economic, and social activity which the public must be educated to pursue in a manner consistent with sound sporting and conservation practices.

The purposes of IGFA, as set forth in the early bylaws, are "to encourage the study of game fishes for the sake of whatever pleasure, information, or benefit it may provide; to keep the sport of game fishing ethical, and to make its rules acceptable to the majority of anglers; to encourage this sport both as a recreation and as a potential source of scientific data; to make such data at the disposal of as many human beings as possible; and to keep an attested and up-to-date chart of world-record catches."

My firsthand knowledge, confidence, and recognition of the organization's worldwide work comes from my experience of being, for many years, an IGFA representative in New England.

Longlines

The longline is a highly effective and devastating method of capturing fishes. Although intended to harvest tuna, marlin, and swordfish, longline fishing is wasteful because it attracts indiscriminately to the baited hooks other species of fishes that are thrown back dead into the sea.

Basically, the longline system consists of the main line, supported by buoys. Radar reflecting devices, lights, and beepers are located at certain points on the line to facilitate tracking down the line by the electronics operator aboard the commercial fishing vessel. The method is especially resourceful because short lines, attached to the main stem and spaced apart so that they don't tangle, are of varying lengths; consequently, the baited hooks are presented to fishes swimming at different depths. The system becomes even more wasteful when harvesting is delayed through ineptitude, breakdown of equipment, or storms that make retrieving the lines impossible.

The longline is appropriately named because it is indeed "long." Used with great expertise by the Japanese, the lines are known to extend for more than fifty miles in the open ocean. Longlines (and drift nets) are of great concern to conservationists and a constant bone of contention politically between countries participating in marine commercial fishing. Not least of the ongoing feuds are the bitter attitudes displayed between sportfishermen and commercial interests.

Well-observed, documented, and publicized outstanding examples of uncontrolled decimation of stocks of some of our most important food and game fishes have been and are presently taking place. The Japanese for years have been employing a longline fishery involving bluefin tuna populations in the Gulf of Mexico, where the tuna spawn.

Another classic example of depletion of a stock or race of fish brought to the brink of extinction through overfishing by longline is the swordfish fishery off the southeast coast of the United States and the Gulf of Mexico. Shortly after the discovery of swordfish off the coast of Florida in 1975, recreational anglers came from all over the world for the opportunity to hook a broadbill swordfish off the Florida coast. The unusual success of the sportfishermen was highly publicized in magazines around the world. But, as would be expected, commercial fishing interests were quick to note the abundance of swordfish in the Florida fishery, and soon hundreds of longline boats were drifting up to 10,000 miles of gear, and as many as 100,000 hooks per night, seeking the valuable swordfish. Commercial landings exploded from less than 2 million pounds in 1977 to about 15 million pounds in 1983. After such commercial saturation, sportfishing for swordfish fell drastically, and activity disappeared as stocks fell so low it became useless for the recreational angler to try.

The most recent "raping of the seas" development (as of this writing) is the severe encroachment of commercial longline and drift-net fishing in Hawaiian waters. Commercial fishing in Hawaii is a well-established and lucrative business, but, as with all commercial depletion of stocks, there is a limit to the harvest that the resource can offer and still remain healthy.

Hawaii's local longline fleet has expanded to about sixty vessels, twice the size of a few years ago. In 1988 the longline catch was about 50 percent greater than in the previous five years, and is expected to increase another 25 percent in the next couple of years.

Hawaiian sportfishing interests were given another blow when it was learned that a local fish export company was increasing its cooperative operations to include servicing ten Japanese longliners. The company will collect and transship tuna (and other species) through Honolulu to Japan.

And more bad news to Hawaiian game-fish stocks is the recent arrival of another fleet of longline vessels from the Gulf of Mexico. The reason for the move is easy to diagnose. In the 1970s, Japanese vessels with their longlines targeting bluefin and yellowfin tunas in the spawning grounds of the gulf depleted the stocks to such an extent that it was no longer profitable to fish there; consequently, they left of their own accord. And in searching for more promising fishing grounds to decimate, Hawaiian waters at present are the most attractive. If the recreational angler feels distraught over the longline affair, the drifting gill-net situation will make him even more concerned (see Drift Nets).

The Longliner's Response

For many years a friend of mine, Ray Dackerman, and I have been officials of the Annual U.S. Atlantic Tuna Tournament. Ray heads Ralboray Inc., and his card reads "A Producer, Exporter and Domestic Supplier of Fresh Quality Tuna." One evening, during a period of relaxation after a day's fishing in the 1989 tournament, I had an opportunity to discuss with Ray, at some length, the longline situation and the general thought that the commercial longliners were responsible for detrimental depletion of stocks of bluefin tuna and swordfish as well as yellowfin and bigeye tuna.

Ray's commercial-fisheries operations reach around the world, including Japan, Indonesia, and the Middle East. He receives a daily report from near and far areas giving the statistics on catches suitable for market. The reports include numbers, weights, species, and condition (freshness, fat content, and color) of the fishes.

The point I am leading up to is this: Ray, being an expert big-game fisherman of long experience in many different waters, is also a conservationist where fisheries stocks are concerned. Because he buys and sells fish around the world he knows where, when, and in what abundance the most desirable fishes are to be found. The target of this story is that Ray Dackerman tells me, most emphatically, that in his opinion there is no great depletion of stocks of bluefin tuna and swordfish and the other large species. Ray says, "The fish are still there and plenty of them. They simply change their migrational route patterns according to existing conditions."

Pothole Fishing

Not many years ago, pothole fishing was not generally known in sport terminology. It is now a popular type of fishing in certain northern areas.

The sharp rise in the number of anglers and the demand for more and better fishing in North America have encouraged the investigation of all types of inland waters for fishing possibilities. In Canada, as in most other areas around the continent, there is much angling pressure on streams and rivers. Therefore, interest increases in developing a large number of shallow lakes for fishing in the North Country.

These small bodies of water, commonly called potholes, are not connected to river systems and maintain their levels by surface drainage and springs. Many of the lakes hold perch and northern pike; native trout are found in some, and minnows and sticklebacks are common to many. Perch and pike are stocked in some of these potholes, but because of the popularity of trout fishing, the feasibility of planting trout in potholes was initiated.

Investigations showed the lakes to be rich in plankton and insect life, which constitute the main diet for young trout. Possibilities of oxygen depletion in the more shallow lakes and consequent winterkill during some severe winters is apparent. An overall look at the situation strongly suggested fingerling planting to fisheries scientists.

In the majority of initial plantings of trout in potholes, which held only a species of minnow, fishing was very successful. For example, a typical plant of trout fingerlings in May resulted in the fish averaging two pounds in weight in August of the next year.

Red Tide

The so-called red tide is a pollutant found in coastal and offshore marine waters; its danger to sea life is a concern of environmental scientists, as are the major pollutants that flow into and contaminate the seas—acid rain, agricultural runoff, garbage from boats and ships, industrial waste, nitrogen, oil spills, mercury, PCBs, pesticides, phosphates, sludge dumping, urban runoff, and waste treatment water.

The red tide (there is also a brown tide caused by another type of alga) gets the immediate attention of anglers, however, because the suffocating and sometimes poisonous blooms of algae that cause the phenomenon regularly infuse the nation's coastal bays and gulfs, causing a trail of dead and dying fishes and contaminated crustaceans and molluscs as well. Some of the more intense coverings of the toxic blooms have resulted in zones of water almost totally depleted of oxygen, known as dead zones. For example, in the summer of 1988 more than a million fluke and flounder were killed when they were entrapped in anoxic water in Raritan Bay, New Jersey.

The real or specific causes of red-tide pollutions still remain a mystery to marine scientists; they are just beginning to delve into the working of the process by which coastal waters are hit by this type of pollution. One of the theories offered is that the problems may begin hundreds of miles from the ocean, where nutrients, such as nitrogen and phosphorus, and contaminants enter rivers from different kinds of sources and mix with waters of wetlands and marshes where fresh water meets salt water. A detrimental mixing occurs.

Algae blooms can occur suddenly, especially in bays where stagnant waters are in evidence. The specific causes for these spurts of algae growth are unknown. They have been noted to start, for example, during long periods of sunny weather after days of heavy rain. It is generally known that agricultural fertilizer runoff helps algae growth. The massed algae form a thick layer of vegetation that displaces other plants; and as the algae expire and rot they draw out enormous amounts of oxygen from the water, asphyxiating fishes.

Whatever the reason or causes of red tide, one fact is for certain: not only is the phenomenon costly to fishes and recreational fishing, but the dead carcasses washed up on shore stink up the beaches.

Reservoirs

Since reservoirs are of great interest to freshwater anglers, let us briefly consider some major conditions affecting fishing in big reservoirs. Temperature is important in relation to productivity and fish behavior. Reservoirs are located in both northern and southern areas; each type requires certain kinds of fish and fish management. Temperatures may cause concentration of fish at certain levels and affect the angler's catch. The temperature of the water, as it is released from the dam, is important in fishery management below the dam or tailwater.

The amount of dissolved oxygen in deeper waters of reservoirs indicates possible stagnation and is of direct importance to fish if the amount of oxygen approaches proportions that may not sustain fish life. Some reservoirs have shown serious oxygen depletion. Suspended silt in large amounts has troubled some reservoirs and is considered a serious problem in others. A dense suspension of silt may be present in the bottom twenty or thirty feet, which is considered especially damaging. Silt may smother food of bottom-living fish or prevent the establishment of potential food organisms. Suspended silt may be partly responsible for density currents (produced by suspension of much fine-grained sediment), which spread stagnant water over large areas of reservoir bottom.

Flushing, which causes very rapid exchange of water in the reservoir within a few weeks, may have a serious bearing on fish management. Plankton may be lost by flushing, especially in the smaller reservoirs.

Fluctuating water levels caused by periodic water release (drawdowns) seriously affect fish that rely on insects and other shallow-water life for food. The sudden release of great amounts of water through the dam lays bare the shore area and wipes out much of the fish food. An entire potential fish stock may be wiped out if the drawdown occurs during the spawning period—eggs are left high and dry. Drawdowns under management can be used as an effective tool in controlling undesirables, such as carp, or an overabundance of bluegills.

Alternative species have been introduced into reservoirs in an effort to save the angling, or as a species replacement, but mostly without success. Fruitless attempts have been made to replace lake trout with rainbow trout. Some attempts to improve the growth of lake trout by introducing the common whitefish have proved useless. Some waters that held good trout fishing are now dominated by whitefish. Lake trout were tried to replace a lost cutthroat fishery, without success.

Tailwater fishing below dams of large reservoirs has become an important point when planning the form and design of the dam. That is, the location of the water outlets has a direct bearing on fishing in the tailwaters and influences fishing in the reservoir. Fishing in reservoirs where dam outlets are deep down is far superior to impoundments where outlets are located close to the top of the structure.

The type of fishing in the tailwaters also depends on the depth from which the water is released through the dam. Water flowing a short distance from the top of the dam usually designates a warm-water fishery, because the released water is drawn from warm top layers of water. Water coming through an outlet situated down deep will usually create a cold-water environment, because the lower-level water is being released.

Fishing is good in the reservoir with deep outlets and very poor in the impoundment with high outlets, because water discharged from the deep outlets gets rid of oxygen-consuming decomposition materials with the colder, deeper waters. This action prevents stagnation and makes maximum amounts of water suitable to sustain fish life. The upper water, so vital to fish production, remains in the reservoir with resulting extensive good fishing. Another result is the transformation of warm-water fish habitat in the river below the dam to a cold-water fish habitat.

The situation is reversed in the reservoir with high outlets. Because the warm top-layer water is being discharged, there is a progressive accumulation of decomposition materials in the colder deep waters, with rapid depletion of the oxygen so necessary to fish life. The fish-producing habitat—warm, oxygenated surface water—is discharged downstream. Poor fishing is the result, and a warm-water fish habitat continues below the dam.

Cold-water release below dams introduces possibilities of extensive tailwater trout fishing where none occurred previously. The situation also creates new problems. Suitable water-discharge features would have to be incorporated in the dam to allow maximum aeration of water. One fact must be considered: maintenance of trout fishing below the dam would mainly depend on artificial stocking with fingerlings or the usual put-and-take of adult fish. Cold-water discharge affects original warm-water river populations. If the warm-water fishing is preferred over trout fishing, water must come from the warm upper layers of water above the dam. In one respect, a warm-water fishery has advantages, because it is supported by natural reproduction.

Solunar Theory

The term "solunar" has been coined from "solar" and "lunar" (sun and moon). As we all know, the pull of the sun and moon in certain positions in relation to the earth creates oceanic tides. For many generations, fishermen have judged the quality of their fishing by the relative positions of the sun, moon, and earth. The reasoning behind the speculation is that the forces of the moon stimulate marine fishes "to go on the feed," although in coastal areas the actual flow, rise, and fall of water levels is considered.

John Alden Knight was the first to study seriously the solunar periods and their effect on the feeding habits of fishes, that is, in association with sportfishing in inland streams and lakes. In 1926, Knight's interest in the subject was triggered by the actions of a highly successful guide, Bob Wall, whom he employed when fishing for largemouth bass in the St. John's River area of Florida. Bob Wall concentrated his fishing time strictly by his "moon chart," on which he recorded the degree of angling success in relation to the "ups and downs" of the moon.

Knight deduced that the pull of the sun and moon affecting marine fishing must exert a similar force on inland freshwater fishes and fishing. He also produced solunar tables, in which he calculated the degree of fishing success in fresh water by association with the time of the rise and fall of the nearest ocean tides and the meridian longitudes of the general area to be fished.

In his book *The Modern Angler* (1936, Charles Scribner's Sons), John Alden Knight devotes three chapters to the description of his solunar theory and gives reasons for justifying its validity.

To the skeptics who immediately and arbitrarily discard the thought of lunar influences on living organisms, may I point out: researchers and aquarists have known for years that clams, housed in glass tanks indoors, are active during periods of high tides occurring in marine waters, and these same clams tighten their shells and slide themselves into the aquarium's sandy bottom when the tide is at low. The same influences of marine tides have been observed in the behavior patterns of saltwater mussels (opening and closing of their shells) when captive in the artificial aquarium environment. The mussel is a marine mollusc that attaches itself to coastal rocks, mostly underwater during high tide.

The well-known word "lunatic" is derived from "lunar," exemplified by countless occurrences of abnormal human behavior during the calendar's full moon. One of the many ways to substantiate lunar influence exerted on human behavior is to review the bookings of any police department. When the moon is in its full phase the jails gather the highest number of inmates of the month. Violent crime also seems to rise during the lunar peak.

I was first introduced to the belief of moon influence many years ago when, as a youngster, I regularly visited Mr. Daddio, a farmer, down the road from where I lived. He allowed me to dig worms in mulch and manure piles and to fish, illegally (as far as the water company was concerned), from the banks of his land that partially bordered Wintergreen Reservoir. Toward evening he would join me along the shore, where we watched and hoped that the red-and-white bobber would be pulled under by a yellow perch or a bluegill. Meanwhile, we talked about subjects of nature, including the planting of his vegetable gardens during times closest to the full moon. Because Mr. Daddio was from "the old country" and spoke faulty English, I mentally attributed his moon beliefs to superstition. If my good friend Mr. Daddio the farmer were alive today I would more deeply value our lakeside chats, and I would not so quickly reject his moon theories regarding his plantings.

In later years, my next notable experience with a "phase of the moon" enthusiast was with Kip Farrington, a well-known pioneer of big-game angling in bygone days. In my many years of association with Kip during committee meetings of the Annual International Tuna Cup Match held formerly in Nova Scotia, he always emphasized the importance of scheduling the three days of fishing as close as possible to the phases of the moon, along with other logistical factors to be considered.

And, a contributor to lunar theory from along the Rio Grande: in a recent visit to Linn, Texas, deep down near the Mexican border, I engaged in moon discussions with longtime friend Duke Guerra, the owner and director of the vast San Vicente Ranch where I am often a "house guest." He informed me that his family has been in the cattle and farming business for generations in Mexico and along the Rio Grande valley of Texas. He cited examples of particular behavior of cattle during specific phases of the moon, but the most convincing case, and one that I believe, because the Duke is a highly intelligent and successful man who has no superstitious tendencies, concerns mesquite, a heavy hardwood tree that grows in Texas and Mexico.

In previous years, mesquite was used extensively as posts for erecting fences. The Duke emphasized his experience. "During my lifetime, so far," he said, "I have been involved in the construction of more than 500 miles of fences intended to contain cattle, and, more recently, big-game animals imported from Africa, Asia, and South America."

Rancher Guerra gives this example and swears by it: "When a mesquite, to be used for fencing, is cut down during the full of the moon it will remain strong and useful for about thirty-five to forty years, but if cut during the dark phase of the moon the mesquite, when secured in the ground as a post, will become soft and useless in three to four years." Asked why, he responds, "The mesquite's sap in the trunk and limbs is retracted into the root system by full-moon forces, resulting in the long-life span of the mesquite post. My guess is that termites are not attracted to mesquite devoid of sap."

My personal opinion, not supported by any scientific experimentation, but strengthened by observable facts of moon influences on marine waters and living organisms, generally and specifically is: I am a strong believer that the moon must have certain controls or influences over fishes and resulting sportfishing.

The angler-ichthyologist can add a most interesting and enjoyable facet to his fishing by adding a notebook to his tackle bag and developing a chart at home to record, that is, to note, after each fishing trip, the relationships involved with the degree of angling success, phases of the moon, and status of the nearest marine tides, if possible.

Sport Fishing Institute (SFI)

The new era of sportfishing in the United States started in the 1940s after World War II. In 1949, the Sport Fishing Institute was conceived, and since then it has made enormous progress nationally toward the conservation and betterment of sportfishing.

The organization, although based in Washington, D.C., is not associated with the U.S. government; it is a nonprofit, professionally staffed fish-conservation agency that has no trade functions and pushes no commercial product. Investments in SFI programs are wholly deductible for federal income tax purposes.

Through years of wise directorship and financial aid from about a hundred industries interested in supporting the welfare of recreational angling, the SFI has advanced the cause of sportfishing in many ways, including working cooperatively with state and federal governments and regulatory agencies in its advocacy role for sportfishing and financially supporting research in many colleges.

One of the most important functions of the SFI is the production of its *Bulletin,* an eight-page monthly fish-conservation publication; it is largely a review, with editorial comment on nationwide fish-conservation activities, problems, and needs.

The *Bulletin* reaches the majority of people in conservation, who exert significant influence over formulations of policies affecting fishery programs. Included in this group are conservation administrators and commissioners, professional fish and game workers, conservation officers (rangers, wardens, etc.), outdoor writers and radio and television sportscasters, legislative groups, outdoor-recreation leaders, and officials of sportsmen's organizations. Without question the *SFI Bulletin* exerts a great influence and affects the thinking of many millions of sportsmen.

A variety of professional conservation services makes up a good portion of the SFI program. The institute publishes periodic reviews of fish-conservation activities carried on by nearly seventy states, provinces, federal agencies, and private organizations in North America.

Occasionally, special reports on specific phases of fishery science, which are of great interest and value to professional workers, are published.

As a clearinghouse for professional fishery workers, which aids both employer and employees, the SFI contributes another important service, and the technical consultation service offered by the institute is often utilized by state fishery agencies.

Because of my work as an ichthyologist over the many years at Yale University I can truthfully attest to the value of the *SFI Bulletin*. I looked forward, and still do, to receiving the publication. During my productive days at Yale the *Bulletin* filled an important gap in keeping me updated on developments in the fields of fishery science and sportfishing.

Sport Fishing Institute offices are located at 1010 Massachusetts Ave, N.W., Suite 100, Washington, DC 20001. Telephone number is (202) 898-0770.

Toxic Elements

Ciguatoxin is a poison produced by a single-celled marine dinoflagellate. The animal attaches to marine algae and is passed up the food chain through small herbivorous fishes, and at the end of the food chain to humans where it is labeled "ciguatera." The toxin occurs in many parts of the world; most United States cases occur off Florida and Hawaii. Ciguatera is not to be confused with scombroid or histamine poisoning, which arises because of bacterial decomposition resulting from bad handling and storage.

Symptoms resulting from ingestion of the toxin include abdominal cramps, nausea, vomiting, diarrhea, weakness, numbness, mouth pain, disturbance of temperature perception and itching. The poison may even cause death. Organized epidemiologic records on ciguatera poisoning do not exist in the United States; estimates, however, read as high as 10,000 annually.

At this time there is no established antidote for the toxin; treatment is symptomatic. The toxin is not affected by cooking, freezing, drying, salting, smoking, or marinating the affected fish.

Apparently the host fish is not affected by the toxin; it can appear in a number of fish species. For example, in Florida it has been detected in amberjack, barracuda, dolphin, groupers, king mackerel, and snappers.

The good news is that a successful treatment appears to have been discovered. Dr. Luis Jain, a Marshall Islands–based medical surgeon, has found a drug that seems to be quite effective.

Dr. Jain first used Mannitol, a drug that relieves brain swelling, to treat ciguatera poisoning in 1983. He successfully treated two Marshall Islanders suffering from an allergic reaction (brainswelling) to eating poisoned fish. Since that time, successful results have occurred on more than fifty patients treated by Dr. Jain and other physicians.

The most comprehensive article published, to date, on ciguatera appeared in the May–June 1990 issue of *Sea Frontiers*; it was written by Daniel G. Bagen, and titled "Toxic Fish."

The advent in 1945 of DDT, a toxic insecticide for agricultural purposes, led the way for the development of an array of new chemical poisons. When first introduced, DDT received much publicity regarding the beneficial aspects of the chemical with specific success stories, such as the fire ant eradication program in southern states. Due to the early success of insect-control projects, large-scale spraying without previous thorough study took place over vast areas. The result was devastation to fish and wildlife. For example, salmon populations in Canada's Miramichi River suffered from aerial distribution of DDT, which covered the watershed in an effort to control spruce budworm infestation. DDT was responsible for an alarming trout kill in Yellowstone National Park. DDT used in Florida's east coast, sand-fly-larvae control program in marshes resulted in complete fish-kill reported from sixty-seven miles of ditches in the area.

Because of the losses to game, songbirds, birds of prey, and fish by DDT and the newer, more powerful chemicals, a reaction of severe criticism came forth from federal wildlife agencies, sportsmen's associations, state fish and game departments, conservationists, outdoor writers, and others. The result of the publicity campaign was positive, and the governmental agencies responsible for initiating the huge programs of grandiose aerial poison-spraying projects slowly curbed them.

DDT is no longer a menace to fish and wildlife because it has been banned by law from American markets. Nevertheless, the letters "DDT" will always be important because it alerted the people and the United States government to the hazards of allowing application of poisonous insecticides without thorough research before use and monitoring the programs after acceptance.

Anglers should be persuaded to be ever aware of the dangers of indiscriminate spraying of high-potency pesticides by public and private individuals, pesticides which often are initiated without adequate knowledge of the immediate and long-range effects upon forms of life other than the insect pests. However, anglers must realize that all aerial spraying *should not* be condemned. Forest-insect control would be an impossible task without the use of good, tried, and proven insecticides. An outbreak of destructive forest insects can spread to thousands of acres, and aerial spraying is the only economically sound method of combating the pests. Many agricultural pests are similarly controlled by aerial application of insecticides.

Mercury chloride is a highly poisonous compound used as an antiseptic, fungicide, disinfectant, and preservative; it is also used in photography and chemical analysis.

About a dozen years ago, in Japan, many people became ill after eating fish that were taken from waters contaminated by industrial mercury that had been dumped in large quantities into a harbor. Panic arose in the United States when a scientist discovered minute quantities in a swordfish. Swordfish inhabit only oceanic waters; there was no relation between the two issues. Nevertheless, the federal government forbad the sale of swordfish. After years of controversy and research the ban was rescinded and swordfish are now eaten without hesitation.

Regardless of the swordfish story, mercury remains an important health hazard in inland waterways where heavy mercury compounds are dumped from industrial waste. In many fine rivers, such as Connecticut's Housatonic, famous in the northeast for its fly-fishing, the law forbids the eating of the trout because of mercury and PCB pollution.

Polychlorinated biphenyls (PCBs) consist of a group of chlorinated carbons developed for commercial use in electric-transformer insulation fluids, extreme-pressure oils and greases, hydraulic fluids, fire retardants, and plasticizers.

In recent years, PCBs have been highly publicized and of great interest to anglers because they are ruinous to fishes and fishing. PCBs, commonly used for several decades by the electric industry, are known carcinogens and contaminate the sediments of many bodies of water in the United States. Millions of pounds of PCBs were used from 1929 to 1977 primarily as a coolant in electric transformers.

PCBs have been found to cause skin disease, lesions of the liver, and reproductive disorders in laboratory animals. In many waters throughout the United States and in some saltwater areas, such as Long Island Sound in the Northeast, where the bluefish is a major game fish, the general public, as well as the anglers, have been warned not to eat the fish at all or to consume one meal per week and only under proper methods of preparation.

Because PCBs accumulate in the fatty tissues of fishes, the advice from researchers is to skin the fish, cut away the belly flaps that contain the abdominal cavity, slice off the fat along the narrow dorsal strip, and cook the meat so that the fat and juices drip off.

Long before PCBs came on the scene, when I prepared fish for cooking, I always skinned them. I also sliced away the "red or dark meat" present along the lateral line on each side of the body. The taste of all fishes is distinctly improved when the skin, dark lateral meat, and belly flaps are removed, especially in the more oily types such as the bluefish. Before freezing a fish for future eating I remove the aforementioned parts of the anatomy and place the body or fillets in a milk carton filled with water and a dash of lemon added to it.

Until recently it was assumed that PCBs were stable and impervious to bacteria and forever a disaster when eating fish containing the toxins. There is now hope that this is not totally the case; in some waters the problem may be reduced. Researchers at Michigan State University reported that oxygen-free bacteria in sediment beneath the Hudson River had transformed toxic PCBs into less harmful PCB compounds with fewer chlorine atoms. Apparently, the resulting types of PCBs do not accumulate in the bodies of these fishes.

It is obvious, of course, that the breakthrough in controlling affects of PCBs is highly encouraging, but continuing research and much time are required before a significant change will take place.

Alloted space in this volume does not permit an in-depth presentation on the subject of PCBs. An unusually realistic appraisal of the recent PCB scare, written by Al Ristori, appeared in the *Salt Water Sportsman* magazine, northeast edition, July 1989.

The term tetraodotoxin sometimes appears in angling literature; it is of special interest to anglers who work marine shore waters where puffers take a bait intended for other species, because tetraodotoxin is a powerful poison.

The name originates from *tetraodontidae*, the scientific family name for puffers and their relatives. This toxin is concentrated in the skin and internal organs of these fishes and when eaten causes severe neurological and gastric symptoms, and often death. Unless puffers are carefully prepared before eating they usually poison the eater. Puffers are considered a delicacy in Japan (I believe they use only the dorsal fillets), where cooks are trained in safe methods of preparation.

Puffers have the ability to swell or "puff up" by swallowing water when threatened by a predator, hoping to discourage its interest. They will also swell in distress when taken out of the water, by taking in air.

As a boy, fishing from a rowboat in Long Island Sound, I fondly remember catching puffers; we called them "balloon fish." After removing the baited hook the puffer was held in one hand and its belly patted with the other until the fish ballooned up to twice its normal size. The puffer was then placed on the surface of the water "upside down" to drift away with tide or wind.

I also recall an article in the local newspaper that warned people not to eat puffers because a woman's cat had died in convulsions after eating one. The cat must have eaten skin, viscera, and all.

8

Scuba and Submersibles in the Study of Fishes

Underwater Exploration: History, Development, and Practice

The sea and underwater world holds a fascination for humans that is deeply rooted and stems, as most scientists believe, from the fact that the first land animals evolved out of sea origins. Not the least of those inquisitive human beings is the angler, with his interest in the quarry he hopes to lure to his hook.

For generations, ichthyologists and fisheries-management researchers were frustrated and stymied in their endeavors to study fishes and the world they live in, especially in the marine environment, because of the simple fact that fishes are underwater inhabitants. Other investigators in zoological disciplines, such as ornithologists and mammalogists, were way ahead of their colleagues whose primary speciality was fish study because they were able to record life histories, that is, habitats, behavior patterns, food, migration, reproduction, and the like.

Their subjects could be seen, tracked, and observed on the ground or in trees, or located by the use of aircraft. In recent years, however, the aquatic sciences have made great strides toward bridging the gap of knowledge between water and land animals. Dramatic, and in some cases seemingly miraculous, discoveries in marine science have become fact through the development of electronic devices and underwater photography, and the advanced ability of humans to stay underwater for long periods of time by the use of SCUBA (self-contained underwater breathing apparatus) and submersibles. All these benefit anglers through the conservation and wise harvest of fishes, both marine and fresh water.

In the 1930s, attempts were made to lower observers into the sea depths in watertight compartments and small submarines, but they proved impractical because the cost was prohibitive and the opportunities for scientific observation were limited and confining. Diving equipment was primitive and dangerous, with long lines and air hoses attached to pressurized suits and helmets. Air was pumped into the helmets from above the surface of the sea.

How well do I remember in 1946, "diving" with a helmet over my head, around Bermuda's coral reefs. Walking on the sea floor carrying an improvised underwater camera, net bag, and chisel, I photographed reefs and collected coral, sea fans, and other materials to be used in the background for a reef-fishes exhibit at Yale University's Peabody Museum of Natural History. My associates were above me in a boat, hand-pumping air into the helmet I wore—equipment loaned to us by Lou Mowbray, then the director of the Bermuda Aquarium. At that time such procedure was considered up-to-date, sophisticated research. We also peered through glass-bottom boxes in order to eliminate surface-water glare while looking over coral reefs and the myriad of fishes living there. On occasion, while collecting live specimens for the aquarium, we spread sardine oil over the water in order to fascilitate (by flattening the ripples) our search for appropriate spots in which to set the traps.

Actually, with only superficial means for underwater investigation available to us at the time, we were afforded the possibility to obtain just a hint of the rich marine life beneath the waves. Today, underwater opportunity for fish study has changed dramatically. With the great improvement in technologies, the chance for meaningful underwater study has advanced to a point considered impossible fifty years ago. Electronics have been perfected, and depth, type of bottom, rate of water flow, fish movement, and migration all can be observed and recorded. Photography associated with fish study is now an advanced science, with the improvement of underwater cameras and lights making possible the production of high-quality color photos. And undoubtedly, one of the most important developments for fish study and underwater photography now available to scientist and the inquisitive angler alike is the use of SCUBA.

Humans are now able to see and breathe in the depths, to remain for hours at a time and travel in the water just like the fish. These new, great advances for formal investigation did not come about through any sudden scientific discovery, but by simple devices invented through the necessity of furthering a sport—the underwater fish hunt with its spear and goggles for the hunter or spear fisherman. Underwater investigation, that is, the discovery of the submarine world, originated along the French Mediterranean coast near Nice on the shores of the Côte d'Azur, where the clear, temperate waters and abundance of fish life were conducive to spearfishing and an influence on the underwater sport enthusiasts to develop and improve their equipment. One of these followers of aquatic hunting was a Russian, Alec Kramarenco, who, after fleeing from Russia in 1917, lived in

Deep Rover, a one-man submersible built by Deep Ocean Engineering Inc., has been successfully used for oceanic studies in depths to 1,000 meters. *Photo by Sylvia Earle.*

Japan for three years where he observed that pearl divers wore goggles to protect their eyes and improve vision in salt water.

Pierre de Latil, in his book, *The Underwater Naturalist* (dedicated to Prince Rainier III of Monaco, a famed amateur ichthyologist), states that in Nice, where he settled down, Kramarenco found that goggles such as the Japanese used were not available, so he decided to make some for himself. In 1937, after many trials and many models, Kramarenco discovered that a pair of glasses, not lying in the same plane, gave a double image underwater. He found a solution that has become general internationally: a single pane to cover both eyes.

Maxime Forjot was another pioneer who contributed to the evolution of underwater equipment. He patented a mask covering the nose as well as the eyes. Consequently, the clip used by most divers to shut off the nostrils from pressure of water at depths was not necessary.

Then came the breathing tube (snorkel) patented by Forjot in 1938. One end of the tube is held in the mouth below the water surface while the other end rises above it, permitting the diver to breathe while he observes what is below him through his goggles or the pane of his mask.

Another Frenchman, Commander de Corlieu, developed foot equipment that greatly aids underwater swimmers today. In 1937 he patented his rubber flippers for swimmers. It was de Corlieu's flippers that led the way to the development of the "frogman," or underwater commando, during World War II.

The most startling advancement in diving science also took place along the Côte d'Azur when lightweight equipment was developed by two French officers at Toulon and Sanary. Commander Le Prieur was the first to experiment successfully with diving equipment, using compressed-air cylinders, the stored oxygen being regulated by the diver. The now famous Jacques-Yves Cousteau, at that time a lieutenant-commander, working with an engineer, Emile Gagnan, a specialist in liquid air, invented the appliance known as the Aqua-lung. The new discovery in underwater equipment made available to divers created a new form of sport along the Mediterranean coast—submarine exploration, now having enthusiastic followers around the world and generally known as SCUBA.

In America, before World War II, direct, meaningful underwater observation of fishes was practically unknown. It was because of the hostilities at sea that the U.S. Navy was forced to enlarge its emergency programs to experiment with underwater apparatus and electronic equipment. The results provided the basis for modified conversion of such equipment into civilian use for the study of life in the seas.

The successful development of underwater apparatus is exemplified by *Alvin,* the world's best-known manned submersible, *Alvin,* named after Allyn Vine, a

Woods Hole scientist and early advocate of manned underwater research, carries a crew of three and can dive to 13,124 feet; it was built with U.S. Navy funds and is operated by Woods Hole Oceanographic Institute.

During many years of its existence (since June 5, 1964), *Alvin* has undergone numerous modification and made more than 2,200 dives. Although *Alvin* has participated in a series of famous, major oceanographic expeditions such as a study of the Mid-Atlantic Ridge, a probe of the East Pacific Rise, and closeup photographs of the hull of the *Titantic,* it also surveyed the Galapagos Rift and revealed strange new life in lightless depths.

(Aside: In 1960 the research bathysphere *Trieste* in the Challenger Deep of the Marianas Trench near the Phillipines reached a record depth of 35,800 feet for a manned submersible).

Today the amateur ichthyologist or inquisitive angler has opportunities through SCUBA, snorkel, and flippers, to investigate and photograph fishes in marine environments undreamed of during my early years as an aquatic scientist. But even more astounding to me, now, is the fact that professional fisheries investigators can delve much deeper into the underwater world than can the SCUBA enthusiast, who is prevented by water pressure from going beyond certain depth limits. Submersibles have been invented and gradually improved to transport the investigator safely along, deep below the surface, and there are underwater enclosures that make it actually possible for the scientist to live with the fishes. Remote-controlled cameras and television monitors are available that can record observations in the most difficult environments to reach, as well as being used to count salmon traveling up fish ladders and dams enroute to spawning grounds.

As a specific example of the great advancement in fish study being made through the use of submersibles I present the following:

One of the most electrifying ichthyological discoveries of all time occurred when a coelacanth, a "living fossil," once considered to have become extinct about 60 million years ago, was caught by a native fisherman in the Indian Ocean off the Comoro Islands. It was spotted by the legendary naturalist Marjorie Courtenay-Latimer in a trawler's catch at the South African port of East London in December 1938. Recognizing the fish as something extraordinary, she sent a sketch of it to Professor J. L. B. Smith, a noted ichthyologist at Rhodes University in Grahamstown, South Africa. Smith identified it as a coelacanth, but different in genus and species from any recorded as fossils, and named it *Latimeria chalumnae* in honor of its discoverer. The mouth of the Chaluman River was the area of capture. Since then, many others have been caught and studied in laboratories by ichthyologists and other scientists, including Americans, French, and British.

One of the most electrifying ichthyological discoveries of all time occurred when a coelacanth, a "living fossil," once considered to have become extinct about sixty million years ago, was caught by a native fisherman in the Indian Ocean off the coast of South Africa in 1938. In subsequent years other specimens were caught and studied. The model pictured here was reproduced from a plaster mold of a specimen that arrived frozen at Yale's Peabody Museum of Natural History. Ralph Morrill, a well-known museum technologist at Peabody, created the model. *Photo by David Henry.*

As an aside point of interest, I recall with some nostalgia when, as a student at Yale, I studied ichthyology, oceanography, and comparative anatomy under the tutelage of Professor Daniel Merriman (well known for his work on the striped bass). Dan, as we all addressed him, one day stepped up to the lecture podium visibly excited; that morning he had received word through scientific channels that a living coelacanth had been captured off the coast of East Africa. He reconveyed to the class that the fish was identified by Professor Smith, but the distinguished ichthyologist was dismayed, and so was Dan Merriman, when it was reported that the fish was sent to a taxidermist, who saved only the skin. The internal organs were discarded, thereby making them unavailable for scientific study.

About ten years later, in 1949, I was in the happy position of being a paid ichthyologist collecting fishes in the Indian Ocean during a Yale East African expedition based on the shores of Shimoni, about sixty miles south of Mombassa, Kenya. In association with the expedition's objectives I corresponded with Professor Smith, whose huge volume, *The Sea Fishes of Southern Africa,* I referred to constantly for fish identification of the region. I admired J. L. B. Smith because of his extensive works in ichthyology. At the termination of the Yale expedition I had hoped to meet him in Grahamstown at Rhodes University and also to visit the Comoro Islands, but I was able to travel only as far southward as Pemba and Zanzibar Islands.

Recently, an extremely important discovery rekindled great interest in coelacanths, and accentuated the value of submersibles for use in oceanographic research when Hans Fricke, a marine geologist with Max Planck Institute for Animal Behavior in West Germany, photographed and filmed these strange, perplexing creatures at a depth of 550 feet. In a two-man submersible he became the first to find and photograph these extremely primitive fishes in their natural habitat.

Any angler interested in the study of fishes should read a detailed account by Hans Fricke covering the story of the coelacanths that had endured through such a prodigious amount of time with so little change. The article titled *Coelacanths: The Fish That Time Forgot,* with photographs by the author, appeared in the *National Geographic Magazine* in its issue of June 1988.

Excellent, lifelike examples of coelacanths reproduced in plastic from a mold taken over an original, dead specimen were reincarnated by Ralph Morril, one of the best of museum technologists. Specimens (models) are now exhibited at the Yale Museum, in the Smithsonian National Museum of Natural History, and in the Philadelphia Academy of Science.

Although the development and employment of submersibles has drawn worldwide attention because of spectacular deep-water discoveries, it is the use of SCUBA, easily available to serious students and to inquisitive recreationists, that has been contributing so much in recent years in the study of fishes. As a case in point: my friend and fishing companion, Eric Shultz, who has recently earned his doctorate in marine biology at the University of California, has reiterated and emphasized to me the importance of SCUBA as a tool in his research efforts. His list of publications is already impressive, several of which could not have come to fruition without the use of SCUBA in his observations and collections.

Because of his vast experience in the underwater study of fishes I have asked him to submit some of his thoughts on the subject. He has responded with the following:

What is this Underwater Breathing Apparatus all about? To get the answer you need do little more than hie yourself to a dive shop, sports shop, or even the phone book, to find the nearest NAUI (National Association of Underwater Instructors) certification classes. No great initial investment is required. If you have been snorkeling, you probably have all the equipment you need already; the rest can be rented. In addition to the mask, fins, snorkel, and wetsuit, you now will put on a weight belt, a scuba tank on a harness; an inflatable buoyancy-controlling device, probably as part of your harness. The regulator has a mouthpiece, the same as your snorkel's. Nobody has figured out how to deliver the air in a more direct fashion. For the time being, we must envy the fish.

SCUBA diving once had an image problem, viewed as a sport only for those hairy of chest and steely of nerves. In fact, it is not particularly strenuous, and rather safe once you are aware of the adjustments that must be made when you go to higher pressures, and then return to low pressure. You must be properly trained to dive safely. There is no substitute for a good certification course!

So what do people do while they are underwater? Several organized activities have developed, to busy those who are not content with merely sightseeing. One of these activities is, of course, fishing. In many parts of the world, divers collect their next meals with simple tools. Fish may be impaled with a three-prong spear, or if you wish for greater power you may take along a proper spear gun, in which the spear is propelled by the force of relaxing rubber or escaping air. In any case, hunting fish for dinner while diving is a challenging sport. This is a good way to learn about the animal, by the way: hunger is an excellent teacher.

You may find, depending on the location, that free diving, without a SCUBA tank, is a more effective way of spearfishing. To explain why, I'll tell a fishing story. In my first years of diving I was full of scorn for those

Present-day elaborate underwater cameras are used by scientists to record fish behavior. The diver enticing an oceanic white-tip shark with food so as to get a close-up photo is Dan McSweeney. *Photo by Al Giddings, Ocean Images, Inc.*

SCUBA makes possible the underwater studies of the great white shark initiated by John McCosker, director of the Steinhart Aquarium. Rodney Fox, protected by the cage, is feeding the shark. *Photo by Al Giddings, Ocean Images, Inc.*

Aquatic scientist and SCUBA diver Eric Shultz photographs a French angelfish. *Photo by Foster Bam.*

The great profusion of fishes in the surroundings of coral reefs is observed by SCUBA diver Sallie Baldwin. *Photo by Foster Bam.*

Every angler is naturally interested in decorative or trophy mounts, but only the rare fisherman can point out the specifics that separate a poor taxidermic effort from a good one. The pictured 7½-pound 27-inch Quebec brook trout is a perfect reproduction in polyester resin created by Ralph Morrill, the father of modern fish taxidermy at Yale University's Peabody Museum.

A superb wood carving of a red-breast sunfish and a yellow perch by Joe Swaluk. Present-day gifted artist-craftsmen, using wood as a medium, are capable of producing models of game fishes that outclass skin mounts; and some of the better ones are equal to plastic casts in anatomical accuracy and lifelike appearance.

More of the extraordinary work of Joe Swaluk: the Atlantic salmon is an exact replica of a 20-pound Atlantic salmon caught in Iceland by Edward Calesa. The smallmouth bass chasing baitfish is an exceptionally fine work.

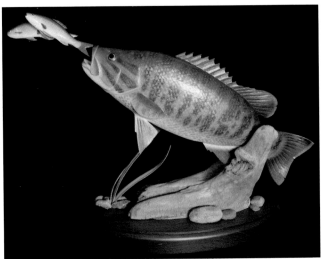

who went underwater armed. I discovered the practice as a matter of necessity, in one of those times when the considerations of survival crowd out the niceties of personal philosophy.

A few years ago I was a member of a team doing research on sex-changing wrasses. We were stationed at a remote Caribbean location; a visit to a proper grocery store was several months away. The indigenous folk liked white rice and white bread. All I had to do was look at one of the locals and I began to feel protein-starved. A night or two of futile fishing off the dock, followed by a late meal of canned beans, and our resident cat started to hide from me. I dreamed of laughing fish, woke up thinking "No more Mr. Nice Guy," and oiled up a borrowed spear gun.

An adept in our group took us out to one of his second-favorite spots that day. "No SCUBA tanks," he said. Then we dropped over the side of the Whaler and I looked down. The bottom was at 40 feet! I gave him an enquiring look and he instructed me: "Just relax, take a couple good breaths, go to the bottom, and wait there very still for as long as you can." Right. I had two objections: (a) no way; (b) there were no fish around anyway, any fool could see that from the surface. Well, we went our separate ways, and I tried what he said. I could reach the bottom, and "relax" there for 15 seconds or so, returning gasping to the surface. Of course I didn't see any fish. Imagine my surprise, upon returning to the boat, to find several snapper with neat holes in their sides, and here was my companion coming back with another!

My friend was kind enough to shoot enough for all of us that day, and the next. I kept at my breath-holding. Reasoning that this was a battle between my stomach and my lungs, I conditioned myself by holding my breath while staring at snapper fillets on my dinner plate.

On the third day, it was up to me; everybody else was busy doing science. I cruised out to a shallow spot, where the 30-foot bottom fell away suddenly into deeper water. A few lazy kicks and good breaths, and I planed easily to the bottom (no kicking, that costs oxygen). I settled into a depression, facing deep water, and filled my mind with serene thoughts.

Then there was this eye. And the eye had a long, silvery body attached to it, with a toothy face. Moving slowly, (except for my racing heart), I raised the gun and pulled the trigger.

The safety was on. The fish spooked. Over our meal of beans that night, I was given the lesson from the master: "Snapper may come back, jacks sometimes circle around, grouper just sit there and act stupidly territorial, but barracuda never return."

I learned, finally. I brought the buck fever under control, learned how to aim, and could hold my breath for a long time, especially when hungry. Snapper (4 species), jacks (2 species), barracuda (big, bigger, enormous), mackerel. Stingrays if nothing else was around (easy as a doormat to shoot, not too bad with a sweet and sour sauce). I never managed to shoot a permit, but scored a first for our field station by bringing in a little tuna one day with a lucky shot.

The point of this story is simple: on the surface, you are being watched. As you paddle around, looking at the little fish and coral, there are other beasties nearby you just don't see. This goes as well for the SCUBA diver, who creates a commotion with air bubbles. You want to see? You want to eat? Lie on the bottom in a nook or cranny and wait.

So now the fishes are swirling around you (incidentally, "fish" means just one, and "fish" also means many of the same kind, but one is supposed to say "fishes" when one means different kinds). There are 20,000 or so species of fishes in the world. Unless you are so desperate for water that you are diving in a motel's kiddie pool, or crazy enough to be looking at Arctic ice from the underside, you will probably see at least a few fish species on a dive. Please learn their names. Buy a field guide to the local fish fauna, and wear it out. Take it along in your dive bag. Drip water on it, go ahead. Write notes on the pages (yes, use waterproof ink). There are even some waterproof books for this, but most that I've seen are designed to be compact and they lack detail. I suggest books that give common and Latin names, with plenty of background information on size range, habitat, and especially pointers on how to distinguish them from look-alikes.

There are several reasons I am insistent regarding field identification. We are a classifying species, it's just one of our persistent habits. We give names to things, usually constructing relationships among the things as we name them. So be a good human and learn the names. That's the appeal of duty. A more effective appeal perhaps is that it really is fun and the critters tend to be more interesting when you know what to call them. Finally, there's the appeal of sympathy. Somebody went to quite a deal of trouble to give these animals proper names. Believe me, I know. We're talking about month after month in poorly ventilated museum collections, with just the silent specimens for company. I am not asking too much: learn the Latin names, even. Don't worry about the pronunciation, there are no Romans around to correct you. Here again, the best way to pursue good pictures is to let them come to you. Settle into a spot where you like the background, and more likely than not the fish will start to pose for you. I have noticed that the really good photographers get more dive time out of a single tank of air than anyone else. They just sit there and breathe easily, while the rest of us charge around sucking our tanks dry.

If you find that you are coming back from a dive with a head full of the fishes you encountered, but can't decide what species you had seen when you look at the book, you either (1) saw a bunch of species hitherto unknown to science; or (2) you got mixed up. Consider taking notes while you are swimming along. Now don't laugh, this is easier than may first appear. We like to use sheets of white PVC, about 8"x10", and ⅛" thick. The surface should be thoroughly buffed so that it is rough enough to catch some pencil lead as you write. Round the cut edges, drill a hold in one corner for the string that holds your pencil, and you have constructed an underwater notebook. To erase, just scrub with some Ajax.

I should say something about photography before I finish. I'm not an avid practitioner of this art form, but I know some who are. This is another good way to learn about the animals. My spectator's observation on the hobby is that it is most fun before obsession sets in. With obsession comes the need for a great deal more equipment, and the certainty that things will refuse to work except when you are testing them. Keep it simple. You can get great images with a waterproof camera such as a Nikono, maybe two lenses, and a strobe flash. If you already have a camera, you may be able to get a waterproof housing for it.

Well-known names associated with water exploration, researching and underwater discoveries are William Beebe, originator of the bathysphere; Edwin Link, designer of submersibles; Jacques-Yves Cousteau, co-inventor of the Aqua-lung; Harold Edgerton, designer of many camera systems used in the ocean; George Bass, archeologist; George Bond, pioneer of saturation diving; Rachel Carson, who wrote *The Sea Around Us;* William Hammer who, in 1971, was the first to use SCUBA in observing plankton in its own habitat; and William Longley, who, working along with the National Geographic Society staff member Charles Martin at the marine laboratory of the Carnegie Institution in Florida, took the first underwater photographs in color.

All the persons listed above have made significant contributions to the underwater sciences, but I, as a professional ichthyologist, must also take my hat off to the following:

Along with Eric Shultz, other U.S. world-class divers, who, through the daring use of SCUBA and submersibles, are making important contributions to the knowledge of the underwater world are Sylvia Earle, Eugenie Clark, John Mc-Cosker, Hans Fricke, Rick Sammon, John C. Fine, and a representative amateur, Foster Bam.

Sylvia Earle is the best known of the deep-water divers. Wallace White, a writer for *The New Yorker* magazine, produced a lengthy article in the July 3, 1989, issue giving a history of her background and accomplishments in projects below the ocean waves; it should be read by anyone seriously interested in the study of the ocean and the life within it. In part, Wallace writes, "She is a renowned marine explorer, who has dived all over the world in all kinds of miniature submarines, or submersibles, and has set a number of records during more than three decades as a biologist, a leader of scientific expeditions, a resident of underseas habitats, a pilot of advanced subaquatic vehicles, and a pioneer of experimental marine equipment. Moreover, fellow oceanographers recognize her as one of the most experienced, most versatile, and most intrepid divers in the history of underwater exploration."

In 1973 and 1974, Eugenie Clark, another noted ichthyologist and underwater researcher, through the use of SCUBA made an important study that added to the knowledge of shark behavior. Off the coast of Mexico's Isla Mujeres, Mexican divers found caves where sharks appeared to be resting on the bottom, motionless, contrary to the theory that sharks need to move constantly in order to breathe. Eugenie Clark, meeting face to face with potentially dangerous sharks in the caves, confirmed that the sharks indeed were lying on the bottom and appeared to be asleep or in a state of stupor, one theory being that fresh water seeping into the caves lowers salinity and possibly tranquilizes the sharks.

John McCosker is director of the Steinhart Aquarium in San Francisco, and, as an ichthyologist, has chosen the white shark, the one known to the public as the infamous "man-eater," as his favorite aquatic creature to investigate. McCosker is an expert in aquarium science who has used SCUBA in studying and collecting fishes for display tanks, but his interest in the white shark has made him famous with the public. Some of his exploits in the waters of South Australia have appeared on film, and photos of him in an underwater cable-suspended cage observing shark behavior (like the shark chewing the bars on his cage) have been published in magazines.

The greatest publicity McCosker and the Steinhart Aquarium received was in 1980 when he retrieved a white shark entrapped in a fisherman's net at Tomales Bay, California. The shark was transported in a tank-truck to the aquarium where it was displayed as the first healthy white shark ever kept alive in captivity.

She (it was a female) was the greatest attraction in the history of the aquarium and drew more than 40,000 visitors in three days. She was featured in *Life* magazine, made front-page news around the country, and appeared on national television.

Rick Sammon, an accomplished underwater photographer and a fellow member of The Explorers Club of New York, is currently president of CEDAM International, the nonprofit organization dedicated to conservation, education, diving, archeology, and museums. His cooperative projects include the Galapagos Project with the Charles Darwin Foundation, on a ten-year marine study; Belize Project with the New York Zoological Society, on setting up marine parks; and the Red Sea Project, collecting fishes for the New York Aquarium.

Sammon's recent article in *The Explorers Journal,* June 1989 (an official quarterly of The Explorers Club), especially caught my attention. The piece, entitled "Conservation on the East African Coast: Exploring Kenya's Marine Parks," described Sammon's group photographing the coral reefs' flora and fauna for the Kenya Marine Management and CEDAM. My interest in the article was whetted by its information that the Kenya government has taken great strides to protect its coral reef ecosystem by establishing marine national parks off the shore of Lamu, Malindi, Mombassa, and Shimoni. As stated previously, during the Yale East African expedition, based at a camp in Shimoni, I studied, photographed, and made plaster molds of fishes collected along those Indian Ocean shores of Africa.

John C. Fine, another member of The Explorers Club, is a biologist, underwater photographer, and a lawyer involved with the protection and conservation of ocean resources. His book *Creatures of the Sea* received the 1989 Silver Medal from the Hellenic Federation. His most recent work, "Groupers in Love: Spawning Aggregations of Nassau Groupers in Honduras," published in *The Explorers Journal* (Fall 1990), is a report on his findings, through the use of SCUBA, that add importantly to our knowledge of fish behavior.

His article describes the event of Nassau groupers gathered in the thousands in a mating congregation formed into a dense ball or cone at a site where the water was 100 to 120 feet deep. The fish ranged from the bottom to about fifty feet below the surface. Nassau groupers are demersal, that is, they live near the bottom most of the time and are territorial and therefore assumed to spawn in separate pairs.

However, the recent belief by fisheries scientists that some grouper congregations are the main mating and reproduction means of these usually solitary fish is highly important to both commercial and sportfishing interests. It becomes obvious that such mass, condensed gatherings of groupers become overwhelmingly vulnerable to commercial overharvesting, thereby subjecting the population of groupers to the verge of possible extinction in any particular zone if not controlled by law.

Foster Bam, an avid fisherman in both marine and fresh waters, is an excellent example of an amateur ichthyologist with the field experiences of a professional. He is a trustee of the American Museum of Fly Fishing and the Bermuda Biological Station for Research; for ten years he served as chairman of the board of trustees of the Oceanic Society. His lifetime fascination with fishes lured him underwater the better to see and know the fishes he loves. Mr. Bam has become an amateur marine biologist and a proficient underwater photographer; his photos rank with the world's best. He contributes time and photos to advance the work of the Oceanic Society and the California Academy of Sciences. One of his favorite SCUBA projects is collecting living specimens for San Francisco's Steinhart Aquarium.

As I look back at my many years of service to Yale University as a museum curator of fish exhibits, I would have considered the availability of today's clear, accurate photos of live fishes and their natural environment, such as produced by Foster Bam, as priceless in reference to underwater physical formations and true coloration of fishes.

Before leaving the subject of SCUBA it should be brought to the attention of the inquisitive angler that diving with the aid of an underwater breathing apparatus is not an activity restricted to the academic study of life in the seas. Recently, Marian Rivman, a spokeswoman for the Diving Equipment Manufacturers Association, stated that 3 million people make an average of ten dives a year, and she estimates the number of people certified last year at half a million, up from 350,000 five years ago (the standard considered for certification is four weeks of training). Most SCUBA activity is recreational, an excuse to get out into the sun, warm water, exercise, and see what one can see.

Other statistics: *Skin Diver Magazine* (Los Angeles), in a survey, found that 65 percent of its readers are male and 35 percent are female. Also, 84 percent have attended college: 73 percent hold owner, managerial, technical, sales, or professional positions.

Aside from the natural allurement, improved equipment is attracting new divers: easy-breathing regulators; better buoyancy-compensator vests that keep divers stable; smaller tanks that hold more air, and diving computers that tell the diver how long it is possible to stay down at a given depth.

Professional diving instructors charge in the neighborhood of $150 for twice-a-week diving lessons; rental equipment and personal gear can range from $800 to $1,500. Many travel agencies offer Caribbean diving trips, for example from $500 to $1,500 for all expenses, including air fare, lodging, and food. Exotic trips to distant areas may cost $3,000 to $5,000.

Instruction in SCUBA diving can be had at much less expense when taken in school and college programs, YMCAs, and municipal recreation departments. Tanks and all other equipment can be rented.

Also, to enjoy diving and the study of fishes, one need not travel expensively to spectacular and faraway places. For example, in the states, Florida is the most popular area with many SCUBA and sport shops offering various trips at different prices. Although the Keys and both the Atlantic and Pacific coasts receive most of the diving activity, freshwater areas such as Florida Springs receive much attention. And sites farther inland are getting more attention; the flooded Bonne Terre mine in Missouri is now considered a mecca for SCUBA participants. The mine is still cluttered with machines and tools. Another example is Lake Mead in Las Vegas, where underwater parks are developed by the construction of artificial reefs with dead trees and other materials to attract fishes.

Related Reading

Clark, John R. 1985. *Snorkelling: A Complete Guide to the Underwater Experience.* New York: Prentice Hall.

Cousteau, Jacques-Y. 1986. *The Silent World.* New York: Lyons and Burford.

Earle, Sylvia A., and Al Giddings. 1980. *Exploring the Deep Frontier.* Washington, DC: National Geographic Society.

Humann, Paul. 1989. *Reef Fish Identification.* Orlando, Florida: New World Publications, Inc.

Pacheco, Antony L., and Susan E. Smith. 1990. *Marine Parks and Aquaria of the United States.* New York: Lyons & Burford.

Ocean Realm Magazine. (Quarterly) Winter Beach, Florida: Raku, Inc.

Underwater Magazine. (Quarterly) Chicago, Illinois: Helix, Ltd.

Skin Diver Magazine. (Monthly) Los Angeles, California: Peterson Publishing Company.

9

Fish Taxidermy and the Angler

Many anglers of my acquaintance would like to have an unusual catch preserved for display in a lifelike position on a wall or as a tabletop mount. The inducement to create such a taxidermic effort may spring purely from the desire to enhance the décor of a certain room or area, or to look at, time and again, to recall fond memories of a great fishing trip. More likely, however, the reason would be, consciously or unconsciously, to present bragging opportunities in front of fellow anglers and other friends.

I have yet to walk into a tackle store, bait shop, fish market, seafood restaurant, charter-boat dock, or a fishing-trip travel agency where fish mounts were not prominently displayed. In other words, mounted specimens are surprisingly common and are found under a variety of circumstances. The fish-taxidermy business seems always to be good; to prove it, an angler has only to ask the taxidermist when to expect his trophy to be completed—it invariably takes months.

I do not expect the general public who view examples of fish taxidermy to be able to distinguish between a good mount and a poor mount, because people who are not anglers cannot even identify the fish. And because I have been a museum scientist with a specialty in fish collection, preservation, and exhibit display, I assumed that the discerning sportfisherman, that is, the inquisitive angler, being familiar with the anatomical appearance of game fishes, would naturally recognize the difference between a poor fish mount and an excellent one. The fact that my assumption was incorrect was brought pointedly to my attention recently during a visit of several hours to the World Fishing and Outdoor Exposition held annually in Suffern, N.Y. Expo, as it is commonly called, is one of the largest shows of its kind devoted almost exclusively to sportfishermen and hunters. The show includes many booths advertising fishing tackle, fishing camps, guide services, and commercial taxidermy studios. Many of the cubicles, of various sizes, displayed mounted fishes on their walls. I enjoyed stopping at the booths to judge, mentally, the fish mounts—*atrocious, bad, poor, good, excellent.* There were representatives of each category or rank of judgment in the total collection. The specimens displayed various materials and techniques of workmanship—skin mounts, plastic replicas, bas-relief casts, freeze-dried trophies, and wood carvings.

As I was walking down one of the aisles at the show, jammed elbow to elbow with enthusiastic outdoorsmen, I bumped into Gardner Grant and Ernie Schwiebert, fellow members of The Anglers' Club of New York and well known in the fly-fishing world as experienced trout and salmon fishermen. After exchanging the usual amenities, Gardner said, "Ed, you must come over to the next aisle. I want to introduce you to some incredibly well-done wood carvings of fish." I responded, "I'll bet you're referring to Joe Swaluk's creations, and I agree with you, because I became acquainted with Joe at last year's Expo and I have again spent some time at his booth to study his new batch of carvings." The three of us made another stop at Mr. Swaluk's cubicle, where we sipped a bit of white wine served to us discreetly in small paper cups. During the conversation Gardner mentioned that he possesses one of Joe's carvings, an exact replica of a trophy-size brown trout he caught at the Beaverkill. He brought the freshly caught specimen to the Swaluk Studio in Spotswood, New Jersey, where photos, measurements, and color notes of the prize were taken and later used as guides to copy in the carving.

While discussing methods of workmanship, Joe remarked that he had taken my advice, offered last year, to use discretion when a mounted fish was to be used as a model for carving. Gardner's immediate reaction was "Why?" I explained to

Joe Swaluk's wood carving of striped bass chasing minnows is another excellent example of art in wood carving. *Photo by Joe Swaluk.*

Gardner and to Ernie that anatomical inaccuracies were incorporated in the work of some commercial taxidermists, especially in skin mounts, and it would be a mistake to repeat them in a fine carving. Then, I asked them if they knew what specifics to look for in order to recognize the quality, or to judge a mount, a carving, or any other artificial reproduction of a living fish. They both freely admitted that they did not, but the question aroused their curiosity. The next day at my desk I reasoned that if Gardner and Ernie, two sophisticated and intelligent anglers, appreciated having brought to their attention some of the taxidermic misconceptions displayed in commercially mounted fishes, then the subject should be of interest to all inquisitive anglers.

Evaluating a Mounted Fish

There is no excuse for poorly mounted and unattractive fish mounts produced by taxidermists. True colors of a live or freshly caught fish are easily recorded with today's fine cameras and variety of color films. The greatest boon to the art of fish

The brook trout (*above*) and the largemouth bass (*below*) are excellent
examples of exaggerated or distorted anatomical features produced by some
taxidermists into unnatural or grotesque effects. *Photos by author.*

taxidermy was the advent of plastics and other synthetic materials. Any fish can be molded in plaster and cast in durable materials.

Before passing judgment on lifelike reproductions of fishes in plastics or skin mounts, it is important to know what a live fish really looks like in detail. This is not a ridiculous statement, for I have been surprised to see that, when detail of fish anatomy is involved, good artists and illustrators, and even some trained scientists, fail to observe intelligently.

Body

The most common fault in fish mounts, and one that taxidermists insist on perpetuating, is the contorted body. To twist a fish's body dorsoventrally, from topside to bottomside, does not depict true action. The fish is no longer a delight to look at; its back is broken and its curvatures are crippled. The fish appears to be in agony.

Watch a fish in an aquarium; its body movements are from side to side, not from top to bottom. Look at a photograph of a fish jumping; again, the body is bent laterally. Next time you see a film of a salmon, marlin, or any other fish jumping, note that its head and tail swing from side to side, not up and down. In other words, it is physically impossible for a fish to bend in violent curves that bring its head and tail down or up at extreme angles. The anatomy of the fish will not permit it. A *slight* downward or upward bend in the tail region is acceptable, and any mount will show plenty of action by turning its head or tail away from the wall.

Fins

With the proper angulation and curvature placed on the fins, any type of action desired in a mount can be imitated. But the fins should not be stretched to their extreme width and they should not be forced unnaturally away from the body. It is unusual to find a skin mount that does not have its fins dried flat, stretched to their fullest and away from the body. The fish appears to be frozen with fright—like a cartoon that shows a man's hair standing straight up when he sees a ghost. When a fish is stationary or swimming, its fins are undulating in movement; they do not open and close like a Japanese fan. The astute taxidermist who wishes to portray his creation in a swiftly swimming action will place the fins in a pleasing position, pointing backward and closer to the body. Fishes use their tail and pre-tail areas primarily for locomotion; fins are mostly stabilizers.

Mouth

Here again, the average craftsman tries to attain dramatic effect by exaggerating the open mouth beyond its anatomical restrictions. This fault is especially conspicuous in the largemouth bass, pickerel, northern pike, and musky. It is a rarity to see any of these fishes that does not have its mouth pushed out and set to distortion and its gill covers opened forcefully wide.

Eye

The eye of a mounted fish is nearly always too large. Next time you see a fresh fish or observe one in an aquarium, pay close attention to its eye. Notice that the eye is a movable ball that fits into a socket. Also note that the extreme width all around the eye is not as wide in diameter as the eye socket. A taxidermist removes the eyeball and replaces it with a glass eye that fits exactly into the entire socket and which, of course, is much bigger than the original eye. To do a good job on the eye of a mounted fish, a portion of the eyeball should be reconstructed and the width of the eye alone measured. A glass eye of the correct color and measurement should be inserted.

Color

Some knowledge of fish physiology is required in order to judge the paint job of a mounted fish. First, most species go through different shades of intensity of coloration depending on environment, time of year, and stress or excitement. Often two species of the same type inhabiting waters only a few miles apart will be different in intensity of coloration; this is especially true of trouts and of salmons, depending upon length of time they have come from the sea. If an angler is accustomed to fishing in a certain area, he may consider a mount of the same species taken from another area as being inaccurately painted. Second, a mounted fish is not easy to paint. Any taxidermist expecting to do a professional job must have a natural artistic ability, plus accurate knowledge of the coloration of the live fish and the technical know-how of applying the paints.

Different Types of Taxidermy

Whether the fish is intended to be a trophy or a decorative piece, the angler should be aware that there are different types of taxidermic methods from which to choose. Knowledge concerning the different systems will influence the selection of a particular taxidermist to do the job; that is, the one who only mounts fish skins or the one who produces an accurate and pleasing plastic cast. Although there are several methods of producing fish models for display—wood silhouettes, medallions, plaster casts, wax casts, rubber casts, freeze-dried specimens—the most prominent or common ways are skin mounts, plastic reproductions, and, most recently, wood carvings or wood sculptures.

The Skin Mount

In a skin mount the prepared skin is draped and secured over an artificial mannequin resembling in size and form the original body. The mannequin is shaped out of balsa wood, styrofoam, or other material. Or the skin is placed in a plaster mold of the fish and filled with a pastelike mixture that dries and hardens.

Some anglers prefer the skin mount because they feel that the original skin of their trophy should be there. Also, the taxidermist may prefer to mount a skin rather than to make a cast because it is less expensive in materials, takes less time, and does not require as much expertise in workmanship. The result, however, is inferior in many ways to the plastic cast.

Plastic Reproductions

The advent of easily obtainable, durable, plastic materials that can be cast in plaster molds without requiring intense heat has been the most important contribution to the art of creating lifelike replicas of fishes for museum displays or trophies for sportfishermen. By far the best plastic to date is polyester resin, a popular item for repairing boats. It is available in paint shops and hardware stores, as well as through boat-supply dealers. It is a liquid that will set in less than half an hour when properly mixed with a few drops of hardener. When set, through its natural chemical action at room temperature, it becomes a hard material that will not shrink or change its form, nor will it be affected by weather changes. Furthermore, it will never crack, peel, ooze grease, or appear wizened, as do most skin mounts. Actually, it is indestructible, unless, of course, the mount is dropped onto a hard surface and a fin is chipped or broken off. Even then, another fin can be cast in the same material to replace the damaged one without the slightest change in appearance.

Wood Carvings

Any discourse concerned with fish taxidermy and fish models must include wood carvings. Present-day gifted, artist-craftsmen using wood as a medium are capa-

These skin-mount fishes were photographed by the author as they were
displayed in various booths at an outdoor sportsmen's show. Every
inquisitive angler should recognize such specimens of poor taxidermy.

The plastic reproductions of a largemouth bass and Atlantic salmon
pictured here are examples of the highest quality of fish taxidermy;
the true-to-life forms were created by Ralph Morrill, father of modern fish
taxidermy at Yale University's Peabody Museum.

ble of producing models of any game fish, replicas that will outclass in anatomic accuracy, color rendition, and artistic presentation the best of skin mounts, and thereby challenge plastic casts for supremacy in the world of fish models—at least in the eyes of the inquisitive angler. I have been convinced of that fact after closely scrutinizing, with the eye of a critic, about a dozen creations of one such artist, Joe Swaluk, mentioned previously in this chapter. I have counted fin spines, noted color accountability, checked for markings within realistic limits, and so on. I could find only minor distractions (to me) in two of his earlier carvings: one occurs in a striped marlin whose lower jaw is incorrect in that, if it was closed, the tip end of the mandible would be too widely separated from the bill as it appears in the real fish; the other is a well-painted brook trout whose caudal peduncle, where it meets the tail fin, is too heavy with a bulge—a trait common in skin mounts of a fine, well-known taxidermist.

I have chosen a few photos of Joe Swaluk's work to portray here and to substantiate or add credibility to my opinions. The photo of the Atlantic salmon included in my choice of illustrations is of special interest to me because *Salmo salar* is my favorite freshwater game fish, and because it depicts a carving of a twenty-pound specimen caught by fly-fisherman Edward Calesa in Iceland's Hofsta River. Joe Swaluk produced the life-size carving from a penciled outline drawing of the fish. The beautiful carving, with which I could not find fault, remains as an artistic and decorative object to be displayed with sophistication, aside from being a trophy of Mr. Celesa and a cherished reminder of a great day of fishing in Iceland.

Also, the Hofsta salmon carving attracted my interest with a direct bearing on my advice to anglers. I have fished Iceland's Grimsa River during each season for the past seven or eight years. Two years ago, on one of my favorite beats, I caught a handsome, sixteen-pound buck salmon. I was so pleased that it had taken a fly I tied, besides performing magnificently in runs downriver while resisting rod and reel, that I immediately decided to take that splendid specimen home as a trophy. Consequently, I gave our favorite guide Sveinbjorn (Sven) Blondal specific instructions on how to place the fish in the lodge freezer, all of which brought facetious remarks from my friend and fishing companion, Foster Bam, who witnessed the entire episode with amusement.

The custom at the Grimsa is to fish a half day at the end of the week, Sunday morning, the day of departure for the Keflavik airport. Fishing until the last moment always creates a problem—time-consuming struggling out of waders, peeling off thermo-underwear, removing other paraphernalia, and then dismantling rods and packing duffle bags in time to be ready when the minibus arrives to pick up the anglers.

Sven retrieved my pride and joy from the freezer and delivered it to my room, where I was prepared to incorporate it into my luggage. I wrapped the fish with newspaper (an excellent insulator) and proceeded to stuff clothes around it in my longest traveling bag. Sven's parting admonition was, "Don't be late for the bus." After some pushing and pulling I found, to my dismay, that the salmon's tail and caudal peduncle, all of about seven inches, protruded beyond the confines of the bag. Meanwhile, close by my bedroom window in the small parking area, Magnus, the genial bus driver, was exhorting the guides to start loading the luggage. Time was growing short for departure. To search for a box, tape, and twine to accommodate the salmon was out of the question. I panicked. The situation called for drastic measures. To settle my nerves I finished the last shot of bourbon from the bottle sitting like a beacon on the dresser, and made a decision. I pulled off my pants, shoes, and socks, placed the salmon in the bathtub, and with pocket knife in hand followed the salmon into the tub. On my knees, with a towel over the ice-cold fish, I frantically began the tough job of sawing off the tail end of the frozen trophy.

While the fish scales were sprinkling over the bottom of the tub, I finally cut through the salmon skin, meat, and bone. Just then I heard Foster, who was standing by the bus, yell to Sven at the loading platform waiting with all the other guides to say good-byes to the departees, as is the custom in all fishing camps. "Where the Hell is Ed?," voiced Foster. "He must be goofing off somewhere as usual."

I expected the knock on my door. I shouted, "Come in, Sven." He opened the door and exclaimed to the empty room, "How did you know it was me?" I replied, "I'm psychic. I'm in the bathtub. Come on in, I need your help." He approached hesitatingly and peeked in as I stood in the tub with the salmon's tail in one hand, the knife in the other and the rest of the fish at my feet. Before I could explain, he stared at me, gulped, and softly said, "Yayzus."

After I told him not to call Foster for help, because I had not lost my mind, I commissioned him to clean up the mess in the tub before the fish scales dried adhesively to the enamel and before the maids came in to prepare the room for the next guests; otherwise they would quickly spread the news that Mr. Migdalski was a real nut. I inserted the tail into the long plastic bag with the body of the salmon, rewrapped it all with newspaper and smiled when the bag zipped up without a hitch.

Sven carried my rods and other bags to the bus in which sat impatient passengers. I lugged the last piece, containing the salmon, to the lodge door as fast as

I could. Then I slowed down and nonchalantly placed the heavy bag on the platform. As I straightened up I could feel the sweat break out on my forehead.

Sequel

The salmon arrived home still perfectly frozen. In my basement workshop, several months later, I prepared the salmon for molding in plaster. First, positioning the fish in a bed of wet, fine sand I pressed the tail end tightly against the body from which it had been severed, and then flowed the mixed-with-water plaster over it.

Because of the medicinal benefits of bourbon that Sunday morning in Iceland I turned a seemingly acute disaster into a successful and satisfying experiment in producing a plastic mount as a trophy fish, showing a distinct vertical wound across its caudal peduncle, a blemish I could have repaired, but I did not do so because it gives me pleasure when I view that scarred replica of my sixteen-pounder and recall the morning of panic on the banks of the Grimsa.

Related References

The chapter "Fish Taxidermy and the Angler" is not a treatise on "how to do it" in fish taxidermy. For additional information, however, for the inquisitive angler who may be interested in delving deeper into the art and science of taxidermy, I list the following:

Billard, Ruth. 1984. *Ralph C. Morrill's Museum Quality Fish Taxidermy.* Bill Art Publications, P.O. Box 124, Rowayton, Connecticut 06853.

McFall, Waddy F. *Taxidermy Step by Step.* (Available from The Modern Taxidermy Magazine.)

Migdalski, Edward C. 1981. *Fish Mounts and Fish Trophies.* New York: John Wiley & Sons, Inc.

Phillips, Bubba, and Archie Phillips. 1979. *How to Mount Fish.* Archie Phillips Publications, 200 52nd St. Fairfield, Alabama 35604.

Tinsley, Russell. *Taxidermy Guide.* (Available from The Modern Taxidermy Magazine).

The Modern Taxidermy Magazine. 1-21 Bruchac Drive, Greenfield, New York 12833.

Wide World of Taxidermy Magazine, P.O. Box 3538, North Fort Myers, Florida 33903.

The National Taxidermist's Association holds an annual convention and exhibition. For information, write to them at P.O. Box B, Greenfield Center, New York 12833.

Index

Acidity of water, 132
Acid rain, 159–60
Acre foot, 133
Affluent of a lake, 133
Agassiz, L., 14
Age of fishes
  determination of, 50–51
  growth and, 46–50
Aging of a lake, 133
Air bladder, 24, 61–62
Air-breathers, 57, 59

Algae, 133
Alkalinity of water, 133
Alluvium, 133–34
Alpine lakes, 134
Alvin (submersible), 186–87
Amberjacks, 93
Anadromous fishes, 73
Anatomy and physiology of
  fishes, 19–80. *See also*
  Taxidermy
  age and growth, 46–50

age determination, 50–51
body form, 19–21
circulatory system, 62–64
coloration, 30–31
digestion, 55–57
fins and locomotion, 23–
  25
fishing and, 145–57
  anatomical advantages
  and restrictions, 145–
  49

foul-hooked fishes, 155–
57
  lactic acid buildup, 151–
  52
  releasing for survival,
  149–51
  resistance to rod and
  reel, 152–53
food and feeding, 54–55
heart, 62–64
muscles, 21–23
reproduction, 72–76
respiration, 57–62
scales, 26–30
senses, 64–70
  color perception, 66–67
  hearing, 67–69, 70–71
  lateral line, 70–71
  pain, 71–72
  sight, 64–67
  smell, 69
  taste, 69–70
  touch, 70, 71
sex determination, 76–77
size and weight, 32–46
  determination of weight,
  41–44
  freshwater fishes, 36–38
  saltwater fishes, 38–39
  weight loss, 44–46
skeleton, 21
skin, 26
sleep, 67
speed, 25–26
teeth, 51–54
Anchor ice, 134
Anderson, Jack, 155–56
Angelfishes, 21
Animal kingdom, divisions

of, 8–9
Annuli, age of fishes and,
  50
Aphytal zone, 134
Aquaculture, 160–61
  farm ponds, 168–69
Aqua-lung, 186
Aquatic plants, 134, 138
Arapaima, 35
Archerfish, 65
Aristotle, 6
Artedi, Peter, 6
Artificial lakes and ponds,
  134
Artificial Reef Development
  Center (ARDC), 163
Artificial reefs, 161–65
Atlantic Coast Fishes, 11

Backwash, 134
Bacteria, 134–35
  lake and pond, 134–35
Bam, Foster, 194, 196, 208,
  209
Barracudas, 21
  teeth of, 51
  temperature tolerances of,
  125
Basin, 135
Bass, George, 193
Basses. *See* striped bass;
  temperate basses
Bathymetric maps, 135
Beaver pond, 135
Beebe, William, 193
Berg, Leo S., 14, 15
Billfishes, 83–84
  temperature tolerances of,

125
Bioluminescence, 66
Blondal, Sveinbjorn (Sven),
  208–10
Blood, 62–64
Bluefish, 21, 90–91
  teeth of, 51
  temperature tolerances of,
  125
Bluegills, growth rates of,
  47
Body form, 19–21
  of mounted fish, 203
Body temperature, 54
  lateral line system and, 71
Bond, George, 193
Bonefish, temperature tol-
  erances of, 125
Bonitos, 87
Boulenger, G. A., 14
Bowfin, 100–1
Breathing, 57–62
Brown trout, 47
Browsers, 55
Burbot, 109
Bush, George, 160

Calesa, Edward, 208
Camouflage, 31
Carbon dioxide, 140–41
Carps, 106–7
  eggs of, 76
Carrying capacity of fish-
  eries, 135
Carson, Rachel, 193
Cartilaginous fishes, 81–82
Cataracts, 71
Catfishes, 107–8

freshwater, 25
oxygen demands of, 57
sea, 76
CEDAM International, 195
Celsius (centigrade) system, 128
Chars, 103–4
Charts and maps, 131–32
Cichlids, 111
Circulatory system, 62–64
Clark, Eugenie, 194
Classification of fishes, 12–16
Classification of Fishes, Both Recent and Fossil, 14
Coastal and inshore fishes, 90–98
Codfishes, 109
temperature tolerances of, 123
Coelacanth, 187–89
Cohen, Daniel M., 14–16
Coliform bacillus, 135
Coloration of fishes, 30–31
Color of fishes
mounted fish, 204
sexual differences and, 77
Color of lake water, 135
Color perception of fish, 66–67
Contour maps, 132
Coral reefs, 165
Corlieu, Commander de, 186
Cornea, 65
Courtenay-Latimer, Marjorie, 187
Cousteau, Jacques-Yves, 186, 193

Croakers, 91–92
Current canal thorough weed beds, 136
Currents
in lakes and ponds, 136
ocean, 116–21

Dackerman, Ray, 171–72
DDT, 180
Deeps (trenches)
in oceans, 115
in lakes, 136
Density of seawater, 115
Depth of the ocean, 115
Destratification, 136
De Sylva, Donald, 49–50
Diatoms, 136
Digestion, 55–57
Dissolved oxygen in water, 136–37
Diving. *See also* SCUBA
recreational, 196–97
Dolphins, 85–86
temperature tolerances of, 124
Donaldson, Ivan, 32, 48
Douglas, John, 11
Drawdown, 137
Drift nets, 165–67, 170
Drop-off, 137
Drums, 112
marine, 91–92
Dugout pond, 137

Earle, Sylvia, 194
Eating fish, toxins and, 179–82

Edgerton, Harold, 193
Eels, 21, 23, 109
migration, 79–80
spawning, 75–76
Effluent, lake, 137
Eggs, 72. *See also* reproduction; spawning
Electricity, 71
Enriched lakes, 137–38
Epilimnion, 138
Eschmeyer, William N., 11
Esophagus, 55
Estuaries, 167–68
Explorers Club of New York, The, 195
Eyes, 64–65
electrical currents and, 71
of mounted fish, 204

Fall overturn, 142
Farm ponds, 168–69
Farrington, Kip, 177
Fathom, 128
Feeding, 54–55
Fertilization, 76
Fine, John C., 194, 195
Fins, 21, 23–25
of mounted fish, 203
Fisheries, artificial reefs and, 161–65
Fishes of the Western North Atlantic, 14–15
Fishing (sportfishing)
anatomy of fishes relative to, 145–57
anatomical advantages and restrictions, 145–49

foul-hooked fishes, 155–57

lactic acid buildup, 151–52

releasing for survival, 149–51

resistance to rod and reel, 152–53

limnological factors in. *See* Limnology

ocean currents and, 118–21

pothole, 172

water temperature and, 122–23

Fishkill, 138

Flatfishes, 92

Flounders, 92

temperature tolerances of, 123

Flukes, 92

Flying fishes, 24–25

Food chain, 54

Food cycle, upwelling and, 125–28

Food for fishes, 54

Forjot, Maxime, 186

Fossil fishes, 9–10

Foul-hooked fishes, 155–57

Four-eyed fish, 65–66

Freezing of seawater, 128–29

Freshwater Fishes of North America, 11

Fricke, Hans, 189, 194

Gage, Charlie, 156–57

Gagnan, Emile, 186

Game fishes, 81–112

freshwater, 98–112

bowfin, 100–1

catfishes, 107–8

cichlids, 111

codfishes, 109

drums, 112

eels, 109

families of, 99

gars, 100

herrings, 101

minnows and carps, 106–7

mooneyes, 105

paddlefish, 100

perches, 111

pikes, 106

salmons, 101, 104–5

smelts, 105

suckers, 107

sunfishes, 110–11

temperate basses, 109–10

trouts, 101–4

whitefishes, 101–2

marine, 81–98

barracudas, 90

bluefish, 90–91

bonefish, 91

coastal and inshore fishes, 90–98

cobia, 91

cods, 91

corakers and drums, 91–92

dolphins, 85–86

families of, 82–83

flatfishes, 92

greenlings and lingcod, 93

grunts, 93

jacks, 93–94

mackerels, 86–88

open-ocean fishes, 83–90

porgies, 95

sailfishes and marlins, 83–84

scorpion fishes, 95–96

sea basses, 94–95

sharks, 88–90

snappers, 96–97

snook, 97

surfperches, 96

swordfish, 85

tarpons, 94

temperate basses, 95

tripletail, 97–98

wrasses, 98

Gars, 100

Genus, 12

Gill nets, 165–67

Gill rakers, 59

Gills, 57–61

Glacial flow, 138

Goodrich, E. S., 14

Grant, Gardner, 200

Grayling, 101, 102

Grazers, 55

Greenlings, 93

Greenwood, P. Humphrey, 15

Grimsa River, 208–9

Groupers, anatomy relative to fishing, 147

Growth of fishes, 46–50

Grunion, migration of, 77–78

Guerra, Duke, 177

Gulf Stream, 116–17

Haddock, 91
 temperature tolerances of, 123
Halfbeaks, 24
Halibuts, 92
 temperature tolerances of, 123
Hamman, Howard, 11
Hammer, William, 193
Hatch, 138–39
Hawaii, longline and drift-net fishing in, 170–71
Hearing, 67–69, 70–71
Heart, 62–64
Henshall, John, 152
Herald, Earl S., 11
Herrings, 101
Hewitt, Edward R., 42–43
Holding a fish, 150
Homing instinct, 79
Hubbs, Carl L., 14
Hypolimnion, 139

Ichthyology, 5–16
 amateur, 7–8
 beginnings of, 6
 books on, 11, 12, 14–17
 classification of fishes, 12–16
 divisions of animals, 8–9
 fossil fishes, 9–10
 identification of fish, 10–11
 meaning of, 5
 names of fishes, 11–12

 professional, 6–7
Ichthyotoxins, 139
Identification of fish, 10–11
Incubation, 75
Inlets, 139–40
Insecticides, 180
Insects. *See also* pesticides
 aquatic, 138–39
International Game Fish Association (IGFA), 11, 44, 169
Intestine, 55–57
Iris, 65
Istiophorids, 83–84

Jacks, 93–94
Jain, Luis, 179–80
Jordan, D. S., 14
Jumps, 24–25

Kittredge, Benjamin F., 42
Knight, John Alden, 175–76
Knot, 129

Lactic acid, 151–52
Ladyfish, 94
Lagler, Karl F., 14
Lakes. *See also* limnology
 artificial, 134
 distinction between ponds and, 141
 stratified, 141–42
Lampreys, 59
Large intestine, 55
Largemouth bass

 anatomy relative to fish-ing, 147
 color perception, 66
 sexual maturity of, 46
 spawning, 74
Lateral line, 70–71
Latil, Pierre de, 186
Latin names for fishes, 12
Leaps, 24–25
Lens, 64–65
Le Prieur, Commander, 186
Limnology, 131–44
 abyssal depth, 132
 acidity of water, 132
 acre foot, 133
 affluent of a lake, 133
 aging of a lake, 133
 algae, 133
 alkalinity of water, 133
 alluvium, 133–34
 alpine lakes, 134
 anchor ice, 134
 aphytal zone, 134
 aquatic plants, 134
 artificial lakes and ponds, 134
 backwash, 134
 bacteria, 134–35
 basin, 135
 bathymetric maps, 135
 carrying capacity of fish-eries, 135
 charts and maps, 131–32
 coliform bacillus, 135
 color of lake water, 135
 current canal thorough weed beds, 136
 currents, 136

deeps, 136
destratification, 136
diatoms, 136
dissolved oxygen, 136–37
distinction between lakes
    and ponds, 141
drawdown, 137
drop-off, 137
dugout pond, 137
effluent, 137
enriched lakes, 137–38
epilimnion, 138
fishkill, 138
glacial flow, 138
hatch, 138–39
hypolimnion, 139
ichthyotoxins, 139
inlets, 139–40
offshore winds, 140
onshore winds, 140
oxygen and carbon diox-
    ide, 140–41
sediments, 141
silting, 141
stratified lakes, 141–42
temperature tolerances of
    fishes, 143
turbidity, 143–44
undercut bank in rivers,
    144
water temperature, 142–
    43
wetlands, 144
Lingcod, 93
Link, Edwin, 193
Linnaeus, Carolus, 6, 12
List of Common and Scientific
    Names of Fishes from the

United States and Canada,
    A, 12, 15
Locomotion, 23–25
Longley, William, 193
Longlines, 169–72
Lungfishes, respiration in,
    59, 62

McClane, A. J., 11
McCosker, John, 194–95
Mackerels, 86–88
Mako sharks, 89–90
Mantas, 25
Marine factors. See
    Oceanography
Marlins, 35, 83–90
    temperature tolerances of,
    125
Martin, Charles, 193
Matching the hatch in fly-
    fishing, 138–39
Mercury, 180–81
Merriman, Daniel, 188–89
Meyers, G. S., 15
Migdalski, Edward C., 11
Migration, 77–80, 123
Minnows, 106–7
Modern Angler, The, 176
Mooneyes, 105
Morril, Ralph, 189
Mouth of mounted fish,
    204
Mowbray, Lou, 150, 184
Müller, Johannes, 14
Muscles, 21–23
    eye, 65
Muskellunge (musky), 106

age and growth of, 47–48
Myomeres, 21

Names of fishes, 11–12
National Marine Fisheries
    Service (NMFS), 163
National Oceanic and At-
    mospheric Administra-
    tion (NOAA), 167
Needlefishes, 24
Nervous system, 64. See also
    Senses of fishes
    pain and, 71–72
Nests, 74
Nets, drift, 165–67, 170
Nitrates, 114
Nutrition, 54

Oceanography (oceanic
    factors), 113–129
    composition of, 113–14
    currents, 116–21
    density of seawater, 115
    depth of the ocean, 115
    salinity of seawater, 114
    sunlight, 115–16
    tides, 117–18
    upwelling and the food
    cycle, 125–28
    water temperature, 114,
    122–25
Offshore winds, 140
Onshore winds, 140
Oxygen, 57
    dissolved in, 136–37
    in lake and pond water,

140–41
in water, 114
Oxygen demands, 57

Pacific Coast Fishes, 11
Paddlefish, 100
size and weight of, 35
Pain, 71–72
Parasites, 55
PCBs (polychlorinated bi-
phenyls), 181–82
Pelagic spawning, 73
Perches, 111
white, 95
Peterson Field Guide Se-
ries, 11
Petroleum platforms, as
artificial-reef material,
164–65
Phosphates, 114
Photography, underwater,
184–85
Physiology of fishes. *See*
Anatomy and physiology
of fishes
Pikes, 106
anatomy relative to fish-
ing, 147
Pirarucu, 35
Plants, aquatic, 134, 138
Plastic reproductions of
fishes, 205
Poisoned fish, 179–82
Pollock, 91
temperature tolerances of,
123
Pollution. *See* Acid rain;

Red tide; Toxins
Polychlorinated biphenyls
(PCBs), 181–82
Pompanos, 93
Ponds
artificial, 134
beaver, 135
distinction between lakes
and, 141
dugout, 137
farm, 168–69
Porgies, 95
Pothier, Israel, 40–41
Pothole fishing, 172
Predators, 54
Puffers, 56
Pyloric caeca, 55
Pylorus, 55

Rain, acid, 159–60
Ray, G. Carlton, 11
Rays, 25, 59
Recreational diving, 196–
97
Redds, 73
Red tide, 173–74
Reefs
artificial, 161–65
coral, 165
Regan, C. T., 14
Releasing for survival, 149–
51
Reproduction, 72–76
sex determination and,
76–77
spawning, 72–76
sperm and eggs and, 72

Reservoirs, 173–75
Respiration, 57–62
Rips and races, 118–19
Ristori, Al, 182
Rivers. *See also* Limnology
turbidity of water in, 143–
44
undercut bank in, 144
Rivman, Marian, 196
Robbins, C. Richard, 11
Rock bass, 95
Rockfishes, 95–96
Romer, Alfred S., 14
Rosen, Donn E., 15

Sailfishes, 83–84
age and growth of, 49–50
temperature tolerances of,
125
Salinity of seawater, 114
Salmons, 101, 104–5
leaping of, 24
spawning, 73, 75, 78–79
species of, 105
*Saltwater Fishes of North
America,* 11
Sammon, Rick, 194, 195
Sawfish, 21
Scads, 93
Scales, 26–30
Schmidt, Johannes, 79
Schwiebert, Ernie, 200, 201
Scofield, Eugene, 48–49
Scombrids, 86–88
Scorpion fishes, 95–96
SCUBA, 184–97
books on, 197

instruction in, 196–97
recreational, 196–97
Sea basses, 94–95
Sea Fishes of Southern Africa,
The, 189
Sea horses, 76
Sea lamprey, 59
Sea temperature, 114–15,
122–25
Seatrout, temperature tolerances of, 125
Seawater. *See also* Water
temperature
composition of, 113–14
Sediments, 141
Sella, 40
Senses of fishes, 64–70
color perception, 66–67
hearing, 67–69, 70–71
lateral line, 70–71
pain, 71–72
sight, 64–67
smell, 69
taste, 69–70
touch, 70, 71
Sexual dimorphism, 77
Sexual maturity, 46
SFI Bulletin, 178–79
Sharks, 88–90
anatomy relative to fish-
ing, 145, 147
respiration in, 59
size and weight of, 35
Shultz, Eric, 189–93
Sight, 64–67
Silting, 141
Size and weight of fishes,
32–46
determination of weight,

41–44
freshwater fishes, 36–38
saltwater fishes, 38–39
weight loss, 44–46
Skates, 59
Skeleton, 21
Skin mount, 205
Skin of fishes, 26
Small intestine, 55
Smell, sense of, 69
Smelts, 105
Smith, J. L. B., 187, 189
Snappers, 96–97
Snook, 97
temperature tolerances of,
125
Soles, 92
Solunar theory, 175–78
Spawning, 72–76
migration and, 77–80
sex determination and,
76–77
Spearfishing, 185–86, 190–
91
Species of fishes. *See also*
Classification of fishes
number of, 15–16
Speed of fishes, 25–26
Sperm, 72
Sportfishing. *See* Fishing
Sport Fishing Institute
(SFI), 163, 178–79
Spring tides, 118
Steinhart Aquarium, 194–
95
Stickleback, 76
Stomach, 55–56
Stone, Richard B., 163–64
Strainers, 55

Stratified lakes, 141–42
Striped bass, 21, 95
lengths of various age
groups, 48–49
length-weight relationship,
49
spawning, 73
temperature tolerances of,
125
Stunted population, 46–47
Sturgeons, 99–100
eggs of, 76
size and weight of, 32–35
white, age of, 48
Submarines, 184
Submersibles, 186–87
Suckers, 55, 107
Sunfishes, 110–11
Sunlight, sea life and, 115–
16
Surfperches, 96
Swaluk, Joe, 200, 208
Swim bladder. *See* Air
bladder
Swordfish, 35, 85
sportfishing for, 170
temperature tolerances of,
125

Tarpons, 25, 94
temperature tolerances of,
125
Taste, sense of, 69–70
Taxidermy, 199–210
bending a fish, 203
books and magazines on,
210–11
color, 204

evaluating a mounted
fish, 201, 203
eyes, 204
fins, 203
mouth, 204
plastic reproductions, 205
skin mount, 205
types of, 204–5
wood carvings, 205, 208–
10
Taxonomy of fishes, 12–16
Teeth, 51–54
Temperate basses
freshwater, 109–10
marine, 95
Temperature. *See* Body
temperature; Water tem-
perature
Temperature tolerances
marine fishes, 123–25
freshwater fishes, 143
Tetraodotoxin, 182
Thermometer, water, 132
Tide-running, 78
Tides, 117–18
Tomcod, 91, 109
Tongue, 55, 69–70
Touch, sense of, 70, 71
Toxins, 179–82
Trenches, deep, 115
Tripletail, 97–98
Tropical fishes, 76
Trouts, 101–4
spawning, 74, 75
Tuna, 19–20, 86–87
bluefin
anatomy relative to fish-

ing, 147, 149
aquaculture of, 161–62
migration, 77
size and weight of, 40–
41
temperature tolerances
of, 125
speed of, 25–26
Turbidity, 143–44
Turbots, 92

Undercut bank in rivers,
144
Underwater exploration,
183–97
Underwater Naturalist, The,
186
Upwelling of waters, 125–
28

Vertebrate Paleontology, 14
Vision, 64–67
Voss, Gilbert, 49

Wahoo, 87–88
temperature tolerances of,
124
Wall, Bob, 176
Ward, William H., 42–44
Water temperature
celsius (centigrade) sys-
tem, 128
freezing of seawater, 128–
29

lakes and ponds, 142–43
migration and, 78
of seas, 114–15, 122–24
specific tolerances of
fishes, 123–25
sportfishing and, 122–23
Weakfishes, 91
Webster, Dwight, 160
Wedgeport tuna fishing
area, 119, 120
Weed beds, current canal
through, 136
Weight loss in fishes, 44–46
Weight of fishes. *See* Size
and weight of fishes
Weitzman, Stanley H., 15
Wetlands, 144
White, Wallace, 194
Whitefishes, 101–2
White perch, 95
Winds
offshore, 140
onshore, 140
Winterkill. *See* Fishkill
Wood carvings, 205, 208–
10
Woodward, A. S., 14
World Fishing and Out-
door Exposition (Suffern,
N.Y.), 200
World Record Game Fishes,
11, 12
Wrasses, 98

Zone of Influence Theory,
79